NORTHERN CALIFORNIA
TRAVEL ✦ SMART®

W9-BNW-203

How to Use This Book 1
Suggested Itineraries 2
Using the Planning Map .9
Mileage Chart 12
Why Visit Northern California? 13
Practical Tips 23
❶ San Francisco 35
❷ Marin County 59
❸ The East Bay: Berkeley and Oakland 73
❹ The South Bay and the Peninsula Coast 85
❺ The Monterey Peninsula 101
❻ Big Sur 113
   ☆ Scenic Route: Nacimiento Road 122
❼ Wine Country 123
❽ The North Coast: Sonoma and Mendocino 141
❾ The Redwood Parks .157
   ☆ Scenic Route: The Mattole Road 172
❿ Volcanoes 173
   ☆ Scenic Route: The Lava Loop 185
⓫ Sacramento and the Central Valley 187
⓬ Gold Country 199
   ☆ Scenic Route: High Sierra Pass Roads 214
⓭ Lake Tahoe 215
⓮ Owens Valley and Mono Lake 227
   ☆ Scenic Route: June Lake Loop 238
⓯ Yosemite 239
⓰ Sequoia and Kings Canyon National Parks 251
   Appendix 259
   Index 262
   Map Index 264

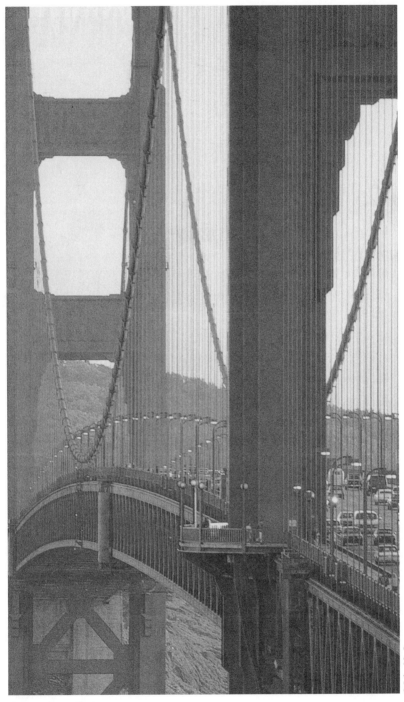

Golden Gate Bridge

NORTHERN CALIFORNIA

TRAVEL ✦ SMART®

Second Edition

Paul Otteson

John Muir Publications
Santa Fe, New Mexico

For Mary, my partner in all things.

Also, thanks to my many friends around the state who support me with information, ideas, opinions, corrections, and good times. Thanks also to my mother, my top sales rep in Phoenix—she's beginning to believe.

John Muir Publications, P.O. Box 613, Santa Fe, New Mexico 87504

Printed in the United States of America.
Second edition. First printing October 1998

ISSN 1098-5999
ISBN 1-56261-422-3

Editors: Marybeth Griffin, Chris Hayhurst
Graphics editor: Tom Gaukel
Production: Nikki Rooker
Design: Linda Braun
Cover design: Janine Lehmann
Typesetting: Linda Harper
Map style development: American Custom Maps–Albuquerque, NM
Map illustration: American Custom Maps–Albuquerque, NM
Front cover photo: *large*— ©Leo de Wys, Inc./Jon Hicks
                small— ©Leo de Wys, Inc./Steve Vidler
Back cover photo: ©Photo Network/Ron Schwager
Printing: Publishers Press

Distributed to the book trade by
Publishers Group West
Berkeley, California

HOW TO USE THIS BOOK

This *Northern California Travel•Smart* guidebook is organized in 16 destination chapters, each covering the best sights and activities, restaurants, and lodging available in that specific destination. Thanks to thorough research and experience, the author is able to bring you only the best options, saving you time and money in your travels. The chapters begin with San Francisco and follow in geographic sequence so you can follow an easy route from one to the next. If you were to visit each destination, you'd enjoy a complete tour of the best of Northern California.

Each chapter contains:

- User-friendly maps of the area, showing all recommended sights, restaurants, and accommodations.
- "A Perfect Day" description—how the author would spend his time if he had just one day in that destination.
- Sightseeing highlights, each rated by degree of importance: ✮✮✮ Don't miss; ✮✮ Try hard to see; ✮ See if you have time; and No stars—Worth knowing about.
- Selected restaurant, lodging, and camping recommendations to suit a variety of budgets.
- Helpful hints, fitness and recreation ideas, insights, and random tidbits of information to enhance your trip.

The Importance of Planning. Developing an itinerary is the best way to get the most satisfaction from your travels, and this guidebook makes it easy. First, read through the book and choose the places you'd most like to visit. Then, study the color map on the inside cover flap and the mileage chart (page 12) to determine which you can realistically see in the time you have available and at the travel pace you prefer. Using the Planning Map (pages 10–11), map out your route. Finally, use the lodging recommendations to determine your accommodations.

Some Suggested Itineraries. To get you started, six itineraries of varying lengths and based on specific interests follow. Mix and match according to your interests and time constraints, or follow a given itinerary from start to finish. The possibilities are endless. *Happy travels!*

SUGGESTED ITINERARIES

With the *Northern California Travel•Smart* guidebook you can plan a trip of any length—a one-day excursion, a getaway weekend, or a three-week vacation—around any special interest. To get you started, the following pages contain six suggested itineraries geared toward a variety of interests. For more information, refer to the chapters listed—chapter names are bolded and chapter numbers appear inside black bullets. You can follow a suggested itinerary in its entirety, or shorten, lengthen, or combine parts of each, depending on your starting and ending points.

Discuss alternative routes and schedules with your travel companions—it's a great way to have fun, even before you leave home. And remember: Don't hesitate to change your itinerary once you're on the road. Careful study and planning ahead of time will help you make informed decisions as you go, but spontaneity is the extra ingredient that will make your trip memorable.

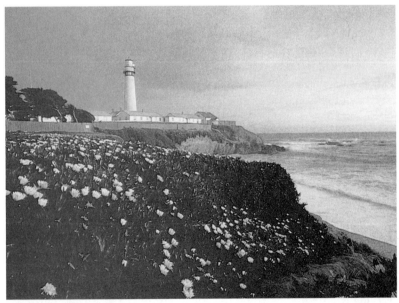

© Robert Holmes/California Dept. Tourism

Pigeon Point Lighthouse

Best of Northern California Tour

If you've got a couple of weeks to spend touring Northern California, this route will show you the best the area has to offer—from beaches to forests and big cities to small towns.

❶ **San Francisco**
❷ **Marin County**
❸ **The East Bay: Berkeley and Oakland**
❹ **The South Bay and the Peninsula Coast**
❺ **The Monterey Peninsula**
❻ **Big Sur**
❼ **Wine Country**
❽ **The North Coast: Sonoma and Mendocino**

❾ **The Redwood Parks**
❿ **Volcanoes**
⓫ **Sacramento and the Central Valley**
⓬ **Gold Country**
⓭ **Lake Tahoe**
⓮ **Owens Valley and Mono Lake**
⓯ **Yosemite**
⓰ **Sequoia and Kings Canyon National Parks**

Time needed for this trip: 2 weeks

Nature Lovers' Tour

For an unforgettable road trip, drive a full loop on CA 1, U.S. 101, CA 299, CA 89, and U.S. 395. Scenic priorities should include Big Sur, Yosemite and Mono Lake, Lake Tahoe, Lassen and Shasta, and a redwood park.

- ❻ **Big Sur**
- ❺ **The Monterey Peninsula** (Seventeen-Mile Drive, Monterey Bay Aquarium)
- ❹ **The South Bay and the Peninsula Coast** (Año Nuevo State Reserve)
- ❷ **Marin County** (Marin Headlands, Point Reyes)
- ❽ **North Coast** (state parks and beaches)
- ❾ **The Redwood Parks**
- ❿ **Volcanoes** (Lassen Volcanic National Park)
- ⓭ **Lake Tahoe** (D. L. Bliss State Park, Emerald Bay State Park)
- ⓮ **Owens Valley and Mono Lake** (Ancient Bristlecone Pine Forest)
- ⓯ **Yosemite**
- ⓰ **Sequoia and Kings Canyon National Parks**

Time needed for this trip: 2 weeks

Arts and Culture Tour

Use San Francisco as a home base for day trips to the museums, universities, historic sites, and cultural enclaves of the Bay Area. Two- to three-day tours to the north or south offer scenic splendor, fine restaurants, delightful inns, wonderful galleries, and charming towns.

❶ **San Francisco**
❷ **Marin County** (Tiburon, Sausalito)
❸ **The East Bay: Berkeley and Oakland** (University of California at Berkeley)
❹ **The South Bay and the Peninsula Coast** (Stanford University, San Jose)
❺ **The Monterey Peninsula** (Seventeen-Mile Drive, Carmel)
❻ **Big Sur** (galleries)
❼ **Wine Country**
❽ **The North Coast: Sonoma and Mendocino** (Mendocino)
⓫ **Sacramento and the Central Valley**

Time needed for this trip: 1 week (or a lifetime)

Family Fun Tour

For a pleasant family trip, the key is to make sure the kids get hands-on fun, variety, and short drive times. Concentrate your trip in the crescent that runs from Monterey through San Francisco, Sacramento, and Yosemite.

- **⑤ The Monterey Peninsula** (Monterey Bay Aquarium)
- **④ The South Bay and the Peninsula Coast** (Paramount's Great America, Santa Cruz)
- **① San Francisco** (Alcatraz, Exploratorium)
- **② Marin County** (Bay Model, Point Reyes)
- **③ The East Bay: Berkeley and Oakland** (Lawrence Hall of Science)
- **⑦ Wine Country** (Marine World and Africa U.S.A.)
- **⑪ Sacramento and the Central Valley** (Old Sacramento, WaterWorld USA)
- **⑫ Gold Country** (mines and caves)
- **⑬ Lake Tahoe** (gondolas)
- **⑮ Yosemite**

Time needed for this trip: 10 days

Best of the Bays Tour

There's enough to keep anyone busy for weeks on California's central coast. Marine attractions include whale watching, kayaking, and observing elephant seals. The state's past is preserved in historic homes, missions, and museums. You can hike in redwood groves or immerse yourself in urban culture.

❻ **Big Sur** (Hearst Castle, parks, Point Lobos State Reserve)
❺ **The Monterey Peninsula** (Carmel, Monterey State Historic Park, Monterey Bay Aquarium)
❹ **The South Bay and the Peninsula Coast** (Año Nuevo, Stanford University, San Jose, Santa Cruz)
❶ **San Francisco** (Alcatraz, Chinatown, Golden Gate)
❷ **Marin County** (Marin Headlands, Sausalito, Point Reyes National Seashore)
❸ **The East Bay: Berkeley and Oakland** (Berkeley, Oakland, Mount Diablo)
❼ **Wine Country** (Sonoma, Napa Valley, Calistoga)

Time needed for this trip: 1 to 2 weeks

High Sierras Tour

You can avoid the cities altogether and enjoy some of the nation's most spectacular places by staying in the high country. To the east and north, stay close to U.S. 395 and CA 89. To connect Yosemite and Lake Tahoe, meander through Gold Country on historic CA 49. Beautiful roads cross the range at several points, including CA 120 in Yosemite, CA 88 south of Tahoe, and CA 70 through the Feather River canyon.

- ❿ **Volcanoes** (Lassen Volcanic National Park)
- ⓬ **Gold Country**
- ⓭ **Lake Tahoe** (D. L. Bliss State Park, Emerald Bay State Park)
- ⓮ **Owens Valley and Mono Lake** (Ancient Bristlecone Pine Forest)
- ⓯ **Yosemite**
- ⓰ **Sequoia and Kings Canyon National Parks**

Time needed for this trip: 10 days

USING THE PLANNING MAP

A major aspect of itinerary planning is determining your mode of transportation and the route you will follow as you travel from destination to destination. The Planning Map on the following pages will allow you to do just that.

First, read through the destination chapters carefully and note the sights that intrigue you. Then, photocopy the Planning Map so you can try out several different routes that will take you to these destinations. (The mileage chart that follows will allow you to calculate your travel distances.) Decide where you will be starting your tour of Northern California. Will you fly into San Francisco, Oakland, or Sacramento, or will you start from somewhere else? Will you be driving from place to place or flying into major transportation hubs and renting a car for day trips? The answers to these questions will form the basis for your travel route design.

Once you have a firm idea of where your travels will take you, copy your route onto the additional Planning Map in the Appendix. You won't have to worry about where your map is, and the information you need on each destination will always be close at hand.

© Robert Holmes/California Dept. Tourism

High Sierra from the Alabama Hills

Planning Map: Northern California

You have permission to photocopy this map.

N

Nevada
California

Sierra Nevada

395

395

395

Yosemite
National
Park

14

15

41

49

120

99

88

49

Sacramento

5

580

80

7

Oakland

880

101

101

4

San Jose

1

San Francisco

1

2

3

Santa Cruz

Monterey

68

5

6

1

101

5

180

41

99

Fresno

Sierra
National
Forest

Kings
Canyon
National
Park

16

Sequoia
National
Park

180

Sequoia
National
Forest

Bakersfield

Pacific Ocean

0 SCALE

75
KILOMETERS

75
MILES

ROAD

INTERSTATE HIGHWAY

AREA BOUNDARY

NORTHERN CALIFORNIA MILEAGE CHART

	Alturas	Chico	Crescent City	Eureka	Fresno	Lake Tahoe	Modesto	Monterey	Oakland	Red Bluff	Redding	Sacramento	San Francisco	San Jose	Santa Cruz	Sequoia N.P.	Stockton	Susanville	Ukiah
Chico	216																		
Crescent City	375	292																	
Eureka	301	228	84																
Fresno	471	267	542	448															
Lake Tahoe	265	155	461	395	291														
Modesto	377	173	448	364	94	197													
Monterey	517	329	476	392	177	346	180												
Oakland	404	195	371	287	160	198	66	113											
Red Bluff	176	41	251	187	245	210	201	357	192										
Redding	145	72	220	156	326	241	232	388	223	31									
Sacramento	307	103	382	294	164	120	70	226	92	131	162								
San Francisco	392	188	360	276	196	204	77	118	11	216	247	85							
San Jose	448	232	407	323	149	233	110	69	44	288	319	136	47						
Santa Cruz	478	269	437	353	177	255	140	41	74	318	349	166	77	30					
Sequoia N.P.	554	350	615	531	83	367	177	243	378	409	164	247	279	253	260				
Stockton	347	143	418	334	124	160	30	195	73	171	202	40	84	117	147	207			
Susanville	110	106	356	292	373	279	414	313	105	136	209	345	375	456	375	309			
Ukiah	327	166	240	156	302	258	208	236	131	156	187	138	120	167	197	385	62	178	
Yosemite	399	280	548	484	97	231	107	226	166	297	328	166	184	137	207	180	253	126	300

WHY VISIT NORTHERN CALIFORNIA?

Northern California is a land of superlatives. You'll find the world's tallest, oldest, and most massive living things in its wonderful forests. The Sierra Nevada boasts the tallest mountain in the lower 48, visible from a highway through the nation's deepest valley. The country's most spectacular seacoast stretches for 80 miles south of Monterey. Great lava plateaus cover the northeast and are guarded by Mount Shasta, the second tallest volcano in the contiguous United States.

The region's two premier vacation spots are located above a foothills region imbued with the history of the Gold Rush. Yosemite Valley in Yosemite National Park draws over 3 million visitors annually. To the north, the clear blue waters and forested mountains of the Lake Tahoe basin attract skiers in the winter and outdoor enthusiasts the rest of the year.

Capital city Sacramento anchors the huge Central Valley, the source of most of California's nation-leading agricultural production. The major rivers of the Sierra feed thousands of miles of canals and aqueducts to sustain the acres of pasture, grains, cotton, fruits, nuts, and vegetables. Wildlife refuges dot the valley, serving as bird oases along the Pacific flyway.

Northern California's heart is the San Francisco Bay Area, home to 6 million people. The East and South Bay regions support two premier universities, the cities of Oakland and San Jose, and the high-tech Silicon Valley. To the north, Marin County is home to the active, wealthy, and politically correct—and possibly more therapists per capita then anywhere else in the world. The Wine Country, North Coast, and Monterey Peninsula surround the bay with a reservoir of scenic beauty, arts, culture, and cuisine.

The center of it all is the incomparable city of San Francisco—America's favorite. No California visit is complete without a stroll through Chinatown, a trip to Alcatraz, and a walk on the Golden Gate Bridge. Don't miss what the late columnist Herb Caen called the "Baghdad by the bay."

You will taste the blended spirit of Northern Californians as you explore. It's a region that's close in time to its roots, close geologically to both splendor and destruction, close technologically to the cutting edge, and close culturally to just about everything.

HISTORY

Before European explorers arrived, about 250,000 Indians inhabited California, living in small, hunter-gatherer tribes. They spoke many different dialects, which prevented extensive interaction. Most subsisted on the natural bounty of their home and migratory territories—fish, shellfish, and birds along the coast; acorn meal, deer, and small game farther inland.

In 1542 Juan Rodríquez Cabrillo and his crew were the first Europeans to see what would become the western United States when they sailed north along the coast from Spanish-ruled Mexico. Though Cabrillo died on the way, his crew mapped the coast and claimed it for Spain. The claim changed hands when English pirate Sir Francis Drake sailed into a coastal bay for repairs—probably Drakes Bay south of Point Reyes—and claimed the area for Queen Elizabeth. The Spanish returned in 1602, landing in Monterey and reasserting sovereignty.

Settlement began in 1769 when Father Junipero Serra and Gaspar de Portola led an expedition to found missions along the coast. By 1823, 21 missions had been established, most separated by "a hard day's travel" along *El Camino Real* (the King's Highway). Military garrisons, or presidios, were created to secure Spanish control. Ultimately the missions brought more death than salvation by introducing disease to the Indian population.

In 1833, 13 years after Mexico's independence from Spain, state support for the missions ended and they fell into disuse. To encourage settlement, Mexico issued huge land grants to ranchers who produced hides and tallow for export. In the same period, American opportunity seekers trickled in by sea, and Russian sea otter hunters operated along the northern coast.

American settlers began arriving in the 1840s via overland routes devised by Captain John C. Fremont, Kit Carson, and others. In 1846, hearing that the U.S. had declared war on Mexico, settlers in Sonoma staged the Bear Flag Revolt. They seized the home of an unresisting General M. G. Vallejo, raised the Bear Flag over the square, and created the California Republic. The republic was soon disestablished and the Bear Flag exchanged for the Stars and Stripes. U.S. troops occupied the presidios, and California became an American territory.

On January 24, 1848, James Marshall was working on John Sutter's sawmill in the Sierra foothills when he discovered gold in the millrace. The news quickly spread, and within two years California's population swelled from 15,000 to 100,000—the Gold Rush was on. San Francisco blossomed as a center of trade, wealth, and power. California gained statehood in 1850 and, through political power plays, divided up many land grant rancheros, making them available to speculators and settlers. California was well established by the time the boom faded—agriculture picked up the slack when the easy gold and silver were gone. The Civil War had little impact on the state, save to encourage economic self-reliance.

High hopes following the completion of the transcontinental railroad in 1869 were dashed in the 1870s. Inflated land prices, cheap eastern goods, and an oversupply of labor led to the "Black Friday" of April 26, 1875, when the Bank of California shut its doors to stop a run. Recovery was gradual, but the rich resources of the state fueled continuing expansion.

By the dawn of the twentieth century, San Francisco had risen to a peak of wealth and gilded corruption. All the glory came crashing down at 5:12 a.m. on April 18, 1906, when the first "Big One" hit. A devastating earthquake led to fires that destroyed about three-fourths of the buildings in the city. San Franciscans still live with the heritage of community and industry that rebuilt the city, knowing all along that another "Big One" will come some day. The Panama Pacific International Exposition of 1915 celebrated the return of San Francisco, grander than ever.

Several waves of immigration swelled California's population. From 1910 to 1920, Mexicans fleeing revolution moved to the state in large numbers. The depression years brought refugees from dust bowl states. During World War II, thousands of defense workers came to the Bay Area and stayed. After the war, thousands of soldiers elected to remain as well.

Recent history is as complex as 10 million people living in such a diverse region might produce. San Francisco has welcomed Beat poets, flower children, immigrants, and gays. Berkeley has hosted the Free Speech Movement, anti-war protests, and social reform activism. Silicon Valley has grown into the world's high-tech leader. César Chávez led farm worker unionization in the Salinas Valley. Environmentalists have battled farmers over water rights issues and loggers over forest preservation. Suburban sprawl has eaten up rural land while creating traffic nightmares. And still, Northern California grows, struggles, and triumphs.

ARTS AND CULTURE

From afar, the Northern California culture seems singular and distinctive. The image of laid-back, post-hippie liberals sipping wine and lattes in the "land of fruits and nuts" is a widespread caricature. The truth, of course, is far more complex—though, thankfully, those who feed the stereotype can be found in relative abundance.

San Francisco is undoubtedly the capital of "culture." High society money and taste sustain the excellent symphony, ballet, opera, and fine arts museums. The chief newspaper still runs a society column with photos showing who's who chatting with who-else-is-who at fundraiser socials. In and around the city, there is no shortage of wealth, along with its antiquated habits and its thoroughly posh lifestyle.

The gay community in San Francisco, though not a monolithic culture, explodes the blandness of stodgy old money. Few can experience a Gay Pride parade without gaining respect for the extremes of personal expression. The ongoing fight of gays and lesbians for equal rights, acceptance, and an end to AIDS shows in the efforts of independent filmmakers, writers, and artists.

Many in the largely Hispanic Mission District have lived close to political and economic struggle for years. The Mission is also a hip area to live for the young and visionary—hip with an edge. Political sentiment is left-leaning, and the art, poetry, and theater born in the area often express that sentiment. The city's best and most passionate murals are found on Mission walls.

Chinatown is a city within a city, and the heart of the rich Chinese culture of San Francisco. Many here are direct descendants of the workers who came to build the transcontinental railroad in the 1860s. The Chinese New Year Parade in February, and other celebrations, are bright spots in San Francisco's calendar of events.

In general, the cultural core of San Francisco, Oakland, Berkeley, and Marin integrates a rich variety of arts and people with great aplomb. Black-tied connoisseurs, beer-bellied bigots, green-haired skaters, politically correct vegans, Harley-riding dykes, pocket protector nerds, Beemer cruising homeys, baggy pants grungers, tie-dyed freaks, and just plain folks rub elbows daily—and they like it that way.

San Jose, Sacramento, and many smaller cities have fine symphonies, dance and theater companies, and ethnic enclaves of their own. Details are found in the regional chapters, and through local periodicals, tourist literature, and Web sites.

Move away from the city scene, and the arts and culture sort themselves out a bit. Artistic centers like Carmel and Mendocino yield calmer works, usually inspired by nature. Popular music shifts from heady and angst-draining, to friendly, lyrical, and folksy.

Small, rural communities far from San Francisco resent their dependency on distant politics and economics. The outward friendliness of a culture may hide much, as in Humboldt County, where the two main sources of income—marijuana growing and logging—are both under constant pressure. Yet, some of the most spiritually centered art comes from more isolated regions of the state. Of course, so do chainsaw-carved redwood bears.

CUISINE

As a whole, Californians consume as many Big Macs and Diet Pepsis as anyone. The cities and suburbs are home to the same fast-food joints and convenience stores that we all know and love. The region is firmly in the grip of contemporary pop cuisine. However . . .

When you step above the standard fare, the picture is bright indeed! The region is blessed with a wealth of fine foods, including the best produce around. When these ingredients are provided to a thoroughly international cadre of chefs and restaurateurs, the results range from darn good to spectacular. San Francisco, Berkeley, Oakland, Marin County, the Wine Country, North Coast, and Monterey Peninsula are all rich in quality eating opportunities, ranging from fine to funky.

The most interesting restaurants and cafés offer a marvelous synthesis of styles unique to the region. Sometimes, the best you can do in categorizing a menu is to apply terms such as "mixed grill," "eclectic cuisine," or "fusion cooking."

At Chez Panisse, in Berkeley's "Gourmet Ghetto," chef Alice Waters pioneered "California cuisine," an ideal blend of French basics, international contributions, health consciousness, and inspiration. Individual dishes may have various ethnic roots, but are generally on the lighter side, featuring liberal use of fresh produce, which is often locally grown or regionally authentic. Vegetarian alternatives are strongly represented on many menus, and artful presentation is stressed.

The influence of California cuisine has spread to most nonethnic and nontraditional menus in the state. You'll often find Euro-style or

Asian treatments of meat, seafood, and pasta, along with a rice or exotic grain side dish, multigrain bread, and designer salad. Marvelous omelet and frittata breakfasts may feature ingredients you simply can't find in Kansas. Lunch sandwiches and salads are the greenest anywhere.

Competition is stiff enough up and down the coast that Denny's-grade food can only be found at Denny's. The rest of the state is less enlightened, although islands of creativity can be found everywhere.

FLORA AND FAUNA

Since the end of unregulated exploitation, California sea mammals have enjoyed a vigorous recovery. Gray whales migrate south in December and January, returning north from February through April. The beach at Año Nuevo is rarely empty of elephant seals, with peak concentrations present during mating and calving from mid-December into March. Seals and sea lions congregate on rocks or isolated beaches along the coast. South of Santa Cruz, sea otters can be seen floating beyond the surf, preening, and cracking shellfish.

Ocean fisheries are struggling, but several sea life reserves protect rich ecosystems. At low tide you can find starfish and anemones in tidal pools, as divers search for abalone in the shallows.

On shore, beach grasses and duneland creepers give way to coastal meadows and shrubby scrub. On the central coast, Monterey cypress and pine shape themselves to shed the wind. Jackrabbits, mice, and ground birds hide from searching coyotes and soaring raptors. In coastal wetlands, algae and eelgrass yield to cordgrass, pickleweed, and heath. Shorebirds are plentiful.

The "fog fence" divides the moisture-loving coastal forest from the drier interior ecosystems. Redwood-dominated, mixed-evergreen forest thrives in the wet north. As you move south, the redwoods concentrate into cooler valleys while the coverage of pine, oak, and madrone increases. Deer are plentiful, as are raccoon, skunk, fox, and other small mammals.

Inland from the coast, oak-dotted, grassy hills ring the Central Valley. Fields of California poppy, goldfields, and lupines paint the hillsides in spring, while summer turns all to brown and gold. Thick oak and chaparral concentrate into steep defiles defended by poison oak, while shiny-leafed manzanita blends into the mountain forests above. Mountain lions stalk their prey in the remote high country.

In the Central Valley, the sea of grass that once hosted antelope and herds of tule elk is long gone. Native species have been displaced by aggressive alien species, overgrazing, and cultivation. Tule reed wetlands have been drained, and rivers diked and channeled. Only isolated areas resemble what once was, though the valley plays host to thousands of resident and migratory birds. Egrets, herons, cranes, ducks, swans, and geese frequent wildlife refuges, wetlands, and the Sacramento delta.

Ponderosa pine dominates lower Sierra slopes, with sugar pine, incense cedar, and fir growing higher up. Sequoia groves are found between 5,000 and 7,500 feet. While the grizzly bear displayed on the state flag is now extinct in California, black bears are numerous. They forage through the woods seeking plants, berries, small animals, and carrion. Higher still, a subalpine forest of red fir and lodgepole pine climbs toward the tree line where gnarled foxtail pines cling to life. Above this, marmots whistle among the lichen-covered granite while hikers photograph the diverse wildflowers and tundra-like vegetation of alpine meadows.

White fir, Jeffrey pine, and quaking aspen are common on the dry, eastern slopes of the Sierras and Cascades. Pinyon-juniper forests appear in the middle elevations, while pungent sagebrush spreads throughout the semiarid eastern basins. Above it all, herds of bighorn sheep graze the high vales.

Forests of redwood and Douglas fir grow in the wet and mountainous northwest. Remnant herds of Roosevelt elk can be found grazing in national park lands. Moving eastward, the land dries in stages. The forest changes to pine and pinyon-juniper, and then into range land, sagebrush basins, and barren alkali flats.

THE LAY OF THE LAND

Northern California offers distinct landforms on a scale you won't find elsewhere. Dominating the state is the vast pairing of the Sierra Nevada range with the great Central Valley at its feet. Together they are almost 400 miles long and more than 100 miles wide—a geologically simple range and valley combination as large as the state of Pennsylvania!

The Sierras rise gradually from the Central Valley up to the high peaks on the eastern side of the range. From there the mountains drop sharply into valleys and basins. In the Owens Valley, the elevation drops two vertical miles, from 14,495-foot Mount Whitney to the valley floor. To the east, the White Mountains with their sparse crown of ancient bristlecone pines also reach to more than 14,000 feet, adding to the spectacular scale of the valley below.

The high elevations of the western Sierras feature U-shaped, glacier-cut valleys. The most famous are Kern Canyon in the wilderness of Sequoia National Park, Kings Canyon (the nation's deepest) in Kings Canyon National Park, and Yosemite Valley. As the mountains fall westward, the valleys sort themselves into deep-cut watersheds with long, gradual ridges in between.

The Sierra rivers drain into the Sacramento River in the north and the San Juaquin in the south, both of which flow through the Central Valley and into the Sacramento delta. Here, sluggish waters pass through a thousand miles of canals and sloughs before eventually emptying into San Francisco Bay, then flowing beneath the Golden Gate and into the Pacific.

The mountains of the Coast Range are lower than the Sierras, rising to forested heights of 6,000 feet or more in a few spots, but generally running in long north-south ridges with 1,000- to 3,000-foot summits. The valleys provide warm homes for towns, farms, and vineyards, while hillside pastures host sheep and cattle.

Moving northward, the peaks of the Sierras dwindle, those of the Coast Range rise, and the southern reaches of the Klamath and Cascade Ranges intrude. The landscape becomes rugged and confused, rivers cut tortuous paths to the Pacific, and forest cover increases. The land is wet and wild, drying in steps as you move eastward, with successive peaks and ranges blocking the flow of moisture.

The northeastern corner of the state is a land of volcanic cones, broad plateaus with exposed lava fields, and the beginnings of the basin and range landform which dominates Nevada. Mount Shasta rises like a glacier-capped sentinel. Mount Lassen—which blew its top in 1915— marks the southern end of the Cascade Range. The northeast offers wide forests, broad valleys, lonely lakes, and primeval geology to the intrepid traveler.

OUTDOOR ACTIVITIES

California's extensive public lands offer great hiking opportunities. Day hike destinations include the summit of Mount Lassen, the passes and summits above Lake Tahoe, the Methuselah Trail in the

Ancient Bristlecone Pine Forest, the Redwood Mountain Grove Trail in Sequoia National Park, Paradise Valley in Kings Canyon National Park, Mono Pass in the Yosemite high country, Yosemite Falls and the north rim of the valley, and Calaveras Big Trees State Park. In the west, many good hikes are found in the coastal Marin wildlands, Tomales Point in Point Reyes National Seashore, several state parks on the North Coast, Punta Gorda Lighthouse on the Lost Coast, the Bull Creek Trail in Humboldt Redwoods State Park, Redwood Creek Trail in Redwood National Park, and Fern Canyon in Prairie Creek Redwoods State Park. There are many others of merit. In coastal and foothill areas, follow tick prevention advice and watch out for poison oak!

Extended backpacking and horse pack trips can be enjoyed in several areas, the most spectacular being the High Sierras. Together with some smaller protected areas, the Golden Trout Wilderness, Sequoia National Park, Kings Canyon National Park, John Muir Wilderness, Ansel Adams Wilderness, and the southern half of Yosemite National Park preserve the lower 48's largest contiguous roadless area. North of Yosemite, great wilderness areas include the Desolation Wilderness, located above Lake Tahoe, and the lake and granite country of the Emigrant Wilderness. The Trinity Alps Wilderness and Marble Mountain Wilderness are the best of the northern mountains. At the crest of the Coast Range, east of Big Sur, the Ventana Wilderness features highland forest hiking with volcanic summits. The Pacific Crest Trail runs the length of the Sierras, crosses west to the Klamath Mountains, and then turns east again to the southern Cascades.

Mountain biking was invented in Marin County and is immensely popular throughout the region. Areas featuring miles of marked and mapped trails, good rental shops, and lots of riders include the west Marin wildlands, the East Bay hills above Berkeley and Oakland, the peninsula hills from Santa Cruz to San Francisco, the Lake Tahoe basin, and the Mammoth Lakes region. Road biking is also popular in the state. Backroads and minor highways in the southern Coast Range and Sierra foothills offer great rides through open rolling country.

Climbing options abound in the Sierras. While the faces of Yosemite are legendary, the same hard granite appears throughout the range. Other popular destinations include Castle Crags State Park and Pinnacles National Monument. Mountaineers enjoy various routes in the Sierras and the Trinity Alps, and Mount Shasta attracts fans of glaciers and exposed summits.

Rafting and kayaking are particularly popular in the rivers that drain the Sierras. The various forks of the Feather, Yuba, Tuolumne, and other rivers are well served by rental shops and guide outfits. The American River is a particularly good choice for novice river runners. In the northern mountains, the Klamath, Eel, and Trinity Rivers offer good runs, while the Salmon River is renowned for white-water challenge. For a one-stop inquiry, call Whitewater Voyages, (800) 488-7238, a large company that offers a variety of trips on several rivers. Canoeing is popular on quiet segments of rivers such as the Russian and Eel, as well as in the calm waters of lakes and estuaries.

Ocean sports are enjoyed up and down the coast, though cold water and rough surf offer stiff challenges along many stretches. Surfers frequent several areas along the peninsula between Santa Cruz and San Francisco and also in Humboldt County on the North Coast. Windsurfers enjoy the stiff breezes and modest swells of San Francisco Bay. Sea kayaking is newly popular in the region. Diving locations, instruction, and equipment rental shops can be found in Monterey and on the North Coast.

Soaring and hot-air balloon trips can be enjoyed in the Napa Valley and elsewhere. Tahoe is a good location for both paragliding and parasailing. Certain bluffs on the peninsula coast are popular with hang gliders.

Rivers and lakes in the northern mountains offer the best trout and steelhead fishing. Wild populations are strong above the dams in the Sierras and in some coastal rivers. Stocked waters are options elsewhere. The salmon situation is grim. A California fishing license can be purchased for $27 at California Fish and Game offices or fishing stores.

PRACTICAL TIPS

HOW MUCH WILL IT COST?

Travel in Northern California tends to be somewhat expensive. Gasoline prices are generally higher than elsewhere due to strict emissions laws, high state taxes, specially formulated gasolines, and some price inflation in the cities. Even though an oil glut in early 1998 led to prices well below $1 per gallon in many states, California prices remained higher, with San Francisco drivers paying over $1.30. In a vehicle averaging 20 mpg at a gas price of $1.25 per gallon, a 2,000-mile state tour will cost $125. In a 5-mpg motor home, the same trip comes to $500.

Expensive lodging can be found almost anywhere, but even budget prices are inflated in certain areas. Wine Country, the Russian River Valley, the coasts of Mendocino and Sonoma, Lake Tahoe, parts of the Gold Country, Big Sur, the Monterey Peninsula, and San Francisco all tend to be pricey. In vacation areas, room rates climb between 10 and 30 percent in the summer, and between 20 and 50 percent on summer weekends. Inns and bed-and-breakfasts will often have two-day minimum stays for Friday and Saturday nights from May through September. Private campgrounds may show similar changes. This occurs because accommodations are generally booked solid in these peak periods and locations, and often well in advance.

Basic campsites generally range from $10 to $25, sites with hookups from $15 to $35. Motel 6–style and private budget motels list double occupancy rates from $35 to $60. The range for mid-grade places is broader, but expect to pay from $50 to $100 in the off season or off the beaten track, $70 to $160 at other times. In popular areas, the nice inns, bed-and-breakfasts, and hotels with history or character usually range from $80 to $150. Spa suites with views can climb toward $250, while Euro-style rooms with a shared bath may be as low as $50. Fine hotels range from $130 to outer space. Note, too, that most counties have some variation of a bed tax that adds about 10 percent to the bill.

Dining costs are also somewhat inflated in the popular destinations, although stiff competition and consistently hungry locals assure that good budget choices are generally available everywhere. The egg, potato, burger, fries, and pasta-style budget traveler, who opts to eat every meal out, will spend about $25 to $40 dollars a day, tax and tip included. Switch to an omelet breakfast, lunch special, and fish dinner with wine, and you're talking $40 to $70. Clearly, free or light breakfasts and picnic lunches will save you money while fine-dining blowouts have the opposite effect.

In sum, two people—driving about 150 miles per day in an average car, mixing camping with average lodging and the occasional charming inn, blending average meals with picnics and the occasional splurge, paying admissions fees at various sites, and buying the odd souvenir—could spend about $1,100 per week. You'll have to determine your own niche.

Note: For the most part, only regular adult admission prices are included with regional chapter listings. Student, senior, and child prices for the majority of attractions are discounted from 10 percent to 50 percent. Very young children are often admitted free. Savings can be substantial.

CLIMATE

For the most part, Northern California offers pleasant weather throughout the year, particularly in the coastal regions south of Eureka. Rain amounts rise and fall in a steady bell curve, peaking in December and January while leaving most of the region bone-dry in July. Extended rainy periods are possible any time from October through March. The winter of 1997–98 saw the effects of El Niño, which produced rain for weeks on end. Floods and mudslides were common—a good reason to make sure coast and mountain roads are open before you use them (use the road information number at the end of this chapter).

In the warmer months, the Bay Area enjoys a remarkable and complex system of microclimates. Prevailing westerly winds send cool air flowing through the Golden Gate on most days of the year. This air chills the tip of the city, then flows across the bay and washes up onto the hills above Berkeley and Oakland. Move up or down the bay away from this tongue of air, and the temperature rises dramatically. When it's 68 degrees Fahrenheit on Alcatraz, it can be 85 degrees Fahrenheit in San Jose.

Fog and low rain clouds follow similar patterns. Fog occurs year-round along the coast, though it is particularly common through the nights and mornings of the summer, burning off briefly in the afternoons. By choosing an inn a little higher on the hill or a campsite on the inland side of the ridge, you might enjoy a beautiful sunset or dry tent instead of a dank sea of gray. In San Francisco, someone in the fog zone might experience hundreds more hours of fog in a year than a friend over the hill, just a few blocks away!

Cross over the last ridge east of the coast, and you enter the Central Valley. Here—and in several other inland valleys with low elevation—it is notoriously hot in the summer. While San Francisco is balmy, the San Jose basin and the Napa Valley can be oppressive, simply because coastal mountains block ocean-cooled air from moderating the temperature. Though it's milder in the winter, the Central Valley often experiences "tule fog"—a thick-as-pea-soup blanket that causes serious, chain-reaction car wrecks every year.

Heavy snows close several main roads through the Sierra Nevada all winter long, though Yosemite Valley and the highways to Lake Tahoe are open year-round. Anyone traveling the mountainous areas of California in winter is required by law to carry chains or to drive a four-wheel-drive vehicle with snow tires. High-mountain weather is generally mild in the summer, though occasional storms can cause delays and road problems. The lower slopes and foothills can be almost as hot as the Central Valley.

The far northwest approaches rain forest conditions in certain coastal areas. Moisture that amounts to little more than a half-day fog in Monterey gathers into persistent, drizzly masses around Eureka. These conditions, however, are natural for the magnificent redwood groves. At the cost of wearing a rain jacket, you will enjoy the forest at its finest.

In the northeast, it's dry, though rain or snow falls with fair frequency on the high western slopes of the mountain ridges that march eastward into the basin and range country of Nevada.

WHEN TO GO

With the variety of destination and activity choices available in Northern California, there's a case to be made for visiting at any time of the year.

In the winter, rain is more frequent, but it follows the vagaries of the jet stream and can be absent for weeks at a time. Unlike most areas of the country, California begins to "green up" as soon as the rains come. The coastal hills are particularly beautiful when the new grass pushes through the old—something that can begin to happen as early as December! Winter sports are an obvious option in the mountains. You can count on easy traveling in cool to mild temperatures everywhere else—though all bets are off when El Niño is in effect. If the weather has been wild for awhile, check on your route using the road conditions phone number listed at the end of this chapter.

Spring can bring the best of all possible worlds. The rainy season is over, coastal hills are lush and green, and the summer fogs haven't arrived—nor have the crowds of visitors that arrive with them. Water from melting snow gushes over waterfalls and provides peak thrills to rafters. Spring skiers can enjoy a day on the slopes above Tahoe, then sit by the lake in shorts and watch the sailboats. You'll enjoy shoulder-season lodging prices and availability until mid-April, when things begin to tighten up.

In summer, the hills turn gold, the beaches are warm (though the water stays cold!), and the tourists arrive. While the valleys get hot, the high mountain areas open up for exploration. Spring conditions come late to the high country so that hikers and bikers are greeted by fresh growth and wildflowers. If your visit must be in summer, focus on coastal and mountain areas and save the valleys and foothills for another time. Plan on doing more advance work reserving rooms and campsites—and plan on spending more money. Note also that traffic floods out of urban areas on Friday afternoons and then floods back in again when the weekend is done.

Things quiet down again after Labor Day. Cooler days and crisper nights return, prices drop, availability rises, and travelers go back to work or school. The mountains offer ideal conditions for backpacking since passes are open and streams are low and easy to cross. Fall colors are particularly enticing along the eastern slope of the High Sierra, and in the aspen-tree zones high up on the western slope.

CALIFORNIA SESQUICENTENNIAL

When to go" is not just a question of climate and crowds. Those who visit Northern California at the turn of the millennium will have the chance to share in the events and exhibits of the state's three-year-long sesquicentennial celebration. The year 1998 marks the 150th anniversary of the discovery of gold in the Sierras, while 1999 is the year to recognize the inrush of the forty-niners—the first major wave of immigrants from around the world to the state. And on top of all else that will be going on, the year 2000 will be California's 150th birthday!

Sacramento, San Francisco, Oakland, and many other communities will be hosting special ceremonies and celebrations to mark various events of California's early days. While there are many local events going on, they may not be well coordinated or publicized at the state level. It is worth it to inquire directly regarding the specific areas you plan to visit. The best central resources for up-to-date information on what's happening are the Web site and publications offered by California State Parks (1416 Ninth Street, Sacramento, CA 95814, 916-653-6995, www.cal-parks.ca.gov) and the California Sesquicentennial office (1020 O Street, Suite 301, Sacramento, CA 95814, 916-653-9599, www.gocalif.ca.gov). Other sources of information include chambers of commerce, county museums, historical societies, and tourism Web sites.

NORTHERN CALIFORNIA CLIMATE

Average daily high and low temperatures in degrees Fahrenheit, plus monthly precipitation in inches.

	San Francisco	Sacramento	Truckee	Eureka
Jan.	55/42	53/39	38/16	54/41
	4.5	3.8	5.6	6
Mar.	62/45	65/44	46/21	55/43
	3	2.8	4.3	5.3
May	67/50	80/52	60/36	58/48
	.5	.3	1.2	1.4
July	72/54	95/59	81/43	61/52
	.1	.1	.4	.1
Sept.	74/54	90/57	73/37	62/51
	.3	.4	.9	.9
Nov.	64/46	65/44	52/24	58/45
	2.5	3	4.4	6.4

TRANSPORTATION

Car Travel

Three key highway corridors provide access to the best sights of Northern California with the least amount of extraneous driving: CA 1 with U.S. 101, CA 49, and CA 89 with U.S. 395.

CA 1 and **U.S. 101**: These two highways parallel each other through coastal California, from below Big Sur until they merge near Eureka. The Coast Highway, CA 1, is a slow, winding, sometimes tortuous two-lane road that hugs the edge of the continent. But this is the route for enjoying the spectacular California coastline. U.S. 101 parallels the coast, about 20 miles or so inland, until it becomes the coast highway north of Eureka. It provides the most direct access to the Bay Area, Wine Country, and redwood parks.

If time is tight and you'll pass through the coastal region only once, drive the Big Sur Coast on CA 1 from San Luis Obispo to Monterey. Cut in to U.S. 101 to see San Francisco and the Wine Country, then take CA 128 through the Anderson Valley and back out to CA 1 for the Mendocino Coast.

CA 49: Numbered in honor of the forty-niners of Gold Rush days, CA 49 winds through the Sierra foothills from Oakhurst, south of Yosemite, to Nevada City. It then follows the Yuba River Valley up and over the mountains toward Nevada. The road passes through numerous historic towns that are well worth a look. With Gold Rush sesquicentennial events and exhibits featured throughout 1998–99, CA 49 is of particular interest to visitors.

Many good loops incorporating segments of CA 49 are possible. All three western access roads to Yosemite cross CA 49, as do four High Sierra pass roads, Interstate 80, and CA 89. From Oakhurst at the southern end of CA 49, Fresno and the access to Sequoia and Kings Canyon National Parks are temptingly close. If time is short and history is not a priority, skip CA 49 as a general route and head for the high mountains. You can use information in the "Gold Country" chapter to choose a spot or two to visit near your route through the foothills.

CA 89 and **U.S. 395**: This route is to the mountains what CA 1 is to the coast, though it is generally much faster. CA 89 starts at the foot of Mount Shasta, runs south through lonely forest country, and reaches an altitude of 8,000 feet as it winds through Lassen Volcanic

National Park. Continuing past Lake Almanor, it passes through lovely high valleys, along the scenic western shore of Lake Tahoe, and through gorgeous mountain passes before it meets U.S. 395 and ends. Continuing south, U.S. 395 passes through jumbled volcanic terrain, past amazing Mono Lake, on through hot springs country near Mammoth, and down into the spectacular Owens Valley.

Except for the Tahoe area, this corridor is relatively lightly traveled. Side roads take you to lovely High Sierra valleys, Yosemite National Park, the Ancient Bristlecone Pine Forest, and Bodie State Historic Park. Loops are hard south of Yosemite, but easy to the north.

Air Travel

San Francisco, San Jose, Sacramento, and Oakland are busy hubs of interstate travel. Most major airlines have long-distance routes to San Francisco. Several, including Alaska, American, Reno Air, Southwest, and United Shuttle, offer frequent discount flights to various western cities.

While San Francisco International Airport (SFO) provides the most direct access to the city, the Oakland Airport is more relaxed and easier to navigate. Staying in the East Bay can be easier and a bit cheaper than San Francisco. Shuttles link both airports with the Bay Area Rapid Transit system (BART). Take the SAMTRANS 3X bus from SFO (15 minutes, $1), or the AirBART shuttle from Oakland (20 minutes, $2).

Rail Travel

Though the heyday of passenger trains is long past, there's still nothing that can compare to the relaxed magic of rail travel. Imagine sipping a cool drink in the dome car as you gaze into a canyon, or dining on fresh eggs and toast as stunning Mount Shasta slides slowly by.

Two great Amtrak trains make daily runs through California. The *California Zephyr* leaves Oakland for Chicago in the morning, climbs over Donner Pass, and arrives in Reno in the early evening. The westbound trip arrives in Reno in the morning, Oakland in the afternoon. The *Coast Starlight* goes from Los Angeles to Oakland during the day, runs through the Central Valley at night, passes Mount Shasta in the morning, then travels on to Seattle. Southbound, it's Mount Shasta in the evening and Oakland in the morning. The timing is right on both of these runs for optimal daylight scenery viewing (though short daylight hours in the winter trim viewing time).

Amtrak also has shorter, more frequent runs with stops in the Central Valley, as well as private connector bus service that will take you to such places as Yosemite and Sequoia National Parks. Travelers to the Bay Area can transfer directly to BART (see below) at the Richmond station. Call (800) 872-7245 for reservations.

Urban Transit

San Francisco, Berkeley, Oakland, and several other communities are linked by the excellent BART (Bay Area Rapid Transit) system. In San Francisco, you can step off the BART and onto a cable car at the Embarcadero or Powell Street stations.

The MUNI bus and trolley systems in San Francisco cover the city like a blanket. AC Transit in the East Bay, SAMTRANS on the peninsula, and Golden Gate Transit in Marin County are all very good. Several ferry companies travel to San Francisco from Oakland and Marin County. CalTrain has frequent commuter train service on the peninsula between San Jose and San Francisco. In the Bay Area, parking can be expensive and the traffic, heavy. Consider a BART-based mass transit day of exploration.

San Jose and Sacramento both have light-rail and bus systems, though they are of more use to commuters than travelers. Attractions in these cities are generally in the central downtown area.

CAMPING, LODGING, AND DINING

With over half of Northern California protected in public lands of one kind or another, there is no shortage of quality campgrounds. U.S. National Forest campgrounds are renowned for providing beautiful, private sites for about $10 to $14 dollars. National and state park sites are often as good at an average price of $13 to $17. Private camping is much more varied in quality—you can find bad sites for $30 and great ones for $10—but RV and fifth-wheel campers will find hookups and pull-through sites more consistently available at private campgrounds.

The common problem of low availability on weekends and during peak season is magnified in the Northern California region. Mild year-round weather encourages weekenders to camp when the sun is out, even in the off season. In late spring and summer, Californians fleeing the city quickly jam campgrounds in popular areas. Call the park in which you hope to stay and ask if there are likely to be sites open at your arrival time. If not, use a reservation system to secure a spot. (Reservation numbers for the most frequently used campsites are listed under "Resources" at the end of this chapter.) Fees are charged by some services. While most or all state park sites may be reservable, National Forest sites are reservable only at certain popular campgrounds, with some sites always left for first-come, first-served use.

Free camping is legal in dispersed campsites on Bureau of Land Management and Forest Service lands, as well as at certain highway pullouts. It's also fairly common wherever hidden turnouts on unused roads suggest that a quiet sleep won't ruffle any feathers.

Northern California is blessed with scores of wonderful lodging options. Bed-and-breakfasts and charming inns abound, particularly in Wine Country and along the coast. Nineteenth- and early twentieth-century historic hotels have been lovingly restored in many towns. Modern resorts and hotels, chain motels, and mom-and-pop options fill out the list nicely. The same availability suggestions apply to any and all lodging alternatives in popular areas: *check ahead and reserve when advised.*

This guide features a varied lodging list, giving special attention to unique, historic, outstanding, or necessary alternatives. In areas where one type of lodging dominates—expensive, romantic getaway inns on the North Coast for example—effort is made to list types appropriate to other budgets and travel styles. All prices listed are for double occupancy. Price ranges reflect basic room to luxury suite differences as well as seasonal variations. Those interested in thorough listings of one type of lodging should consult sources such as a B&B guide. Suggestions are listed below in "Recommended Reading." The reservation and information numbers for several national hotel and motel chains are listed below in the "Resources" section.

With the ocean nearby, the best wines in the country, excellent produce, and a cuisine all its own, California is a fine-diner's paradise. Even budget travel couples should try to reserve an extra $100 (or more) for a one-time splurge. Many fine restaurants are quite casual, so dusty walking shoes and a worn polo shirt won't cause a stir. Listings are usually lunch and dinner places unless specifically noted as breakfast spots. Many restaurants are closed one or two days a week, often Sunday, Monday, and/or Tuesday. This is not specified in the listings, so call ahead.

RECOMMENDED READING

Adventure Cycling in Northern California put out by the Adventure Cycling Association—has an excellent selection of road and mountain bike rides.

California Hiking by Tom Stienstra and Ann Marie Brown—details numerous great hikes throughout the state.

California Historical Landmarks (California Office of Historic Preservation)—records the writing of every historic plaque in the state. It's a good rough historic guide for choosing stops and routes.

Chez Panisse Cooking by Paul Bertolli with Alice Waters—Learn the secrets of one of the world's most famous restaurants.

Gold Rush: A Literary Exploration edited by Michael Kowalewski—This outstanding collection is as good as it gets. Selections include pieces by Bret Harte, Mark Twain, and many others.

The Grapes of Wrath; *Cannery Row*; *East of Eden* by John Steinbeck—Several of Steinbeck's works are set in California.

Ishi in Two Worlds: A Biography of the Last Wild Indian in North America by Theodora Kroeber—tells the story of Ishi, last of the Yahi Indians, who wandered into the town of Oroville seeking help in 1911.

My First Summer in the Sierra (1869), *The Mountains of California* (1894), and *Steep Trails* (1918) by John Muir—Muir led the battle for preservation of Yosemite and other areas.

National Audubon Society Field Guide to California—includes plants, animals, wildflowers, birds, insects, weather, nature preserves and more.

On the Road by Jack Kerouac—a classic of the beat generation.

Oz Clarke's Wine Companion by Oz Clarke and Larry Walker—an excellent map/guide combination for designing your Wine Country journey.

The Valley of the Moon by Jack London—set in the Sonoma Valley. London grew up in Oakland, later working in canneries and on the docks. He lived the last years of his life with his wife near Glen Ellen.

RESOURCES

American Automobile Association: (800) 222-4357, for emergencies only

California Division of Tourism: (800) 862-2543, P.O. Box 1499, Sacramento, CA 95812-1499

California Highway Patrol Road Information: (800) 427-7623 California State Parks: (916) 653-6995, 1416 Ninth Street, Sacramento, CA 95814

Campground Reservation Numbers

California State Parks: (800) 444-7275 (ParkNet—$7.50 fee)

National Forests: (800) 280-2267 ($7.50 fee)
National Parks & Monuments: (800) 365-CAMP
Yosemite National Park: (800) 436-PARK
Lodging Chain Reservation Numbers
  Best Western: 800-528-1234
  Clarion Inn: 800-CLARION
  Comfort Inn: 800-228-5150
  Days Inn: 800-325-2525
  Econolodge: 800-55-ECONO
  Hilton: 800-HILTON-7
  Holiday Inn: 800-HOLIDAY
  Marriott: 800-228-9290
  Motel 6: 800-4-MOTEL-6
  Quality Suites: 800-228-5151
  Ramada Inns: 800-2-RAMADA
  Red Lion: 800-RED-LION
  Sheraton: 800-325-3535
  Sleep Inn: 800-SLEEP-IN
  Super 8: 800-800-8000
  Travelodge: 800-578-7878
National Forest Service: (415) 705-2874, 630 Sansome Street, San
  Francisco, CA 94111
National Park Service Western Region Information Center: (415)
  556-0560, Fort Mason Building 201, San Francisco, CA 94123

Web sites (all begin with http://)
  California Festivals: little.fishnet.net/~eelove/ (lists all the
    fairs and festivals by month)
  California State Home Page: www.ca.gov (many links)
  California State Parks: ceres.ca.gov/ceres/calweb/parks.phtml
  California Travel & Tourism: www.gocalif.gov (lots of info)
  Gold Country Museums: www.malakoff.com/muse.htm
  Historical Landmarks: www.donaldlaird.com/landmarks (fea-
    tures every state historical landmark)
  Museumlink: www.museumlink.com/californ.htm (many links
    to individual museums throughout the state)
  National Parks: www.nps.gov/parks.html
  San Francisco: www.sanfrancisco.com (arts and cultural listings)
  Yahoo: www.yahoo.com/Regional/U_S__States/California (a
    great central source for established California Web sites) good as
    a rough historic guide for choosing stops and routes.

SAN FRANCISCO

Hong Kong offers more glitter and steeper hills. New York has more urban muscle. Paris is grander, Prague more magical, Cairo more ancient, and Venice more romantic. Peoria has less traffic. Every city can claim to have something on San Francisco, but very few can claim, like San Francisco, to have it all.

The "City by the Bay" is both an experiment and a museum. Strong curbs on development make the city appear to stand still, but ideas, art, and culture spin about the place like a cyclone. People come from around the world to reinvent themselves. Only intolerance is not tolerated by the body politic—San Francisco is as much a home to the socially wayward as to the socialites.

Above all, the city is beautiful. Despite the wounds and scars that urban and geological troubles have produced, San Francisco feels balanced and whole. No matter where you go, beauty is always only a glance away. Amazing bridges soar to wild headlands and harbor isles. Artful people stroll past splendid architecture. Fine parks, plazas, and promenades provide space for thought and exercise. The fog plays about the Golden Gate and breaks gently over the hills. Fresh Pacific air wipes the sky clean.

The original San Franciscans were the farthest flung of the pioneers—people who didn't park their wagon or hop off the boat until there was nowhere left to go. They came to the edge to find gold, glory, and freedom, and they stayed. Today, that same spirit is what makes this fabulous city America's favorite. ◼

SAN FRANCISCO

Sights

Ⓐ Alcatraz

Ⓑ Cable Cars

Ⓒ Chinatown

Ⓓ Civic Center

Ⓔ Coit Tower

Ⓕ Fisherman's Wharf

Ⓖ Fort Point

Ⓗ Golden Gate Bridge

Ⓘ Golden Gate Park

Ⓙ Lands End

Ⓚ Mission Dolores

Ⓛ Ocean Beach

Ⓜ Palace of Fine Arts

Ⓝ Presidio

Ⓞ San Francisco Maritime National Historical Park

Ⓟ Twin Peaks

Ⓠ Union Square

Ⓡ U.S.S. *Jeremiah O'Brien*

Ⓢ Yerba Buena Gardens and San Francisco Museum of Modern Art (SFMOMA)

A PERFECT DAY IN SAN FRANCISCO

To fully experience what San Francisco has to offer, you'll need something between a week and a lifetime. If a day is all you have, be ambitious and start early. I recommend walking, but taxis, the MUNI system, and cable cars can fill in the gaps.

Park near Union Square—there's an expensive garage right under the square with others nearby. Information, transit passes, and city maps are available at the city visitor center above Powell on Market. See Union Square, then walk down Grant Street through Chinatown. Enjoy the mix of Beat history, Chinatown, North Beach, and the red-light strip where Columbus meets Broadway. Follow Grant through North Beach, then head up Filbert to Coit Tower. Hit the waterfront via Washington Square. Gaze up Lombard to see the "crookedest street in the world" (walk it or drive it if you wish).

Pick up the Alcatraz tour tickets you reserved ahead of time at Pier 41. Before or after Alcatraz, browse Pier 39, Fisherman's Wharf, Hyde Street Pier, Ghirardelli Square, and the Municipal Pier in Aquatic Park. Catch a cable car at the Hyde Street turnaround and ride it back to Union Square. Visit Yerba Buena Gardens at Mission and Fourth if you have the time.

Pick up your car for an evening tour. Take Geary to Franklin, then Franklin to Bay Street. A left on Bay and a right on Laguna Street take you past Fort Mason and down to the Marina district. Enjoy the homes and views along Marina Boulevard. Turn left on Baker for a look at the Palace of Fine Arts. Back on Marina, bear left to the Golden Gate Bridge. Take the last exit before the toll plaza to reach the viewpoint for a bridge walk. Follow Lincoln west to 25th Avenue and Geary Boulevard, and turn right to reach Point Lobos Boulevard and the ruins of the Sutro Baths. A sunset walk on Ocean Beach followed by drinks and dinner at the Cliff House complete the day.

Follow Fulton to Stanyan for a nighttime drive down Haight Street. Turn right on Divisadero to the Castro, then head west up Market to Twin Peaks Boulevard for an unforgettable city-lights view from Twin Peaks. If you have energy left, pick a nightlife zone from the listings and enjoy.

SAN FRANCISCO NEIGHBORHOODS

For the most part, San Francisco is divided into fairly distinct districts, each of which has a focal area where lodging, restaurants, and nightlife options are centered. In the "Food" and "Lodging" sections of this chapter, listings are arranged by neighborhood.

SIGHTSEEING HIGHLIGHTS

Note that several San Francisco and Marin County sights are within the **Golden Gate National Recreation Area**. They include Alcatraz Island, Point Bonita Lighthouse, Stinson Beach, Muir Woods, the Marin Headlands, Fort Point, Ocean Beach, the Cliff House, Fort Mason, and the Presidio. For general and camping information, call the Pacific West Information Center at Fort Mason, (415) 556-0560.

★★★ **Alcatraz**—The word "Alcatraz" comes from the Spanish word for pelican—a bird that had this rock to itself for years uncounted. Around the time of the gold rush, a military garrison was stationed on Alcatraz to guard the bay. Military prisoners were held here because of the security provided by the cold, powerful tides. In 1933 Alcatraz became a federal prison that hosted Al Capone and the famous "Birdman" among others. The prison was closed in 1963 due to the high cost of service and maintenance. The ruins are now maintained and administered by the National Park Service.

When your boat arrives, you'll be guided up the hill and given a personal walkman for an excellent tape-guided tour of the prison. Outside, the island is alive with native plants and birds. Good walks take you to quiet spots with spectacular views of San Francisco, the Golden Gate Bridge, the Marin Headlands, and the bay. It is the island's location as much as its history that makes it a three-star sight.

The Blue & Gold Fleet offers Alcatraz packages, as well as scenic bay tours, dinner cruises, and other routes. Reserve your boat several days in advance if at all possible. Details: Alcatraz Island, San Francisco Bay; (415) 556-0560 for general information, (415) 705-5444 for Blue & Gold Fleet information, (415) 705-5555 for reservations. Round-trip boat fare is $7.75, tape tour is $3.25; boats depart daily from Pier 41 beginning at 9:30 a.m. Boat trip schedule varies, call for specific hours. (2½ hours)

★★★ **Chinatown**—Grant Street between Bush and Broadway is the heart of Chinatown and should not be missed. Walk along the narrow, crowded street, stepping into shops to search among the tacky souvenirs, intricate artworks, or unfathomable concoctions. Explore the maze of alleys around Jackson, Washington, or Clay Streets, and the less touristy Stockton Street. Pick a restaurant at random and plunge in to enjoy tea, dim sum, and the music of the language. Everything is compressed in Chinatown—slow down to see it well. Details: Grant Street, San Francisco. (1½ hours)

★★★ **Golden Gate Bridge**—Rarely are grace and power blended so perfectly as they are in the magnificent Golden Gate Bridge. Since its opening in 1937, it has stood as the West Coast equivalent of the Statue of Liberty. From all angles it is a wonder. Enjoy it from below at Fort Point or on a boat tour. Enjoy it from above with a drive onto the Marin Headlands. Walk out onto it, perhaps all the way across (a distance of 6,450 feet), to feel its scale and to wonder at the views.

Fort Point and the bridge walk can be reached via the southern view area. Take the last, small exit from U.S. 101 about 500 feet before the tollbooths, or approach via Lincoln Boulevard in the Presidio. The northern viewpoint is at the first exit at the north end of the bridge. To reach the headlands road and viewpoints, take the second exit, at Alexander Avenue, and loop under the highway. Details: Golden Gate

Bridge, San Francisco; open for walking (eastside) and biking (westside) daily from 5 a.m. to 9 p.m. (1 hour)

★★ **Cable Cars**—Cable cars operate by clamping on to a continuously moving steel cable that runs under the street. To stop, the operator releases the clutch lever while applying the brake. In their heyday, hundreds of cable cars operated along 100 miles of routes through the city. After the 1906 earthquake, the severely damaged system never recovered, and, by the middle of the century, they had all but disappeared. Citizens fought for their survival, and today you can ride the recently refurbished system through much of historic San Francisco.

You can buy tickets at the turnarounds or just board the car and pay the conductor. One line runs along California Street from the Embarcadero at the base of Market Street to Van Ness Avenue. Two other lines follow Powell Street from Market Street and Union Square to the Fisherman's Wharf area—one via Hyde Street, the other via Mason Street. Both are often crowded requiring a wait in line.

The **Cable Car Museum** features San Francisco's first cable car, built in 1873, along with other transit history displays. You can observe the power plant that drives the cables for all three lines in the basement. Details: 1201 Mason Street, San Francisco; (415) 474-1887; open daily from 10 a.m. to 6 p.m. (until 5 p.m. November through March). Donations are accepted. (½ hour)

★★ **Civic Center**—The **San Francisco City Hall**, built in 1914, is the centerpiece of this compact zone of government and fine arts buildings. If earthquake retrofitting has been completed, climb the Polk Street steps from the **Civic Center Plaza** for a look inside at the magnificent rotunda. Across the plaza on Larkin Street is the brand new **San Francisco Public Library**. Enter the library for a look at why the critics are raving.

Opposite City Hall, on Van Ness, are three outstanding fine arts performance halls. The opulent **War Memorial Opera House**, built in 1932, holds over 3,000 people and is home to the San Francisco Opera, (415) 864-3330, and San Francisco Ballet, (415) 865-2000. Next door, the **Veterans Building** holds the smaller **Herbst Auditorium**, (415) 392-4400, which features a varied slate of events. Across Grove Street, the **Louise M. Davies Symphony Hall** hosts the San Francisco Symphony, (415) 431-5400.

Details: Call (415) 552-8338 for tour information; combined tours are given on Mondays from 10 a.m. to 2 p.m. on the hour, departing from the Grove Street entrance of Davies Symphony Hall. Tours are $5. (1½ hours)

It should be noted that the Civic Center rubs elbows with the **Tenderloin**, a concentrated area of cheap hotels, porn shops, and homelessness. Though the area is basically safe, a daytime visit to the Civic Center may seem prudent. Details: The Civic Center is bounded by Market, Van Ness, and McAllister Streets, San Francisco. (1 hour)

★★ **Coit Tower**—Perched above North Beach on top of Telegraph Hill, Coit Tower is another enduring symbol of San Francisco. It was built by Lillie Coit in 1934 to honor her husband and his fellow fire-fighters. The top of the 210-foot tower is reached by elevator, and the views are splendid. Inside are historic murals painted by local artists. A small park surrounds the tower, affording pleasant views and a place to relax. It's worth the walk here from North Beach since tourist traffic often moves at a snail's pace up the entry road. You can walk up from the corner of Kearney and Filbert, or up the pretty **Filbert Steps** from Sansome Street to the east. Details: The auto entrance is via Lombard east of Grant, San Francisco; (415) 362-0808; tower open daily from 10 a.m. to 8 p.m. (until 6 p.m. in winter). Admission is $3. (½ hour)

★★ **Fort Point**—Completed in 1861 to defend the entrance to the bay, Fort Point (the name of both the fort and the point) is now a military museum. The southern arch of the Golden Gate Bridge was designed to preserve the structure. Today Fort Point is a popular place to get close to the bridge and to the surging tidal flows of the Golden Gate. There's a wave break around the point that attracts surfers. Joggers and walkers favor the 3½-mile route along the bay to the Marina Green. Details: Access is via Long Avenue from Lincoln Boulevard in the Presidio, San Francisco; fort open Wednesday through Sunday from 10 a.m. to 5 p.m. Admission is free. (1 hour)

★★ **Golden Gate Park**—This thousand-acre park stretches halfway across the city, from Stanyan Street to the sea. Created largely on reclaimed dune lands, it is a popular destination for residents and tourists alike. Sunday is a great day to visit since the inner half of John F. Kennedy Drive is closed to traffic. Walkers, cyclists, and skaters cruise the road and a festive atmosphere prevails. (½ day)

Numerous sights within the park stand as one- and two-star attractions on their own. The graceful **Conservatory of Flowers** was built in Britain, shipped around Cape Horn, and assembled here in 1878. Unfortunately, seismic renovation may take until 2001. Details: Golden Gate Park, San Francisco; (415) 666-7017. (½ hour)

The **California Academy of Sciences** includes the excellent **Natural History Museum, Steinhart Aquarium**, and **Morrison Planetarium**. It's a great option for families. Details: Golden Gate Park, San Francisco; (415) 750-7145; open daily from 10 a.m. to 5 p.m. (9 a.m. to 6 p.m. Memorial Day through Labor Day). Admission is $8.50. (2 hours)

Concerts and ceremonies of various sorts are scheduled in the **Music Concourse** in front of the academy. Across the concourse is the **M. H. de Young Memorial Museum**, (415) 863-3330, San Francisco's finest art museum. You'll find the biggest touring exhibits here, as well as an outstanding permanent collection featuring Renaissance and medieval paintings, tapestries, and sculpture. The **Asian Art Museum**, (415) 668-8921, is associated with the de Young. It features selections from the 10,000-item Avery Brundage collection. Details: Golden Gate Park, San Francisco; both museums open Wednesday through Sunday from 9:30 a.m. to 5 p.m. Admission is $7 and allows entry to both museums. (2 hours)

Just southwest of the museums are two beautiful outdoor attractions. The **Japanese Tea Garden** features lovely, sculpted grounds with pools and bridges. All is balanced and serene. Have tea and cookies at the teahouse where fortune cookies were invented in 1909. Details: Golden Gate Park, San Francisco; (415) 752-4227; open weekdays from 8:30 a.m. to 6 p.m. October through February, 9 a.m. to 6:30 p.m. March through September; open weekends and holidays from 10 a.m. to 5 p.m. Admission is $2.50. (45 minutes)

Across Martin Luther King Jr. Drive is the **Strybing Arboretum and Botanical Gardens**, a wonderful place to stroll among exotic plants or bask on a lawn. Details: Golden Gate Park, San Francisco; (415) 661-1316; open weekdays from 8 a.m. to 4:30 p.m., weekends and holidays from 10 a.m. to 5 p.m. Admission is free. (1½ hours)

Farther down, you can rent a paddleboat or canoe to circumnavigate **Strawberry Hill** on **Stow Lake**, check out the bison at the **Buffalo Enclosure**, or play some par-3 golf at the **Golden Gate Municipal Golf Course**. There are occasional concerts at the **Polo Field**, next to the **Fly**

Casting Pools. Sports fields, picnic areas, and barbecue pits are scattered about. Call (415) 831-2700 for park information. (½ day)

★★ **Lands End**—At the northwest tip of the city, Lincoln Park and the Golden Gate National Recreation Area preserve a headland area that includes Point Lobos and Lands End Point. Point Lobos Avenue becomes the Great Highway as it swings past the walkable ruins of the **Sutro Baths**, the site of a huge complex of indoor pools and baths built in 1886 that burned down 30 years ago. Next door is the **Cliff House**, (415) 386-3330, where you can dine or drink at the edge of the continent. The sunset views will make you smile. On the terrace below is the Musée Mechanique featuring old music boxes, games, and other odd devices. Details: (415) 750-0415, open daily, 11 a.m. to 7 p.m. (weekends 10 a.m. to 8 p.m.). Next door, you can enter the Camera Obscura, the world's largest camera. Details: (415) 750-0415, open daily. Admission is $1. (1 hour)

Lincoln Park preserves most of Lands End. Trails provide access to the park, including a stretch along an abandoned headlands road that didn't stand the test of time. The **Lincoln Park Memorial Golf Course** is a public course with some of the best views around and a reasonable greens fee to boot. At the end of Legion of Honor Drive is the **Palace of the Legion of Honor**. This newly renovated museum has an outstanding collection of European art and is one of the city's finest. Details: 4th Avenue and Clement Street, San Francisco; (415) 863-3330; open Tuesday through Sunday from 9:30 a.m. to 5 p.m. Admission is $7. (2 hours)

★★ **Palace of Fine Arts**—Built for the 1915 Panama Pacific International Exposition that celebrated the city's rise from the ashes of 1906, this ornate dome-and-pillar structure was never intended to last. Saved from the wrecking ball by adoring citizens and strengthened in the 1960s, it is an enduring symbol of the city's sentiment. Take Baker Street from Richardson Street or Marina Boulevard, walk about, and enjoy the swans in the reflecting pool.

Various performances are given at one end of the actual "palace," the curved building behind the rotunda. At the north end, families should check out the **Exploratorium**. This hands-on science museum is one of the best of its kind in the country, featuring scores of fun and educational displays. Don't miss the crawl-through "Tactile Dome." Details: Marina Boulevard and Lyon Street, San

Francisco; (415) 561-0360; open Tuesday through Sunday from
10 a.m. to 5 p.m. (until 6 p.m. in the summer and until 9:30 p.m.
every Wednesday). Admission is $9. (2 hours)

★★ **San Francisco Maritime National Historical Park**—Located
by Fisherman's Wharf, at the bottom of Hyde Street, the park is a
great place to catch the spirit of the city. Ferries once plied the waters
of San Francisco Bay in large numbers, serving Marin County and the
East Bay before the bridges were built. Some of them docked at
Hyde Street Historic Ships Pier, which now serves as home for several historic vessels, including a side-wheeler ferry and an iron-hulled
square rigger. Details: Hyde Street, San Francisco; (415) 556-3002;
pier open daily from 10 a.m. to 6 p.m. (9:30 a.m. to 5 p.m. in winter).
Admission is $4 (may be less if some ships are off limits because of
repair). (1 hour)

At the bottom of Polk Street, the art deco **San Francisco
National Maritime Museum** has a good nautical history collection.
Details: Polk Street, San Francisco; (415) 556-8177; open daily from
10 a.m. to 5 p.m. Admission is free. (1 hour)

The green surrounding the park and the gracefully curved
Municipal Pier are great places to stroll, relax, and people-watch. The
turnaround for the Hyde Street cable car is at the edge of the park—
just look for the long line of tourists waiting for a ride. (2½ hours)

★ **Fisherman's Wharf**—As an *area*, Fisherman's Wharf has a lot to
offer, but the wharf itself is basically a pier with restaurants and fish
companies. It's a great place to get a simple and tasty crab salad, a crab
sandwich, or crab legs. Enjoy them with a glass of wine and some genuine sourdough bread.

Along the three blocks of Jefferson Street, between the wharf and
Aquatic Park, you'll find tourist heaven. **The Cannery** and **The
Anchorage** are shopping and eating complexes fronting the street.
Visit the **Wax Museum**, **Ripley's Believe It or Not! Museum**, or the
Medieval Dungeon, where torture devices are on display. When
you've bought your T-shirts and postcards, move quickly on to Hyde
Street Pier or the boat to Alcatraz.

To the west, above the Maritime Museum on Beach Street, is
Ghirardelli Square. Once home to the Ghirardelli Chocolate Factory,
this one-square-block, historic brick complex now hosts upscale shops,
galleries, and tourist boutiques. It's a good spot to enjoy lunch with a

view or to buy a fancier gift than what you'd find near the wharf. Tasty Ghirardelli chocolate is, of course, available.

Five hundred yards east of the wharf, **Pier 39** is basically a tourist amusement pier lined with souvenir shops and eateries. One feature of interest is the section of floating docks that has been taken over by fat, boisterous sea lions looking for a free lunch—follow the barking. Another feature is the brand new **UnderWater World**, a long acrylic tunnel that runs through an aquarium beneath the waters of the bay. A tape-guided tour is available. Details: Pier 39, San Francisco; (415) 623-5300; open daily from 10 a.m. to 7 p.m. (until 8:30 p.m. Friday through Sunday). Admission is $13. (1 hour)

✯ **Ocean Beach**—Stretching broad, straight, and smooth along San Francisco's western edge, this wonderful beach attracts everyone who needs a dose of salt air and soothing waves. Kids play in the sand, frisbees and kites color the air, sitters sit, joggers jog, and strollers stroll. The water is too cold for all but the briefly brave and the wetsuit set. The advantage is that it's never too crowded, and there are no concessionaires providing excess litter. At night, groups gather here and there around perfectly legal beach fires.

At the south end of the long beach are the rusting gun emplacements of **Fort Funston**. It's a great place to let the dog romp while you watch the hang gliders. (2 hours)

✯ **Presidio**—One of the nation's newest national parks is in the midst of a transition. After decades of occupancy, the military is gone. Various factions have fought their way to a tenuous agreement on public and private use of the many buildings and facilities. It remains to be seen what the future will bring. Lincoln Boulevard winds through the grounds, providing access to **Baker Beach**, the **World War II Memorial**, **Fort Point**, and the **San Francisco National Cemetery**. Ask about **Lover's Lane**, the original mission road. Details: The visitor center is in Building 102 on Montgomery Street, Presidio (not the downtown Montgomery Street); (415) 561-4323; open 9 a.m. to 5 p.m. daily. The main entrances are via Lombard Street to the east (don't turn onto Richardson for the bridge), and Lincoln Boulevard from 25th Avenue to the west. CA 1 and U.S. 101 fly over and through the Presidio as they approach the Golden Gate Bridge. If you're on these arteries or the bridge, stay to the right and get off at the bridge viewpoint just south of the tollbooths. (2 hours)

✸ **Union Square**—Here you'll find the classic retail heart of the city with posh stores and fine hotels surrounding the square. East of the square, the two-block-long **Maiden Lane** extends the chic shopping zone. The city's only Frank Lloyd Wright–designed building is at 140 Maiden Lane. San Francisco's small Theater District is clustered around Geary just southwest of the square. The Powell Street cable car stops at Union Square and ends at Market Street. (½ hour)

✸ **Yerba Buena Gardens and San Francisco Museum of Modern Art (SFMOMA)**—The wondrous new San Francisco Museum of Modern Art has drawn much praise and some criticism for its unique architecture. Located across from Yerba Buena Gardens, the museum is a key element in the revitalization of the city's South of Market district. The touring exhibits are top notch while the permanent collection is improving steadily. Details: 151 3rd Street, San Francisco; (415) 357-4000; open Tuesday through Sunday from 11 a.m. to 6 p.m. (until 9 p.m. on Thursday). Admission is $8. (2 hours)

Across 3rd Street, the lawns and terraces of Yerba Buena Gardens are more of a gathering place than a botanical display. They are quite lovely, however, and provide a place to converse and relax. The **Center for the Arts** is at one end of the garden and the **Moscone Convention Center** is located across Howard Street. (1 hour)

✸ **Twin Peaks**—At Castro Street, arrow-straight Market Street begins to climb and curve as it winds up onto a series of hills in the center of the city. Near the top, Twin Peaks Boulevard cuts sharply off to the right, twisting around until it splits into a one-way road that shapes a figure eight around the two summits of Twin Peaks. On the east side of the north summit, an extended parking area gives access to one of the best day or evening views of any city, anywhere. (½ hour)

✸ **U.S.S. *Jeremiah O'Brien***—This last of the liberty ships spends most of its time moored at Pier 32, just south of the Bay Bridge on the Embarcadero. Hundreds of these transport ships were built in the bay during World War II—only the *O'Brien* remains. If you don't see the gray hulk docked at the broad pier, it might be out on a goodwill mission of some sort. There are great views of the Bay Bridge from both the ship and pier. Details: Pier 32, San Francisco; (415) 441-3101; ship tours given weekdays from 9 a.m. to 4 p.m. Admission is $5. (1 hour)

City Tours—For an organized look at San Francisco's highlights, consider a touring option. The famous **49 Mile Drive** hits all the major sights. The route is highlighted on most city maps and marked by road signs The **Red & White Fleet** offers a variety of land and water tours of the bay, city, and greater Bay Area. They're based at Pier 43½, (415) 447-0597. Scheduled bus and 'motorized cable car' tours are offered by **Gray Line**, (415) 558-9400 or (800) 826-0202. (2 hours to full day)

Mission Dolores—Less than a week after this mission was founded, the Declaration of Independence was signed in Philadelphia. It is the oldest site in San Francisco. The permanent structure was completed in 1783, and the large basilica next door was built in 1913. Of particular interest is the mission cemetery where the graves of Indians and early pioneers can be found. Details: The basilica is at the corner of Dolores Street and 16th Street, the mission is next door, San Francisco; (415) 621-8203; open daily from 9 a.m. to 4 p.m. Admission is $2. (1 hour)

FITNESS AND RECREATION

San Francisco is a city for walking. Walk the 3½-mile promenade from the Marina Green, along Crissy Field in the Presidio, to Fort Point and the Golden Gate Bridge. Enjoy the pounding surf as you walk up and down the miles-long Ocean Beach. Consider a loop through Golden Gate Park with a side trip along Haight Street. You won't move fast down Grant Street in Chinatown, but the diversions make up for the pace. The Embarcadero is particularly nice along the open area between the Bay Bridge and the Ferry Building. A walk down Mission between 16th and 24th gives you a taste of culture and commerce while connecting the BART stations.

FOOD

It has been said that there are enough restaurants in San Francisco to seat the city's entire population at one time. Explore the city for a while, and you'll be tempted to believe the claim. With more restaurants per capita than any other city in the nation and an amazing diversity of menus, San Francisco is a diner's paradise. Clearly, the selections below barely scratch the surface of interesting eating possibilities in this world-class city. Don't hesitate to investigate further if dining is your passion. Restaurants are grouped roughly by neighborhood.

DOWNTOWN SAN FRANCISCO

Fisherman's Wharf
Pier 39
Aquatic Park
Fort Mason
JEFFERSON ST
MARINA BLVD
Pier 23
San Francisco Bay
BAY ST
LOMBARD ST
Telegraph Hill
Russian Hill
UNION ST
BROADWAY
WASHINGTON ST
Nob Hill
CALIFORNIA ST
Embarcadero Plaza
San Francisco - Oakland Bay Bridge
BUSH ST
GEARY ST
Union Square
Pier 32
GOLDEN GATE AV
GROVE ST
FELL ST
HAIGHT ST
Buena Vista Park
MARKET ST
16TH ST
17TH ST
20TH ST
24TH ST
CESAR CHAVEZ (ARMY) ST

DIVISADERO ST
FILMORE ST
VAN NESS AV
HYDE ST
TAYLOR ST
POWELL ST
GRANT AV
COLUMBUS AV
MONTGOMERY ST
BATTERY ST
THE EMBARCADERO
STEUART ST
MAIN ST
1ST ST
MISSION ST
6TH ST
7TH ST
8TH ST
11TH ST
BRANNAN ST
3RD ST
THIRD ST
PENNSYLVANIA AV
CASTRO ST
DOLORES ST
VALENCIA ST
SOUTH VAN NESS AV
FOLSOM ST
LAGUNA ST

101
80
280

N

O SCALE
1.5 KILOMETERS
1.5 MILES
ROAD
INTERSTATE

Food

- **A** Bitter Root Cafe
- **B** Café Flore
- **C** Cypress Club
- **D** Edinburgh Castle Pub
- **E** Empress of China
- **F** Flying Kamikazes
- **G** Fog City Diner
- **H** Green's
- **I** Hamburger Mary's
- **J** Irawaddy
- **K** La Posta
- **L** Lotus Garden
- **M** LuLu
- **N** Masa's
- **O** North Beach Pizza
- **P** Pane e Vino
- **Q** Patio Café
- **R** Rasselas
- **S** Saigon Saigon
- **T** Sanppo Restaurant
- **U** Spaghetti Western
- **V** Stars
- **W** Steelhead Brewing Company
- **X** The Stinking Rose
- **Y** Suppenkueche
- **Z** Swan Oyster Depot
- **a** YoYo

Lodging

- **b** Adelaide Hotel
- **c** The Bed and Breakfast Inn
- **d** Best Western Miyako Inn
- **e** Dockside Boat and Bed
- **f** Fairmont Hotel
- **g** Grant Plaza
- **h** Hotel Bohème
- **i** Maxwell Hotel
- **j** Pacific Tradewinds Guest House
- **k** Queen Anne Hotel
- **l** San Francisco International Hostel
- **m** Sherman House
- **n** Tuscan Inn
- **o** Washington Square Inn
- **p** Westin St. Francis Hotel

The Castro, centered at the corner of Market and Castro Streets, is the heart of gay culture in San Francisco. **Café Flore**, 1815 Market, (415) 621-8579, is a good place to have coffee and peoplewatch in this lively area. Enjoy a retreat into the recesses of Castro society on the crowded patio of the **Patio Café**, 531 Castro, (415) 621-4640.

In Chinatown there is plenty to eat on and around Grant Street and Stockton Street, and most restaurants are reasonably priced. The **Lotus Garden**, 532 Grant Street, (415) 397-0707, serves vegetarian dishes below a Taoist temple. Fine Chinese dining in the heart of Chinatown doesn't get any better than the **Empress of China**, 838 Grant Street, (415) 434-1345.

Hayes Valley, near the **Civic Center**, is home to the famous **Stars**, 555 Golden Gate Avenue and at 150 Redwood Alley, (415) 861-7827, which does, in fact, attract stars and wannabes for its "New American" cuisine. Reservations are recommended. Popular **Suppenkueche**, 525 Laguna, (415) 252-9289, has better German cuisine than you'll find in Germany. For fish, chips, and pints of bitters in a very British setting, hit the **Edinburgh Castle Pub**, 950 Geary, (415) 885-4074.

In the Financial District, the **Fog City Diner**, 1300 Battery Street, (415) 982-2000, has been in a Visa commercial so it must be good. International options surround the classed-up diner fare. If you can get in, you can say you've been there. Step into the **Cypress Club**, 500 Jackson Street, (415) 296-8555, and you'll look around for the stage crew. This place is almost a scenic attraction on its own. The diverse menu is tops, as are the prices.

Fisherman's Wharf offers several touristy places to enjoy seafood, especially crab, right off the dock. Nearby, in the Anchorage, is the **Steelhead Brewing Company**, (415) 775-1795, offering site-brewed beers with great food. The finest in vegetarian California cuisine is found at **Green's**, (415) 771-6222, operated by the Zen Center in a thoroughly redone barracks building at Fort Mason. A meal here is a must for veggie connoisseurs. It's located in Building A of the Fort Mason Center with an entrance at the base of Buchanan Street.

In Japantown many restaurants are located within the Japan Trade and Cultural Center buildings. So if you find yourself staring at a mall-like wall where an address is supposed to be, look inside. Moderately priced fine cuisine in a modest setting attracts those in the know to **Sanppo Restaurant**, 1702 Post Street, (415) 346-3486. Perhaps the best seafood restaurant in town is **YoYo,** 1625 Post Street, (415) 922-7788, which offers Japanese cooking with a French twist.

Lower Haight is located where Haight Street meets Fillmore Street. The scene here is young and lively. Breakfasts are huge in a sub-casual setting at **Spaghetti Western,** 576 Haight Street, (415) 864-8461.

For some rock 'n' roll with very good sushi, head to the **Marina** and the **Flying Kamikazes,** 3339 Steiner, (415) 567-4903. The **Irawaddy,** 1769 Lombard Street, (415) 931-2830, has unusual but excellent Burmese cuisine. Settle into your pillows and enjoy.

In the Mission there's no shortage of Latin American food, and it's hard to go too far wrong. For a dose of the real Mission, try the Mexican dishes and margaritas at **La Posta,** 2891 24th Street, (415) 641-8258. If a mariachi band drops in and you welcome them at your table, you should tip them. The **Bitter Root Cafe,** 3122 16th Street, (415) 626-5523, is a good choice for a meal in the Mission's hip heart. Proving the culinary diversity of the Mission, **Saigon Saigon,** 1132 Valencia, (415) 206-9635, is the place to go for Vietnamese dining. It offers great service at good prices.

North Beach offers great dining hotspots. **North Beach Pizza,** (415) 433-2444, is an area legend. The original location at 1499 Grant Street is a great place to grab a slice, day or night. Garlic is the name of the game at **The Stinking Rose,** 325 Columbus Street, (415) 781-7673, along with great Italian food at a fair price.

The Russian Hill, Pacific Heights, and Cow Hollow neighborhood includes the intimate **Pane e Vino,** 3011 Steiner Street, (415) 346-2111. The mood here would be romantic if not for the vociferous bustle of the thoroughly Italian staff. For Ethiopian food with live jazz on the side, **Rasselas,** 2801 California, (415) 567-5010, has the goods.

In the SoMa (South of Market) area a block from Yerba Buena Gardens, **LuLu,** 816 Folsom, (415) 495-5775, offers outstanding Mediterranean cuisine and features wood-burning oven–roasted meats and great pizza. For a beer and a bite—including worthy burgers—stop at **Hamburger Mary's,** a SoMa original at 1582 Folsom Street, (415) 626-1985.

Good places to eat abound in the area around Union Square and Nob Hill. The most expensive restaurant in San Francisco is probably **Masa's,** 648 Bush Street in the Hotel Vintage Court, (415) 989-7154. The unique blending of French and California cuisine stresses artistic presentation. Make reservations before you leave home. For an affordable, authentic San Francisco lunch, hit the **Swan Oyster Depot**, 1517 Polk Street, (415) 673-1101.

LODGING

The following listings focus on lodgings in San Francisco's central tourist area. Reservations are strongly recommended throughout the entire year.

San Francisco is awash with luxury hotels. The **Fairmont Hotel**, 950 Mason Street at California Street, (415) 772-5000 or (800) 527-4727, features the wonderful Tonga Room, with its artificial tropical storm. The lobby is one of the most fabulous in the city. Rooms start at about $260 and climb from there.

The **Westin St. Francis Hotel**, 335 Powell Street, (415) 397-7000 or (800) 228-3000, is a true city landmark. Large and stately at 1,200 rooms, it has presided over Union Square for decades. Rooms start around $200. Another hotel of particular note is the **Sherman House**, 2160 Green Street, (415) 563-3600. A four-story Victorian mansion and historical landmark with only 18 rooms, it was restored to its pre-1906 earthquake splendor in 1980. The original three-story recital hall, where Enrico Caruso once sang, has become the hotel's lobby. Rooms run from $310 to over $750! It's a splendid place to stay for a select few.

In the budget and moderate range, a number of interesting hotels, inns, and B&Bs stand out. Several are in the close-to-Market-Street zone that includes the Civic Center, Union Square, and Financial District. You can get a clean, decent room two blocks from Union Square for as little as $52 at the **Adelaide Hotel**, 5 Isadora Duncan Court (off Taylor between Geary and Post), (415) 441-2474. You'll have to share a bath, but you'll have friendly folks with which to share it. Old, elegant, and friendly, the **Maxwell Hotel** (was the Raphael), 386 Geary Boulevard, (415) 986-2000, has plenty of creature comforts as well as a personality. It's a good choice in the $145-and-up range.

Inexpensive to moderate options in the Japantown and Pacific Heights zone can also be found. San Francisco's first B&B, fittingly named **The Bed and Breakfast Inn**, 4 Charlton Court, (415) 921-9784, is located on tiny Charlton off Union Street. Rooms start at $75 with shared bath, $125 with private bath. The **Best Western Miyako Inn** (not the Radisson Miyako Hotel), 1800 Sutter Street, (415) 921-4000, offers good value and style with rooms from $83 to

$123. Built in 1890, the elegant **Queen Anne Hotel**, 1590 Sutter Street, (415) 441-2828 or (800) 227-3970, can be a B&B bargain. Rooms start at $120 and climb quickly.

In and around Chinatown, North Beach, and Russian Hill, you'll find even more options. For a bargain, try the **Grant Plaza**, 465 Grant Avenue, (415) 434-3883 or (800) 472-6899. For $60, you get $60 worth, but it's well kept and right in Chinatown. To get a feel for the Beat era, stay at **Hotel Bohème**, 444 Columbus, (415) 433-9111. Rooms are about $125 each. For about $125 (small room), you can have continental breakfast, afternoon tea, and evening wine at the **Washington Square Inn**, 1660 Stockton Street, (415) 981-4220 or (800) 388-0220, a charming B&B in the heart of North Beach.

Budget chain motels and moderate independents are found in abundance near Fisherman's Wharf and on Lombard Street in the Marina District. How about staying on your own moored yacht at the **Dockside Boat and Bed**? You and your matey can ahoy for $95 and up, breakfast included. Individual boats are moored at Pier 39, (415) 392-5526. Up into the high-moderate range is the **Tuscan Inn**, 425 North Point Street, (415) 561-1100. Rooms in this nice hotel run from $140 to $240.

Hostels offer ultra-cheap accommodations and are often located in the heart of things. The **Pacific Tradewinds Guest House**, 680 Sacramento Street, (415) 433-7970, offers a great location, no curfew, no lockout, nice folks, and free coffee and tea. Beds are $14 to $16. The more traditional **San Francisco International Hostel** is located in Building 240 at Fort Mason, (415) 771-7277, and costs $15 per bed.

CAMPING

There is no camping available in the city of San Francisco. Check out the listings in other chapters, including Samuel P. Taylor State Park in Marin County, and Mt. Diablo State Park in the East Bay.

NIGHTLIFE

Nightlife options are as diverse as the culinary offerings of the region. You can stop at an Irish pub after an evening at the opera, then dance to techno music until dawn. If you simply get to the core areas of the neighborhoods, you can soak in the street scene as you browse, trying a few different nightspots on for size. Things can get a little iffy around

DOWNTOWN SAN FRANCISCO

Nightlife

- **Ⓐ Buena Vista Café**
- **Ⓑ Café du Nord**
- **Ⓒ Carnelian Room**
- **Ⓓ Cesar's Latin Palace**
- **Ⓔ Club Boomerang**
- **Ⓕ Club Dread**
- **Ⓖ DNA Lounge**
- **Ⓗ Eagle Café**
- **Ⓘ Elbo Room**
- **Ⓙ Equinox**
- **Ⓚ Ireland's 32**
- **Ⓛ Gordon Biersch Brewery Restaurant**
- **Ⓜ Kilowatt**
- **Ⓝ Lou's Pier 47**
- **Ⓞ Mad Dog in the Fog**
- **Ⓟ Nightbreak**
- **Ⓠ Noc Noc**

- **Ⓡ Paradise**
- **Ⓢ Pearl's**
- **Ⓣ Persian Aub Zam Zam**
- **Ⓤ Pier 23**
- **Ⓥ The Plough and Stars**
- **Ⓦ Specs**
- **Ⓧ Toranado**
- **Ⓨ Tosca Café**
- **Ⓩ Trocadero**
- **ⓐ 20 Tank Brewery**
- **ⓑ Twin Peaks Tavern**
- **ⓒ Vesuvio Café**
- **ⓓ Zeitgest**

the SoMa, Mission, and Haight zones as the night grows old, though the happy crowds in the centers are generally safe and fun.

On Castro Street and Market Street, near their junction, the strolling and people-watching is tops—a thoroughly gay scene. The **Twin Peaks Tavern**, 401 Castro Street, (415) 864-9470, is a great place to people-watch as you sip. The jazz and blues ambiance of the **Café du Nord**, 2170 Market Street, (415) 861-5016, makes for a fun, mixed scene.

In the Financial District, an unbeatable view of the city from atop the Bank of America Building makes the high-priced drinks worth it in the **Carnelian Room**, 555 California Street, (415) 433-7500. For a happy crowd and danceable live music, drop in at the cramped **Pier 23**, on Pier 23 at the Embarcadero, (415) 362-5125. When the press of bodies becomes too much, step out onto the sprawling deck for a long look at the bay. Food is served through the early evening. The **Gordon**

Biersch Brewery Restaurant, 2 Harrison Street, (415) 243-8246, is a touch industrial in decor, but not enough to get your business suit dirty. The site-brewed beers are admired by many, loved by some. There's classy pub grub upstairs.

There's plenty of daytime activity at the Fisherman's Wharf, Pier 39, Jefferson Street, and Aquatic Park area, though the tourists and street performers begin to dissipate as the evening wanes. Live music of the blues variety is found every night at **Lou's Pier 47**, 300 Jefferson Street, (415) 771-0377. Irish coffee allegedly arrived in San Francisco via the **Buena Vista Café**, 2765 Hyde Street, (415) 474-5044. In any case, it's still there. The **Eagle Café** on Pier 39 is a good place for a real drink amid the tourist schlock, (415) 433-3689.

The Lower Haight, right on Haight around Fillmore, is home to a compact and energetic scene that goes until the bars close. The **Mad Dog in the Fog**, 530 Haight Street, (415) 626-7279, is a good place for pints and people. The energy is infectious. For a different perspective, cross the street to the **Noc Noc**, 557 Haight Street, (415) 861-5811, for a quiet drink and a look at the weirdly sculpted interior.

In the Mission the action centers on 16th Street, between Mission and Valencia Streets, and spreads out from there. There's good live music upstairs and a noisy bar downstairs at the **Elbo Room**, 647 Valencia Street, (415) 552-7788. The bikes parked outside should give you a clue about trendy **Zeitgest**, 199 Valencia Street, (415) 255-7505. **Cesar's Latin Palace**, 3140 Mission Street, (415) 648-6611, is the place for salsa dancing.

The intersection of Broadway and Columbus is the center of the very active North Beach scene. Head north on Grant or east on Broadway for some fascinating browsing. Four worthy nightspots cluster at the intersection of Columbus and Broadway. The compact, two-story **Vesuvio Café**, 255 Columbus, (415) 362-3370, is next to City Lights Books in the historic heart of the Beat District. Read your Jack Kerouac over beer or coffee here. Across the street at the **Tosca Café**, 242 Columbus, (415) 391-1244, listen to opera among jaded urbanites and otherworldly artists over coffee. Next door, at historic **Specs**, (415) 421-4112, the diverse crowd has an edge. Late night, the edge can crack. North of Broadway, **Pearl's**, 256 Columbus, (415) 291-8255, offers good free jazz nightly in a civil setting.

In the Richmond, there are pockets of interest on Geary, but the heart of the area is along Clement Street for several blocks west of Arguello. Stop in for a pint of stout at **Ireland's 32**, 3920 Geary

Boulevard, (415) 386-6173. It's named after the number of counties that should be in the republic, so make sure you've got your politics straight before conversing. The **Plough and Stars**, 116 Clement Street, (415) 751-1122, is another popular Irish option. Both pubs have live music.

In SoMa (South of Market), the action continues really late. Eleventh Street between Harrison and Folsom is the main zone, though other clubs in the big district are islands of action. At the corner of 11th and Folsom, the **Paradise**, 1501 Folsom Street, (415) 861-6906, features three stages and a barroom where you can almost hear yourself. Enjoy performance art or poetry upstairs while the place rocks beneath you. The **20 Tank Brewery**, 316 11th Street, (415) 255-9455, offers a good range of site-brewed ales in a warehouse setting. Across the street is the **DNA Lounge**, 375 11th Street, (415) 626-1409, with a loud, dance-til-dawn clientele. Next door is **Slim's**, 333 11th Street, (415) 522-0333, which attracts big names in blues and more, both as acts and drop-ins.

Upper Haight gets a little sketchy as the night progresses, but there are plenty of folk about between Masonic and Golden Gate Park. A block from Golden Gate Park, the **Nightbreak**, 1821 Haight Street, (415) 221-9008, features thrashing rock bands in a featureless box. If it's open, and if the bartender doesn't throw you out for no apparent reason, you can get a martini at the **Persian Aub Zam Zam**, 1633 Haight Street, (415) 861-2545. Take a chance! The **Club Boomerang**, 1840 Haight Street, (415) 387-2996, has live new bands nightly.

2

MARIN COUNTY

Marin County is rich in many ways. Statistically, its residents top the income list of all Northern California counties. The fruits of wealth translate into safe and interesting towns with charming cafés and boutiques, all enjoyable for the visitor. Most of all, Marin is blessed with a system of local, county, state, and federal park lands that encompass about a third of the county and its most scenic areas.

Marin is also rich in a well-earned reputation. It seems that every trendy new-age self-improvement method or spiritual path finds a home in the county. No greater concentration of well-massaged, juice-drinking, hot tub–soaking, spandex-suited joggers in therapy can be found anywhere else in the universe. Then again, the visitor will quickly note that the smiles per capita rate is on par with the Lexus per capita rate—a very high percentage indeed. Marin is the land of the happy yuppie. Of course, as with all such caricatures, the reality is much more complex.

The county is home to famous musicians such as Grace Slick, Bob Weir, and Carlos Santana. George Lucas has studios at Skywalker Ranch, and his Industrial Light and Magic facility is located in San Rafael. Pixar, the animation company that created the movie *Toy Story*, is next door. To the north, much of the county is still devoted to sheep and cattle grazing. Access to Marin is via U.S. 101, CA 1, the Golden Gate Bridge, Interstate 580 and the Richmond–San Rafael Bridge, or CA 37 from the Wine Country. ◼

MARIN COUNTY

Tomales Point

Tomales

Rohnert Park

PETALUMA VALLEY FORD

SHORELINE HWY

TOMALES–PETALUMA RD

BODEGA AV

Marshall

CHILENO VALLEY RD

Petaluma

MARSHALL–PETALUMA RD

PIERCE POINT RD

Tomales Bay

SHORELINE HWY

K SIR FRANCIS DRAKE BLVD

Inverness

PETALUMA–POINT REYES RD

Drakes Bay

Point Reyes

LIMANTOUR RD

Point Reyes Station

101

NOVATO BLVD

Point Reyes National Seashore

Olema

NICASIO VALLEY

Novato

Samuel P. Taylor State Park

J

K

Golden Gate National Recreation Area

L

SIR FRANCIS DRAKE BLVD

LUCAS VALLEY

37

E

Pacific Ocean

1

B

Bolinas

D

Mt. Tamalpais

F San Rafael

Stinson Beach

Mt. Tamalpais State Park

Muir Woods National Monument

H

I

Mill Valley

J Muir Beach

1

580

C 131

N

Tiburon

Angel Island State Park

Sausalito

G **M** **A**

San Francisco Bay

0 SCALE   10 KILOMETERS   10 MILES   —— ROAD   ---- AREA BOUNDARY   ≡ INTERSTATE

N

Sights

Ⓐ Angel Island

Ⓑ Audubon Canyon Ranch

Ⓒ Bay Model

Ⓓ Bolinas

Ⓔ Marin Coastal Wildlands

Ⓕ Marin County Civic Center

Ⓖ Marin Headlands

Ⓗ Mount Tamalpais State Park

Ⓘ Muir Woods National Monument

Ⓙ Nude Beaches

Ⓚ Point Reyes National Seashore

Ⓛ Samuel P. Taylor State Park

Ⓜ Sausalito

Ⓝ Tiburon

A PERFECT DAY IN MARIN COUNTY

Enjoy a bay view over breakfast in Tiburon. Take U.S. 101 north to downtown San Rafael and Fourth Street for a look at the town. Get on Sir Francis Drake Boulevard in San Anselmo and drive through the Samuel P. Taylor State Park to the coast. Choose between a hike on Tomales Point and a visit to Point Reyes Light Station with a walk on the beach. Hit Bolinas for a late lunch, followed by a drive up Mount Tamalpais or a visit to Muir Woods. Splurge on dinner at the Casa Madrona in Sausalito. If it's not too late, follow Alexander Avenue from town, under the freeway, and up onto the headlands for a spectacular view of the Golden Gate.

SIGHTSEEING HIGHLIGHTS

★★★ **Marin Headlands**—Although much of the Marin coastline features beautiful, protected headlands, the area at the southern tip of the county is generally referred to as the "Marin Headlands." Two of the three stars in this rating derive from the splendor of California headlands in general. The third is earned by the world-class views of San Francisco with the Golden Gate Bridge in the foreground. The headlands are largely within the Golden Gate National Recreation Area.

Take the Alexander Avenue exit just north of the Golden Gate Bridge. Alexander Avenue from Sausalito cuts under the freeway and climbs sharply up into the headlands, becoming the Conzelman Road. About ¼ mile up is **Spencer Battery**, just where the road takes a big swing to the right. A short path next to an old gun emplacement leads to a great overlook.

At the top of Conzelman Road are long disused gun emplacements and magazines, along with what is possibly the best roadside view of the Golden Gate Bridge and the surrounding city. The summit behind is called **Hawk Hill** in honor of the thousands of raptors that migrate through from mid-August to mid-December. Continue down a narrow, one-way road to Point Bonita and the **Point Bonita Lighthouse**. Details: Open Saturday and Sunday from 12:30 to 3:30 p.m.

From Conzelman Road take Mitchell Road to reach the Rodeo Valley, and **Rodeo Lagoon and Beach**. There are trailheads and a youth hostel in the valley. Just north of the lagoon, the **California Marine Mammal Center** works to save and rehabilitate injured sea life. Details: (415) 289-7325; open daily from 10 a.m. to 4 p.m. Admission is free. (1 hour)

Information on these and other sites is available at the **Golden Gate National Recreation Area Visitor Center**. Nearby, an old **Nike Missile Site** can be visited Monday through Friday from 12:30 to 3:30 p.m. Details: Intersection of Field and Bunker Roads, Marin Headlands (in the Rodeo Valley); (415) 331-1540; open daily 9:30 a.m. to 4:30 p.m. (2 hours)

★★★ **Point Reyes National Seashore**—Point Reyes is a magnificent blend of forested hills, rugged headlands, rare wildlife, historic ranches, rolling dunes, sandy beaches, golden sun, and blanketing fog. The Point Reyes peninsula rides on the Pacific plate, separated from the main North American land mass by the San Andreas Fault, which runs directly under the Olema Valley and Tomales Bay. The park is slipping away northward at an average rate of 2 inches per year—though it jumped 20 feet in the 1906 earthquake! Details: Access is from CA 1 and Marin County's Sir Francis Drake Boulevard; (415) 663-1092. The Bear Valley Visitor Center, just west of Olema, is open daily from 9 a.m. to 5 p.m. (opens at 8 a.m. on weekends). Admission is free.

There are three broad areas to explore on Point Reyes. The **Philip Burton Wilderness Area** in the southern half of the park features numerous trails through forested hills, many of which lead to the coastal paths and provide access to wild cliffs and beaches. Trail access for good day hikes is easy from Limantour Road, Bear Valley Visitor Center, and Five Brooks (all from CA 1), and the Palomarin Trailhead (via Mesa Road in Bolinas). Primitive, hike-in camping is available in four areas. Most of the $10 sites can be reserved at the Bear Valley Visitor Center or by calling (415) 663-8054. (½ day)

Sir Francis Drake Boulevard passes through open, non-wilderness land on its way out to **Drakes Estero** (or estuary), **Point Reyes Beaches, Drakes Beach**, and **Point Reyes Light Station**. The lighthouse and visitor center are definitely worth a visit, though frequent fog curtails views as it adds mystery. The beaches are sprawling and wild, though it does get crowded near the parking areas on hot summer days. Watch out for riptides and rough surf! Drakes Estero is a good area for bird-watching. The **Mount Vision Overlook** offers a great view of the entire park. It is reached via Mount Vision Road off of Sir Francis Drake Boulevard. (3 hours)

Perhaps the best area is **Tomales Point** and the **Tule Elk Range**, accessed via Pierce Point Road at the northern end of the park. An easy 4-mile trail follows the crest of the peninsula from the parking area to the tip of Tomales Point, where Tomales Bay meets the Pacific. A sizable herd of Tule elk roams freely on the point and is easily viewed. Hawks frequent the bluffs, while owls can be seen perching on small rocky summits at dusk. (3 hours)

⋆⋆ **Angel Island**—The island has been used for many purposes over the years, but it is now a state park with several miles of hiking trails and biking roads. Exploring the island offers fantastic views of San Francisco, Marin, and the East Bay. Walking and biking roads provide access to forts from the Civil and Spanish-American Wars, as well as old missile and gun emplacements. Near the northeastern point of the island is an immigration station that served as San Francisco's "Ellis Island" for a time before being converted to a World War II internment camp for Japanese citizens. Details: The park can be reached by ferry from San Francisco via the Blue & Gold Fleet, which runs two or three boats daily (on weekends only in winter); (415) 705-5555. The fare is $10 round-trip. Better still are the ferries from the waterfront in Tiburon; call for departures, (415) 435-2131. Fares are $6 round-trip,

$1 for bikes. Several campsites on the island can be reserved through Parknet, (800) 444-7275. (½ day)

★★ **Marin Coastal Wildlands**—Through awareness and effort, the people of Marin County and the Bay Area have succeeded in protecting large areas of coastal wilderness only a few minutes from downtown San Francisco. An extensive trail system links the contiguous wildlands of **Golden Gate National Recreation Area, Mount Tamalpais State Park, Muir Woods National Monument, Marin Municipal Water District Watershed, Samuel P. Taylor State Park,** and **Point Reyes National Seashore.**

The **Coastal Trail** through the Golden Gate National Recreation Area can be linked with the **Coast Trail** in Point Reyes' **Philip Burton Wilderness** to make a 40-mile hiking, biking, and riding corridor with lots of side trails and alternate loops. Access to the wildlands is available at many points, including: Marin Headlands roads, Rodeo Valley, Tennessee Valley Road, CA 1 and the Panoramic Highway, Muir Woods, Stinson Beach, Point Reyes trailheads, and Samuel P. Taylor State Park, as well as from fire road trailheads in Mill Valley, Kentfield, Ross, and San Anselmo. (all day)

★★ **Mount Tamalpais State Park**—Mount "Tam" reigns over Marin County and the North Bay. Unforgettable summit views are only a ten-minute hike from the parking area. Access is via the Panoramic Highway, which begins and ends at CA 1, running from the ridgetop above Mill Valley to Stinson Beach. Follow the signs and take Ridgecrest Road to the top. Many well-loved hiking, biking, and horse trails thread through the park and protected watershed lands that surround the peak, including the bed of an old narrow gauge railroad. Details: (415) 388-2070; open from 7 a.m. to dusk. Admission is free, though day-use parking is $5. (½ day)

★★ **Muir Woods National Monument**—Nestled in a narrow, steep valley, the relatively small Muir Woods preserves a grove of ancient redwoods. With its proximity to San Francisco, it receives more visitors than all the other redwood parks combined. There is an easy loop path through the grove along Redwood Creek. If your trip will not include a northward swing, Muir Woods is a three-star, must-see destination. If the North Coast national and state redwood parks are on your itinerary, you might choose to pass up the difficult parking and noisy visitors.

Like most popular parks, however, solitude is just a walk away. Muir Woods is surrounded by public lands, linked together with an excellent trail system. Details: Take Muir Woods Road or the Panoramic Highway from CA 1 north of Mill Valley; (415) 388-2595; open daily from 8 a.m. to sunset. Admission is $2. (1½ hours)

✴ **Audubon Canyon Ranch**—From mid-March through July, the ranch is open for walkers to observe herons and egrets in their nesting environment. As with most Audubon sites, the birds come first, so access is strictly limited and the ranch is closed at sensitive times. The canyon drains into Bolinas Lagoon and is accessible via CA 1. Details: Located 3½ miles north of Stinson Beach on CA 1; call for reservations; (415) 868-9244; open weekends mid-March through mid-July from 10 a.m. to 4 p.m. A $10 donation is suggested. (2 hours)

✴ **Bolinas**—This could be the town that time forgot. At the least, it's a town that many residents would like time and tourists to forget. The highway sign for the Bolinas turnoff from CA 1 mysteriously disappears every time a new one is erected. Turn west on the Olema-Bolinas Road just north of Bolinas Lagoon to reach this relaxed, communally spirited town that harkens to the '60s. Visit the **Point Reyes Bird Observatory** for a bird-banding demonstration. Details: Mesa Road; (415) 868-0655; open sunrise to sunset. Admission is free. Continue to the end of Mesa Road for the **Palomarin Trailhead** and hike into Point Reyes. (1 hour)

✴ **Samuel P. Taylor State Park**—On Sir Francis Drake Boulevard, near the coast, this park preserves old-growth redwoods along Lagunitas Creek, as well as several square miles of Marin wildlands. You can stop at points along the road to enjoy the trees and stream. The campground is one of the more pleasant places to camp within an hour of the city. Details: Take Sir Francis Drake Boulevard west from San Anselmo or east from CA 1; (415) 488-9897. (2 hours)

✴ **Sausalito**—Sausalito has an archetypal, Mediterranean waterfront charm. Fine homes climb the hills behind the bayside shops and restaurants. The boats sliding through the calm waters provide a foreground for the skyline of San Francisco. People stroll casually in the afternoon sun, stopping to enjoy a view or a cool drink. Details: Take the Alexander Avenue or Marin City exit from U.S. 101. Traffic can be thick and slow on the weekends. Consider taking a Golden Gate Ferry, from the Ferry Building in San Francisco, (415) 923-2000, $4.25 one-way; or a Blue & Gold Fleet boat, from Pier 41, (415) 705-5555, $5.50 one-way. Both ferries run about every 1½ hours. (1½ hours)

✿ **Tiburon**—Like Sausalito, Tiburon features bayside relaxation in a thoroughly comfortable setting. As you wait for your ferry to Angel Island, lunch on the deck at a bayside café, where warm sun and cool breezes are balanced to perfection and the burble of voices is interrupted only by the printing of credit card receipts. If you wish, climb the hill for better views and a look at **Old St. Hilary's Church**, built in 1888. Details: Tiburon is reached via U.S. 101 to Tiburon Boulevard (CA 131). Just as for Sausalito, San Francisco ferry service is offered by the Blue & Gold Fleet from Pier 41, (415) 705-5555, $5.50 one-way. Ferries run about every 1½ hours. (1 hour)

Bay Model—In order to study the movement of tides and river flows, the Army Corps of Engineers constructed a huge and topographically correct model of the San Francisco Bay. The model and visitor center are housed in a warehouse-like building a mile north of Sausalito. Call ahead to see when the model will be filled with water—the best time to see it. Details: 2100 Bridgeway Boulevard, Sausalito; (415) 332-3871; open Tuesday through Sunday from 9 a.m. to 4 p.m., 10 a.m. to 6 p.m. on weekends (closed Sundays in winter). Admission is free. (1 hour)

Marin County Civic Center—Frank Lloyd Wright designed this seat of county government shortly before his death. The structure incorporates arched and curved elements in a hillside setting. Details: Look to the east as you drive by on U.S. 101, or take a closer look by taking the North San Pedro Road exit 1½ miles north of central San Rafael; (415) 499-6387; open Monday through Friday from 8:30 a.m. to 4:30 p.m.; call for tour times and prices. (1 hour)

Nude Beaches—Sunbathing in the buff is moderately popular in and around the bay. **Red Rocks Nudist Beach** is more or less officially clothing free. It's located less than a mile south of Stinson Beach. Some out-thrust rocks break up **Muir Beach** into southern and northern sections, and on the northern half clothing is traditionally considered optional. (2 hours)

Tiburon and San Francisco Bay

FITNESS AND RECREATION

Marin County is where Gary Fisher invented the mountain bike, and Mount Tam has always been Fisher's proving ground for new models. The **Marin Coastal Wildlands** are a great place for a ride. For the most part, bikers are limited to fire roads, though miles of good single-track exist. Contact the park visitor center at (510) 437-3134 or visit the many local bike and rental shops for trail maps and other information.

Hiking is also a great option in Marin. For an easy, outstanding hike, walk the ridge path that runs the length of **Tomales Point** at the northern end of Point Reyes. Closer to the city, a loop between **Tennessee Valley** and **Rodeo Valley** provides access to a great stretch of roadless coast. Take the Panoramic Highway from CA 1 to reach trailheads for the summit of **Mount Tamalpais** and coastal routes. Head south along the coast from **Muir Beach** or north from Mesa Road in Bolinas. Whether biking or hiking, always remember to watch out for poison oak throughout the area and to take tick precautions.

MARIN COUNTY

Food

- **A** Angel's Café
- **B** Buckeye Roadhouse
- **C** Casa Madrona
- **D** Gray Whale Pizza
- **E** Hanna's Restaurant
- **G** Horizons
- **F** Lark Creek Inn
- **F** Marin Brewing Company
- **D** Parkside Café
- **F** Piazza D'Angelo
- **E** Royal Thai
- **G** Sam's Anchor Café
- **H** Shop Café

Lodging

- **C** Alta Mira
- **D** Blackthorne Inn
- **C** Casa Madrona
- **I** Marin Headlands Hostel
- **J** Mountain Home Inn
- **E** Panama Hotel
- **K** Point Reyes Hostel
- **O** Roundstone Farm
- **L** Sandpiper Motel

Camping

- **M** Olema Ranch Campground
- **N** Pantoll Station
- **O** Point Reyes National Seashore
- **P** Samuel P. Taylor State Park
- **L** Steep Ravine

Note: Items with the same letter are located in the same town or area.

FOOD

In Sausalito, the **Casa Madrona**, 801 Bridgeway Boulevard, (415) 332-0502, offers a bay view with lunch and dinner dining at its finest. The menu features California cuisine with an international twist. Another great place to dine with a view is **Horizons**, 558 Bridgeway, (415) 331-3232. Sit out on the deck if the weather is nice.

Tiburon has several good eateries. **Sam's Anchor Café**, 27 Main Street, (415) 435-4527, is a popular bayside option with a great deck.

The Buckeye Roadhouse, on CA 1 in Mill Valley, 15 Shoreline Highway, (415) 331-2600, features eclectic dining in bold surrounds. In Mill Valley proper, **Piazza D'Angelo**, 22 Miller Avenue, (415) 388-2000, serves great Italian food. The calzones are especially yummy!

In Larkspur, the **Lark Creek Inn**, 234 Magnolia Avenue, (415) 924-7766, is certainly among the best. The "American" cuisine is stretched well away from the traditional with great success. Service is excellent and the prices are high. Sunday brunch is splendid. Try the **Marin Brewing Company**, 1809 Larkspur Landing Drive, (415) 461-5677, for the county's best site-brewed beers and great food. It's hard to find in the little shopping complex across Sir Francis Drake Boulevard from the ferry dock at Larkspur Landing.

San Rafael has several good restaurants on or near Fourth Street. For great Thai, hit **Royal Thai** at 610 Third Street, (415) 386-1795. **Hanna's Restaurant**, 1700 Fourth Street, (415) 457-6252, offers authentic Italian and Mediterranean at its best.

Try the **Parkside Café**, 43 Arenal (off of CA 1), (415) 868-1272, in Stinson Beach for breakfast or lunch. In Bolinas, the **Shop Café**, 46 Wharf Road, (415) 868-9984, is a rustic and friendly place to eavesdrop on the town news. **Gray Whale Pizza** in Inverness, 12781 Sir Francis Drake, (415) 669-1244, is a good place to stop and feed the family.

If you're heading north on CA 1, stop at **Angel's Café** in charming Tomales, (707) 878-9909, for breakfast. The tasty fare is reasonably priced at $5 to $7 a meal. Kathy, the owner, has been collecting ceramic angel figurines for over 20 years. They watch over you as you dine.

LODGING

Freeway chain motels and budget independents can be found along U.S. 101 from Mill Valley north. Use the phone numbers listed under "Resources" in the Practical Tips chapter to contact any of them.

In Sausalito, the **Casa Madrona**, 801 Bridgeway Boulevard, (415) 332-0502 or (800) 288-0502, is the plush choice with rooms and cottages between $140 and $260. A hot tub and beautiful views are included. The **Alta Mira**, 125 Buckley Avenue, (415) 332-1350, also has a great view and a restaurant. Basic rooms are $80, view rooms start at $110.

At the edge of the wildlands, high above Mill Valley, is the wonderful **Mountain Home Inn**, 810 Panoramic Highway, (415) 381-9000. Rooms are high at $133 to $250 (includes breakfast), but the views alone are worth the price. Trailheads are right out the door. Hikers and mountain bikers commonly stop for refreshments during the day. At night, the lights of the bay twinkle below. If you're going to splurge near the city, this is a great choice.

In San Rafael, the **Panama Hotel**, 4 Bayview Street, (415) 457-3993, has class and character. Interesting and occasionally famous people stay here—a good story might be yours. With shared-bath rooms starting at $55, it can be a real bargain (rooms with private bath are $95 and up).

Stinson Beach has several motels, including the refurbished **Sandpiper Motel**, 1 Marine Way, (415) 868-1632, featuring pleasant rooms not far from the beach from $95 to $135. Olema boasts the **Roundstone Farm**, 9940 Sir Francis Drake Boulevard, (415) 663-1020, a lovely B&B with a ranch setting, views of Tomales Bay, and great breakfasts. In Inverness, try the wonderfully constructed **Blackthorne Inn**, 266 Vallejo Avenue, (415) 663-8621. Plan on spending $130 or more.

On a loop above the main road in Rodeo Valley is the **Marin Headlands Hostel**, (415) 331-2777, a Hostelling International facility. The location is a perfect base for exploring the city and the headlands. It costs $12 for dorm beds, $35 for doubles. The **Point Reyes Hostel**, (415) 663-8811, is a couple hundred yards off Limantour Road, in the heart of Point Reyes National Seashore. Beds are $12.

CAMPING

There are two walk-in campgrounds with a total of only 22 sites in Mount Tamalpais State Park. One is just next to **Pantoll Station** at the junction of Panoramic Highway and Ridgecrest Road. The other is at **Steep Ravine**, 1 mile south of Stinson Beach. Fees for both are $10 to $11. Steep Ravine also has cabins for $30. Call (415) 388-2070 for information and reservations.

Samuel P. Taylor State Park is a great place to camp. Trailers up to 27 feet long can be accommodated. Sites are $11 to $15, and are located west of Lagunitas on Sir Francis Drake Boulevard. Call (415) 488-9897 for information, (800) 444-7275 for reservations. There is a $6.75 fee per reservation. The **Olema Ranch Campground** down the road at the junction of Sir Francis Drake Boulevard and CA 1, (415) 663-8001 or (800) 655-2267, is pleasant enough, with sites from $18 to $25. There are hookups, a store and café, and more. **Point Reyes National Seashore** has only hike-in sites. Call (415) 663-1092 for reservations and information.

NIGHTLIFE

Marin is pretty quiet in the evenings. The main action is on Fourth Street in San Rafael. **New Georges**, 842 Fourth Street, (415) 457-8424, is a great place to see live music. With the concentration of musicians in Marin County, the caliber at this club runs from above average to exceptional. Nearby are a few quiet spots for a break and a chat.

In Mill Valley, the oh-so-tiny **Sweetwater**, 153 Throckmorton, (415) 388-2880, is the place to see the truly famous sitting in with a local favorite. The big shots appreciate the hassle-free fit into the jaded crowd. Get there early, or you'll have to listen to the rock, blues, and jazz through the wall.

For a good, site-brewed ale and a game of pool, stop in at the **Marin Brewing Company**, 1809 Larkspur Landing Circle, near the ferry terminal on Sir Francis Drake Boulevard, (415) 462-4677. The beer may not be as good as the Triple Rock in Berkeley, but second place in this brewpub-happy region is very good indeed.

3

THE EAST BAY:
BERKELEY AND OAKLAND

Berkeley and Oakland rise from the East Bay "flats" to the crest of the hills. They enjoy the bay's best weather, receiving the cool, clean air that flows through the Golden Gate while avoiding the fog and chills of San Francisco. Area residents enjoy thousands of acres of recreational lands in their own backyards.

Oakland gained prominence in 1869 as the terminus of the transcontinental railroad and grew into a center of trade and industry. Today, despite ongoing issues of crime and poverty, the city has a strong economic base and a rich slate of cultural and recreational offerings.

The city of Berkeley exists in a love-hate relationship with the renowned University of California at Berkeley. Some 30,000 students enroll at "Cal" each fall, flooding the city with energy and potential. Intellectually inflated and politically left-leaning, Berkeley is a hotbed of activism—a circus of tie-dyed freaks, espresso yuppies, used-book hounds, pesto critics, street preachers, brewpub bums, rallying students, smoky poets, homeless hustlers, and Nobel laureates.

The rest of the East Bay is a patchwork of commercial and residential zones. Richmond gets a nod as a past powerhouse of industry—scores of liberty ships were built here in World War II. Hayward, Walnut Creek, Concord, Livermore, and the towns between are suburbia at its best and worst. Mount Diablo rises above it all, a bit concerned by the housing tracts that nibble at its skirts. ◣

BERKELEY AND NORTH OAKLAND

580

80

El Cerrito

San Francisco
Bay

CENTRAL AV

Kensington

Albany

AV/S DR

ARLINGTON AV

MARIN AV

SOLANO AV

COLUSA AV

Berkeley
Marina

GILMAN ST

580

O A Q

4TH ST

6TH ST

L

123

S

HOPKINS ST

THE ALAMEDA

P

GRIZZLY PEAK BLVD

HEARST AV

N

UNIVERSITY AV

BANCROFT WY

DWIGHT WY

DERBY ST

7TH ST

M L KING JR WY

SHATTUCK AV

SPRUCE ST

G

H

U

J

University
of California
Berkeley

E

B

ASHBY AV

BANCROFT WY

D

SAN PABLO AV

13

80

T

Emeryville

ADELINE ST

Claremont Canyon
Regional Preserve

TELEGRAPH AV

CLAREMONT AV

R

F

COLLEGE AV

TUNNEL RD

Claremont
Hotel

To C

M I

24

BROADWAY

580

13

K

To Downtown Oakland

To V

0 SCALE

1.5
KILOMETERS

1.5
MILES

ROAD

INTERSTATE

BART SYSTEM

AREA BOUNDARY

N

Sights

Ⓐ Berkeley Marina

Ⓑ Lawrence Hall of Science

Ⓒ Mount Diablo

Ⓓ Telegraph Avenue and Sproul Plaza

Ⓔ University of California at Berkeley

Food

Ⓕ Barney's Gourmet Hamburgers

Ⓓ Blue Nile

Ⓓ Café Intermezzo

Ⓖ Cha'Am

Ⓗ Chez Panisse

Ⓘ Citron

Ⓙ Mel's Diner

Ⓚ Michael's Diner

Ⓛ O Chamé

Ⓜ Oliveto Restaurant

Food *(continued)*

Ⓝ Santa Fe Bar & Grill

Ⓞ Skates on the Bay

Ⓟ Zachary's Chicago Style Pizza

Lodging

Ⓠ Berkeley Marina Radisson

Ⓡ Claremont Resort, Spa, and Tennis Club

Ⓢ Golden Bear Motel

Ⓣ Gramma's Rose Garden Inn

Ⓓ Hotel Durant

Ⓙ Shattuck Hotel

Ⓤ YMCA

Camping

Ⓥ Anthony Chabot Regional Park

Ⓒ Mount Diablo State Park

Note: Items with the same letter are located in the same town or area.

A PERFECT DAY IN THE EAST BAY

After a night in the Claremont Hotel and breakfast at Rick and Ann's in Berkeley, follow Claremont Avenue and Telegraph Avenue to downtown Oakland. Stroll on Broadway to see the city hall and the heart of town, then down 14th to Lake Merritt. Enjoy a lakeshore walk and a look at the Camron-Stanford House. Visit the excellent Oakland Museum and its sesquicentennial exhibits. Head to Berkeley via Telegraph Avenue. Take a walking tour of the campus and then a ride to the top of Sather Tower. Experience Telegraph Avenue and "Berserkeley," then enjoy sunset on the Berkeley Pier and dinner with a view at Skates on the Bay.

SIGHTSEEING HIGHLIGHTS

★★ **Oakland Museum of California**—Just west of Lake Merritt, this outstanding museum is a great place to get a rich overview of the Golden State. The structure itself is an award-winning architectural design by Kevin Roche. The three main sections of the museum offer the visitor a clear, rich perspective on California art, history, and ecology. It is perhaps the best museum of its kind in the state. Details: 1001 Oak Street, Oakland; (510) 238-3401; open Wednesday through Saturday from 10 a.m. to 5 p.m., Sunday noon to 5 p.m. (until 9 p.m. on Friday). Admission is $6 adults, $4 seniors and students. Free Friday evenings after 5 p.m. (2 hours)

★★ **Telegraph Avenue and Sproul Plaza**—Students of human behavior should consider this a three-star destination. Telegraph Avenue links downtown Oakland to the University of California. The avenue ends at the entrance to Sproul Plaza. The administration building and student union glare at each other across the plaza, as activists stir lunchtime crowds with speeches on the issue of the day. Jazz bands play below in front of Zellerbach Auditorium while impromptu bucket drummers beat above.

The five blocks of Telegraph just south of campus are a circus of humanity. Shy, schoolgirl-dressed freshmen from Japan stroll past studded and pierced skaters. Pipe-smoking profs buy espresso, ignoring a request for spare change. Cadres of well-groomed jocks push past clusters of grubby gypsy kids. Street vendors line the avenue selling batik baby clothes, handcrafted jewelry, pro-pot T-shirts, and anti-cop bumper stickers.

The shops on Telegraph are equally interesting. Over 40 cafés and coffeehouses line the row selling an ethnically wide-ranging array of dishes at wonderfully affordable prices. Cody's, Moe's, Shakespeare, Shambala, and Half Price team up in a block-and-a-half-long strip to provide the most concentrated selection of new, used, discount, and spiritual books anywhere.

Just above Telegraph, between Haste Street and Dwight Way, are the trees, vegetable gardens, basketball courts, and lawn of People's Park. The park is university-owned land that was confiscated by local citizens in 1969. The university put up a fence, but the outcry after deadly riots led to its removal. The park has since been a jealously guarded symbol and a site for several protests. The movement, however, is showing signs of fatigue, and the university has recovered authority over part of the parcel. (1 hour)

✻ **University of California at Berkeley**—The beautiful "Cal" campus is great for relaxed strolling and offers a number of attractions to the visitor. Details: The Visitor Services office is located at 2200 University Avenue (at Oxford Street), Room 101, Berkeley. Campus tours are offered at 10 a.m., Monday through Saturday, 1 p.m. Sunday (tours start at the Visitor Services office on weekdays, from Sather Tower on weekends); office open 8:30 a.m. to 4:30 p.m.; (510) 642-5215. (2 hours)

Strawberry Creek flows down from the hills and through the campus. Alongside the creek are lovely paths, redwood trees, a eucalyptus grove, charming bridges, and interesting sculpture. Above campus, Strawberry Creek flows through the beautiful **Botanical Gardens**. Details: Centennial Road, Berkeley; (510) 642-3343; open daily from 9 a.m. to 4:45 p.m. (until 7 p.m. in mid-summer). Admission is $3. (1½ hours)

Several campus museums are worth noting. The **University Art Museum and Pacific Film Archive** features Asian and modern rotating exhibits, as well as various series of art films. Details: 2626 Bancroft Way (also 2625 Durant Street), Berkeley; (510) 642-0808 or (510) 642-1124 for film information; museum open Wednesday through Sunday from 11 a.m. to 5 p.m. (until 9 p.m. Thursday). Admission is $6 (free on Thursday evenings). (2 hours)

In Kroeber Hall, you'll find the **Museum of Anthropology**. Details: Bancroft Way and College Avenue, University of California, Berkeley; (510) 642-3681; open Wednesday through Sunday from 10 a.m. to 4:30 p.m. (until 9 p.m. Thursday), and weekends from noon to 4:30 p.m. Admission is $2. (1 hour)

The **Museum of Paleontology**, in the Life Sciences Building, has skeletons, fossils, and more. Details: University of California, Berkeley; (510) 642-1821; open daily from 8 a.m. to 5 p.m. (opens at noon on weekends). Admission is free. (1 hour)

Sather Tower, the Campanile, is a 300-foot-tall landmark, visible for miles. Those same miles of visibility can be enjoyed from the top of the tower. If you're lucky, you'll be there on a weekday when the carillon is played at noon. Details: University of California, Berkeley; open daily from 10 a.m. to 4 p.m. (until 5 p.m. on weekends), closed from 2 to 3 p.m. on Saturday and Sunday for carillon concerts, last elevator ascends 30 minutes before closing hours. Admission is 50 cents. (1 hour)

☆ **Berkeley Marina**—The marina is a great place to spend an hour.
The **Waterfront Walk** offers a 1½-mile waterside path popular with
walkers and joggers. A sunset stroll out onto the 600-yard-long
Berkeley Pier, the refurbished remnant of a much longer structure,
offers a marvelous view across the bay. The marina is a favored location
for windsurfers and kite flyers. Good lodging and dining are available
in the area. Details: At the end of University Avenue, Berkeley.
(1 hour)

☆ **Lake Merritt**—Without Lake Merritt, downtown Oakland might
seem as drab as any city forced to face off against San Francisco.
Instead, this urban saltwater lake provides a 3-mile stretch of waterfront parkland, affording recreational opportunities and splendid views
of the skyline. At the western end of the lake, the **Camron-Stanford
House** reminds strollers of the Victorian Oakland that once was.
Details: 1418 Lakeside Drive, Oakland; (510) 836-1976; tours are
offered Wednesday from 11 a.m. to 4 p.m., and Sunday from 1 to 5
p.m. Admission is $4. (4 hours)
    On the north shore, **Lakeside Park** features **Children's
Fairyland**, (510) 452-2259, a pleasant creative play area with a
carousel, puppet shows, and farm animals—kids love it. Admission is
$3.25 for adults, $2.75 for kids. The **Nature Center** has a small
museum and educational activities. It's open daily from 10 a.m. to 5
p.m., and admission is free. The **Boat Rental Center**, (510) 444-3807,
offers small craft for exploring the lake. Details: Grand Avenue, Lake
Merritt, Oakland.

☆ **Mount Diablo**—You can see more of the earth's surface from the
summit of Mount Diablo than from any other point on the planet
except Mount Kilimanjaro (if the air is clear). The phenomenon is
related to the shape of the Central Valley. As the world curves away,
sphere that it is, the margins of the Central Valley rise toward the hills
in compensation, exposing more land to the viewer upon Mount
Diablo's summit. In addition, the mountain is isolated at the center of
the long valley. Take a look.
    Mount Diablo State Park offers hiking and biking trails, rock
climbing, and views galore. Details: For the north entrance, take the
Ignacio Valley Road exit from Interstate 680. Follow Ignacio Valley
Road east to a right on Walnut Avenue, which merges into Northgate,
the entrance road. Take Diablo Road from Interstate 680 near Danville

to reach the south entrance. Open 8 a.m. until sunset (except for campers); (510) 673-2890. Day-use fee is $5. (½ day)

✸ **Lawrence Hall of Science**—Located high above the Berkeley campus, this hands-on museum features wonderful exhibits that can be enjoyed by both kids and parents (but mostly kids). Outside the unique concrete structure, children can climb on a full-size model of a whale, while the adults admire the panoramic view. Details: Take Hearst Avenue from Shattuck in downtown Berkeley, turn right into the campus on Gayley Road, left above the stadium on Stadium Way, then left again on Centennial Drive; (510) 642-5132; open daily from 10 a.m. to 5 p.m. Admission is $6, kids $4. (2 hours)

Jack London Square—Where Broadway meets the Inner Harbor in downtown Oakland, this somewhat awkwardly laid out collection of waterfront restaurants, shops, theaters, and nightspots welcomes the visitor. Featured sights include the relocated **Jack London Cabin**, which he once occupied, and London's one-time watering hole, **Heinold's First and Last Chance Saloon.** Built in 1880, the ground under the pub has shifted substantially, leaving it with an intriguingly slanted floor. Details: The foot of Webster Street, Jack London Square, Oakland; open daily; (510) 839-6761.

Look for Roosevelt's yacht, the **U.S.S.** *Potomac*, permanently berthed at the foot of Clay Street. Details: Jack London Square, Oakland; call about the eight monthly bay cruises, (510) 839-8256; dockside tours are offered Wednesday and Friday at 10 a.m. and 2 p.m., Sunday at 11 a.m. and 3 p.m. Tours are $3. (1½ hours)

FITNESS AND RECREATION

The Bay Area is a place to be outdoors. The hills above Oakland and Berkeley are quite wild, protected by a series of regional parks, preserves, and watershed lands. Above Berkeley, **Tilden Regional Park** offers swimming in Lake Anza, strolling in the Botanical Gardens, golfing on a hilly course, and hiking and biking on several miles of trails. Take Centennial Way up through the Berkeley campus, or Claremont Avenue to Grizzly Peak Boulevard, then left to the park.

To reach **Robert Sibley Volcanic Regional Preserve** and **Redwood Regional Park**, take a right on Grizzly Peak from Claremont Avenue. Both have good hiking and biking trails. Sibley preserves a volcanic cone and other formations. The **East Bay Skyline National Recreation Trail** connects Tilden, Sibley, Redwood, and others as it follows the ridge crest. The trail is part of a larger system that circles the entire bay region. Good jogging or walking loops include **Lake Merritt** (3.2 miles), **North Waterfront Park** at the Berkeley Marina (1.3 miles), and **Aquatic Park** at the bottom of Bancroft Way in Berkeley. (2.2 miles)

FOOD

Several good spots are found in the downtown Oakland and Jack London Square vicinity. On the waterfront, you'll find **Il Pescatore**, 57 Jack London Square, (510) 465-2188, with tasty seafood and Italian fare. For authentic and inexpensive Vietnamese fare, **Vi's Restaurant**, 724 Webster Street, (510) 835-8375, is the place—a diamond in the rough. Everyone loves **Zza's Trattoria**, 552 Grand Avenue, (510) 839-9124. The thin crust of the pizza crunches delicately before the toppings melt in your mouth. Aaahhh!

College Avenue through North Oakland is a great stretch for dining. **Citron**, 5484 College Avenue, (510) 653-5484, features intimate dining and top-quality French cuisine. Even with two locations, you may well have to wait in line for the pizza consistently voted the best of the East Bay at **Zachary's Chicago Style Pizza**, 5801 College Avenue, (510) 655-6385, or 1853 Solano Avenue, (510) 525-5950. Their specialty is an amazing deep-dish with a layer of crust baked in between filling and topping. They don't make 'em any better than they do at **Barney's Gourmet Hamburgers**, 5819 College Avenue, (510) 601-0444. The reputation of **Oliveto Restaurant**, 5565 College Avenue, (510) 547-5356, has grown steadily. It has the extra advantage of being across the street from the Rockridge BART station.

The **Café Intermezzo**, 2475 Telegraph Avenue, (510) 849-1128, serves insanely huge salads and sandwiches at great prices. Buy one and share. The **Blue Nile**, 2525 Telegraph Avenue, (510) 540-6777, is one of the bay's top Ethiopian restaurants, with the bonus of exotic ambiance and good prices. Try **Michael's Diner**, 2650 Telegraph Avenue, (510) 548-0600, where can you get a delicious bacon cheeseburger—with no meat or dairy products!

Many good places to eat are located on Shattuck Avenue, which runs through downtown and north Berkeley. For a thick shake with your cheeseburger and fries, try **Mel's Diner**, 2240 Shattuck Avenue,

OAKLAND

Sights

A Jack London Square

B Lake Merritt

C Oakland Museum of California

Food

D Il Pescatore

E Vi's Restaurant

F Zza's Trattoria

Lodging

G Best Western Thunderbird Inn

H Lake Merritt Hotel

I Marriott Park Oakland Hotel

J Washington Inn

K Waterfront Plaza Hotel

(510) 540-6351. Where Shattuck meets Vine Street, Berkeley's "Gourmet Ghetto" is a center of eating and pantry stocking. Still the pinnacle of East Bay dining, **Chez Panisse**, 1517 Shattuck Avenue, (510) 548-5525 (510-548-5049 for the café), helped hatch California cuisine and then raised it to fine art. Bill Clinton always stops by when he's in town. Prix fixe in the downstairs dining room runs from $35 to $70. Upstairs, the café entrées are around $15. It's open for lunch and dinner, closed Sunday. **Cha'Am**, 1543 Shattuck, (510) 848-9664, is a local favorite, offering the best in Thai cuisine.

Several places are near the bay, toward the bottom of University Avenue or around Fourth Street near Hearst. Located in an old train station, the **Santa Fe Bar & Grill**, 1310 University Avenue, (510) 841-4740, has been serving consistently good, high-end cuisine for years. The inspiration at **Skates on the Bay** at the end of University Avenue by the Berkeley Pier, (510) 549-1900, is the marvelous view. Dinner from the varied menu ranges from $12 to $20. **O Chamé**, 1830 Fourth Street, (510) 841-8783, is a terrific, casual, and artful Japanese café—one of Berkeley's best.

LODGING

Chain motels are found along the freeways and near the Oakland Airport. Use the numbers listed under "Resources" in the Practical Tips chapter.

The **Claremont Resort, Spa, and Tennis Club**, Ashby Avenue and Domingo Avenue (you can't miss it), (510) 843-3000, is *the* place to stay in the East Bay. Located in Oakland, right on the Berkeley border, this huge, white, Edwardian palace is visible for miles. The views of the bay from restaurant, bar, and bayside rooms are spectacular. Enjoy a massage, soak, and swim after a long day of walking through the city. Rooms start at $215, view rooms at $260.

In downtown Oakland, the **Lake Merritt Hotel**, 1800 Madison Street, (510) 832-2300 or (800) 933-4683, offers bargain luxury with a lake view. Rooms range from $110 to $180. Continental breakfast is served in the Terrace Room. Also in the city center is the **Washington Inn**, 495 10th Street, (510) 452-1776 or (800) 464-1776, a small, restored hotel built before World War I. The $110 to $140 rooms include breakfast. Across the way is the huge **Marriott Park Oakland Hotel**, 1001 Broadway, (510) 451-4000 or (800) 338-1338. Rooms range from $115 to $150, and some feature terrific views.

At Jack London Square, the **Best Western Thunderbird Inn**, 233 Broadway, (510) 452-4565 or (800) 633-5973, has rooms from $80 to $95 and a pool. Nearby, the **Waterfront Plaza Hotel**, 10 Washington Street, (510) 836-3800, has rooms starting for $165, $185 with nice views across the harbor.

The **Berkeley Marina Radisson**, 200 Marina Boulevard, (510) 548-7920 or (800) 228-9290, has a wonderful location at the Berkeley Marina. Rooms run from $100 to $170. Just above Telegraph Avenue is the **Hotel Durant**, 2600 Durant Street, (510) 845-8981. Rooms start at $110 and offer great access to the campus. **Gramma's Rose Garden Inn**, 2740 Telegraph Avenue, (510) 549-2145, is a pleasant B&B only three blocks from all the action on Telegraph Avenue. All rooms have a private bath, and cost $90 to $165. Downtown you'll find the older, moderately elegant **Shattuck Hotel**, 2086 Allston Way, (510) 845-7300 or (800) 742-8882. Rooms go from $80 to $110 and include a continental breakfast. A clean budget alternative is the **Golden Bear Motel**, 1620 San Pablo Avenue, (510) 525-6770. Rooms are $55. True budgeteers can stay at the downtown **YMCA**, 2001 Allston Way, (510) 848-6800. Tiny singles are $25, and you can use the workout facilities.

CAMPING

There are three campgrounds in **Mount Diablo State Park**, (510) 837-2525. Trailers are limited to 20 feet and motor homes to 24 feet, due to the narrow, winding roads. You must arrive before sunset when the park entrance roads close. Sites cost from $12 to $15. Make reservations ($7.50) through Parknet, (800) 444-7275.

Anthony Chabot Regional Park, (510) 635-0135, has 31 sites for $16, or $21 for RVs. Take Interstate 580 to the Estudillo Avenue exit in San Leandro. Head east into the park on Estudillo, which becomes Lake Chabot Road.

NIGHTLIFE

Compared to the city, East Bay nightlife is pretty tame, ends early, and tends to favor coffee over beer. Several zones are good for browsing, a bite, and a drink up until 11 p.m. or midnight. Bars and clubs close at 1 or 2 a.m. These same areas are more alive during the day.

Near downtown Oakland, the only evening area of much activity is **Jack London Square.** Most are there to eat or see a film, but there are a couple of nightspots, including the tiny, ancient, and sinking **Heinold's First and Last Chance Saloon**, (510) 839-6761. **Shenanigan's**, (510) 839-8333, has a good bar with its restaurant in the square. Farther into town, the **Pacific Coast Brewing Company**, 906 Washington Street, (510) 836-2739, has great brews and food.

College Avenue, between Broadway and Alcatraz Avenue, has much to offer. Toward Broadway, **Bill McNally's**, 5352 College Avenue, (510) 654-9463, is a fine Irish pub. Near the BART station, the **Edible Complex**, 5600 College Avenue, (510) 658-2172, has pricey coffee but serves as a gathering place of good minds. Farther north, College Avenue and Ashby Avenue intersect in Elmwood. At the corner, **Espresso Roma**, 2960 College Avenue, (510) 644-3773, has beer, coffee, pastries, and light entrées, as well as a room with wall plugs that laptop users treasure.

Heading toward the Berkeley campus on Telegraph Avenue from Parker Street, you'll hit the **Bison Brewing Company**, 2598 Telegraph Avenue, (510) 841-7734. A great place to enjoy a site-brewed beer. A pool table, occasional music, good grub, and weird architecture complete the picture. Between Dwight Way and Haste Street, **Cody's** bookstore is open until 10 p.m., **Moe's Books** until 11 p.m., and the **Caffé Mediterraneum** until midnight—there's an evening right there. **Blake's**, 2367 Telegraph Avenue, (510) 848-0886, has food and beer upstairs with live music or deejays downstairs. Monday night is a blues open-mike night with occasional visits by the greats. **Caffé Strada**, 2300 College Avenue, (510) 843-5282, at Bancroft and College is a big draw for students who need espresso (as are a dozen other places).

The happening place is the **Jupiter**, 2181 Shattuck Avenue, (510) 843-1761. Take a pint of good microbrew into the splendid courtyard out back to enjoy top local bands. The best of all spots is the **Triple Rock**, 1920 Shattuck Avenue, (510) 843-2739. This brewpub consistently serves the finest site-brewed beer in the bay. Try the I.P.A., Tree Frog, Stonehenge Stout, or their classic Red Rock. It's a great place to relax and talk. Renowned musician Pete Escobedo opened **Mr. E's**, 2284 Shattuck Avenue, (510) 848-2009, featuring Latin and jazz music with a fair share of top acts.

Elsewhere, the **Albatross** (also the Bird) at 1822 San Pablo Avenue, Berkeley, (510) 849-4714, was the first pub in town—and perhaps still the best. Playing a board game by the fire or reading to classical music at the bar is welcomed. This is the best darts bar in town. For live music, either Irish traditional or jamming electric, the **Starry Plough**, 3101 Shattuck Avenue, Berkeley, (510) 841-2082, is an excellent choice.

4

THE SOUTH BAY AND THE PENINSULA COAST

The South Bay has, in recent decades, been a rapidly growing economic success story. Silicon Valley (the flatlands from Palo Alto to San Jose and around toward Fremont) hosts corporate headquarters for such companies as Apple Computer, Hewlett Packard, Intel, and Sun Microsystems. Stanford University has enjoyed a meteoric rise to rival Harvard as the nation's premier private school. At 850,000, San Jose is now the most populated city in Northern California.

The San Jose metropolitan area has been justly compared to Los Angeles. While the region is a safe, hospitable, and economically vibrant place to live, the South Bay hills can trap smog over the hot, sprawling, strip-malled suburbs with their maze of freeways. For this reason, visitors often choose to breeze through the South Bay.

The hills and coast of the peninsula are a different story. Bitter battles between preservationists and developers have stalled subdivision of the headlands, perhaps permanently. Towns are still small and pleasant; CA 1 is still a winding two-lane road; and coastal vistas are uninterrupted by corporate towers and cookie-cutter housing. While touring the peninsula coast, it is entirely possible to forget that 6 million people are going about their business just over the hills.

Several good parks and public beaches line the coast, including a vital breeding ground for the once endangered elephant seal and the southernmost bastion of old-growth coastal redwoods. ◣

THE SOUTH BAY AND PENINSULA COAST

Sights

Ⓐ Año Nuevo State Reserve

Ⓑ Big Basin Redwoods State Park

Ⓒ Capitola

Ⓓ Filoli

Ⓔ Mission Santa Clara de Asis

Ⓕ Mount Hamilton

Ⓖ Paramount's Great America

Ⓗ Rosicrucian Egyptian Museum
and Planetarium

Ⓗ San Jose City Center

Ⓘ San Juan Bautista

Ⓙ Santa Cruz

Ⓚ Scenic Railways

Ⓛ Stanford University

Ⓗ Winchester Mystery House

Note: Items with the same letter are located in the same town or area.

A PERFECT DAY ON THE PENINSULA

Spend the morning in Palo Alto, having breakfast on University
Avenue and visiting the sights of the Stanford University campus.
Hook up with CA 84 for a winding journey through the hills to the
coast. Visit Año Nuevo State Reserve for a look at the elephant seals. If
time allows, take a longer hike in Año Nuevo, along Waddell Creek in
Big Basin Redwoods State Park, or on the headlands at Wilder Ranch
State Park. Enjoy the Santa Cruz Beach Boardwalk late in the day, then
retire to Capitola for an evening constitutional and bed.

SIGHTSEEING HIGHLIGHTS

★★★ **Año Nuevo State Reserve**—Huge male elephant seals, with
their bulbous probosci, are shameless when it comes to displaying mating behavior and violence in front of the gawking humans at Año

Nuevo. They begin arriving in December and battle for dominance. Later in the month, smaller females begin arriving to give birth, nurse their young, and gather into harems. In January, victorious alpha males mate with their harems while the lesser bulls watch from the sidelines.

In general, there are always at least a few elephant seals to be seen. Stragglers and early arrivals frame the mating season, while the seals return in stages to molt from April through August. Harbor seals, California and Steller's sea lions, and many types of shorebirds can also be seen. Shy bobcats are occasionally sighted in the meadows. For the peak period from December 15 through March, you should make reservations for the popular seal viewing tour. At other times, you can just stop at the park. Only key seal areas have limited access, the rest of this large reserve is open for hiking and other activities. Details: The park entrance is 13 miles south of Pescadero on CA 1; call (650) 879-2025 for park information, (800) 444-4445 for reservations; open daily from 8 a.m. to dusk. Parking is $5, general entry is free, and guided walks are $4. (2½ hours)

★★★ **San Juan Bautista**—A few miles east of U.S. 101 on CA 156, this town of less than 2,000 sits right on the San Andreas Fault. It was an unfortunate place to build the **Mission San Juan Bautista** in 1797, but they couldn't have guessed it at the time. The outer walls of the unusual, three-aisle mission church came down in the 1906 quake, but the interior, dating to 1816, survived. Reconstruction in 1976 restored the outer walls and opened up interior archways that had long been blocked, returning the church to its status as the largest in California. The church and a surviving wing of the original mission are open for self-guided tours. Details: 2nd Street, central San Juan Bautista; (408) 623-4528; open daily from 9:30 a.m. to 5 p.m. (opens at 10 a.m. Sunday). A donation is requested. (3 hours)

The mission sits in wonderful **Old Plaza**, surrounded by several historic Spanish-colonial buildings—all part of the **San Juan Bautista State Historic Park**. The **Plaza Hotel**, built in 1858, once served as a major overnight stop on the stagecoach route. The nearby **Castro House** was built in 1840. These and other structures, including some replicas, combine successfully to create the feel of a bygone era. Details: Second and Mariposa Streets, San Juan Bautista; (408) 623-4881; open daily from 10 a.m. to 4:30 p.m. Admission is $2. (2 hours)

The town of **San Juan Bautista** is a delight for strolling and relaxing—one of my favorite historic towns in the state. Among the old shops on historic Third Street, you'll find the wonderful **San Juan Bakery**, the oldest in the West.

⭐⭐ **Big Basin Redwoods State Park**—This large park in the hard-to-reach heart of the peninsula preserves some of the southernmost stands of old-growth redwoods. Wonderful hikes lead through groves, to the summits, or from the ridge to the sea. Two campgrounds are available. Access is via the twisting CA 236 from CA 9. A narrow finger of the park reaches the Pacific south of Año Nuevo via Waddell Creek. There's a trailhead there, though no road. Details: The headquarters are nine miles northwest of Boulder Creek on CA 236; (408) 338-8860; open daily from 8 a.m. to 10 p.m. Day-use parking is $6. (3 hours)

⭐⭐ **Santa Cruz**—This is a beach, boardwalk, and student town—not a place to get serious. Pacific Avenue is the main street for shopping and strolling.

The **Santa Cruz Beach Boardwalk** was constructed in 1904. While the boards are now paved over, this beachfront amusement park offers good, old-style family fun. An old wooden roller coaster provides a sense of danger not related to speed or height. Strolling, people-watching, and ice cream consumption are standard practice. **Santa Cruz Beach**, immediately below the boardwalk, is one of many that line Monterey Bay.

The **Monarch Butterfly Natural Preserve** within **Natural Bridges State Beach** is the best place in the region to observe up to 1.5 million monarch butterflies wintering in the trees. Butterflies are present from October through February. The rest of the park features a beach, ocean-carved rock formations, and tidal pools. Details: 2531 West Cliff Drive, Santa Cruz; (408) 423-4609; free tours are given on Saturdays and Sundays at 11 a.m. and 2 p.m.—though you can stroll through the grounds at any time. Day-use parking is $6.

The **Santa Cruz City Museum of Natural History** is worth a visit. Marine natural history, geology, and exhibits related to the Ohlone Indians are featured. Details: 1305 East Cliff Drive (across the river from the town center), Santa Cruz; (408) 429-3773; open Tuesday through Friday from 10 a.m. to 5 p.m. Admission is free. (1 hour)

Another museum of note is the **Surfing Museum**. You can imagine what's on display. Down below is a favorite surfing break. Details: In the Mark Abbott Memorial Lighthouse, West Cliff Drive at Lighthouse Point, Santa Cruz; (408) 429-3429; open Wednesday through Monday from noon to 4 p.m. Admission is free. (½ hour)

For a real head shaker, check out the 3-D wax version of *Da Vinci's Last Supper* at the Santa Cruz Memorial Park. Details: 1927 Ocean Street, at the foot of Grant Hill Road, Santa Cruz; call (408) 426-1601 to schedule a visit; open Monday through Friday from 1 to 4 p.m. Admission is free. (15 minutes)

✹✹ **Stanford University**—The campus of Stanford University is the largest in the world, thanks to the wealth and landholdings of its founder and prime benefactor, railroad baron Leland Stanford Jr. A campus tour is a pleasant choice for a morning. Take Palm Drive from the El Camino Real (CA 82) in Palo Alto. Details: Visitor Center is in the lobby of Memorial Hall; (650) 723-2560; open Monday through Friday from 8 a.m. to 5 p.m., opens at 9 a.m. on weekends. Free walking tours daily at 11 a.m. and 3:15 p.m.

The heart of campus is the "Quad." The beautiful **Memorial Church** with its ornate, gilded facade and mosaic-tiled mural presides over colonnaded stone walkways and red tile roofs. Nearby, the 285-foot **Hoover Tower** dominates the scene. A $2 elevator ride to the top affords great views of the campus and South Bay region (open daily from 10 a.m. to 4:30 p.m.).

A wonderful spot for peaceful contemplation is the **Rodin Sculpture Garden** outside of the earthquake-damaged and still closed **Stanford Museum**. Call (650) 723-3469 for updated information. Several rare castings are found in the garden, including the amazing *Gates of Hell*. The new **Papua New Guinea Sculpture Garden** in the Eucalyptus Grove at the corner of Santa Teresa and Lomita Drive features towering totems, one of which was carved on site during a special ceremony.

Other options include a visit to the **Hoover Institution on War, Revolution, and Peace**, a conservative think tank and site of research into international issues; and to the associated **Hoover Library**, repository of President Herbert Hoover's papers. The **Stanford Linear Accelerator**, a 2-mile-long building that passes directly under Interstate 280, offers tours by appointment. Details: 2575 Sand Hill Road; (650) 926-2204. The tour is free. (2½ hours)

✹ **Capitola**—This very charming bayside town is just down the road from Santa Cruz. The narrow streets and Victorian summer homes blend perfectly with the small shops that cater to the vacationers and tourists. So when the glitz of the boardwalk and energy of the students in Santa Cruz get too much to bear, book a room in Capitola. An evening walk along the Esplanade is a pleasant and relaxing way to finish up the day. Details: Take the Capitola exit from CA 1. (1½ hours)

✰ **Filoli**—This historic mansion was the home of the exceedingly wealthy Mr. and Mrs. William B. Bourn II, owners of the Empire Mine near Grass Valley. Built between 1916 and 1919, the 654-acre estate features magnificent formal gardens, a 43-room Georgian Revival mansion, and outbuildings. It was used as the mansion for the television program *Dynasty*. You can reserve a spot on a two-hour morning or afternoon tour. Details: Take Cañada Road from Interstate 280 north of Woodside; (650) 364-8300; open mid-February through October; docent-led tours by reservation from Tuesday through Saturday, self-guided tours from 10 a.m. to 2 p.m. on weekends. Admission is $8. (2 hours)

✰ **Mission Santa Clara de Asis**—Located at the heart of the Santa Clara University campus, the present mission church was built in 1928 as a replica of the 1822 church. The plaza, gardens, and part of one wall are original. Details: 500 El Camino Real, Santa Clara; (408) 554-4023; open Monday through Friday from sunrise to sunset. Admission is free. (1 hour)

✰ **Mount Hamilton**—East of San Jose, the Coast Range bumps up a notch in elevation, reaching a height of more than 4,200 feet. A slow, winding road climbs to very near the summit, affording great views along the way. At the top sits **Lick Observatory**, home to the 120-inch Keck Telescope and several others. Details: from I-680, exit on Alum Rock Road east, turn right on Mount Hamilton Road, and follow it 19 miles to the top; (408) 274-5061; visitor center open Monday through Friday from 12:30 to 5 p.m., weekends from 10 a.m. to 5 p.m. Free tours every half hour. (3½ hours)

✰ **Rosicrucian Egyptian Museum and Planetarium**—This excellent and unusual museum features Egyptian and other ancient artifacts, as well as a replica of an Egyptian rock tomb. It is also the international headquarters of the Rosicrucian order, a group dedicated to philosophical inquiry and education. The museum is and deserves to be San Jose's most popular visitor attraction. Details: 1342 Naglee Avenue,

San Jose; (408) 947-3635; open Wednesday through Monday from 10 a.m. to 5 p.m. Admission is $7, planetarium admission is $4. (2 hours)

☆ **San Jose City Center**—Downtown San Jose is on few tourist itineraries, but it has several points of interest. Though almost all of the oldest structures are gone, San Jose was established in 1777 as the "first civil settlement" in California. It served as the state capital from 1849 to 1851. The center of things is the **Plaza de Cesar Chavez** on Market Street at Park Avenue. To reach downtown, take the CA 87 North exit from I-280 and get off on Santa Clara Street, turning right, then right again on Market Street. Shop and restaurant areas downtown include 1st and 2nd Streets, and San Pedro Street at Santa Clara Street. (½ day)

On St. John Street between Almaden Avenue and San Pedro Street, the **Peralta Adobe**, built in 1797, preserves the last vestiges of El Pueblo de San Jose de Guadalupe that covered much of what is now the city center. Across the street is the **Fallon House**, a fine home dating to 1854. Details: A visitor center for both sites is located at 175 West St. John Street, San Jose; (408) 993-8182; Fallon House tours are Tuesday through Sunday from noon to 5 p.m. Admission is $6 adults, $5 seniors, $4 ages 6–17, under age 5 free. (1 hour)

The **Technology Museum of Innovation** has displays and interactive exhibits featuring, not surprisingly, innovations in technology! It's great for families with older kids. Details: 145 W. San Carlos Street, San Jose; (408) 279-7150; open Tuesday through Sunday from 10 a.m. to 5 p.m. Admission is $6.

Nearby, the **Children's Discovery Museum** makes technology friendly to the younger set. Details: 180 Woz Way, San Jose; (408) 298-5437; open Tuesday through Saturday from 10 a.m. to 5 p.m., and Sunday from noon to 5 p.m. Admission is $6. (2 hours)

The work of contemporary artists is exhibited in the **San Jose Museum of Art**. There's a nice café offering Tuscan cuisine. Details: 110 South Market Street, at the north end of Plaza Park; San Jose; (408) 294-2787; open Tuesday through Sunday from 10 a.m. to 5 p.m. (until 8 p.m. on Thursday). Admission is $7. (2 hours)

Just north of the museum are the unmistakable towers and facade of **St. Joseph's Cathedral**, built in 1875 to replace an older structure. The first church on the site was built in 1803. Details: 90 South Market Street at San Fernando Street, (408) 283-8100, open 7:30 a.m. to 5 p.m. Monday through Friday, 8 a.m. to 5:30 p.m. Saturday, and 8 a.m. to 9 p.m. Sunday. Tours by appointment, (408) 275-6090. (½ hour)

✯ **Scenic Railways**—The **Roaring Camp Railroad**, a narrow gauge line, takes a ½-hour round-trip through the redwoods from Roaring Camp, near Felton. In the summer there are four or five trips daily. The **Santa Cruz, Big Trees, and Pacific Railway** offers a 2½-hour round-trip from the Felton Station, stopping at Roaring Camp and going right to the boardwalk in Santa Cruz. Details: Take CA 17 to Mount Hermon Road, through Scott's Valley, to Felton. Turn left onto Graham Hill Road for Roaring Camp.

Trains depart from the old Southern Pacific Depot in Felton, but are scheduled out of Roaring Camp at 10:30 a.m. and 2:30 p.m. Trains run daily in the summer. Either trip is $15. (½ day)

✯ **Winchester Mystery House**—It's hard to know what to make of this spiritually guided obsession of Sarah Winchester, heir of the Winchester Rifle fortune. She was supposedly directed from beyond to continue adding rooms to her home. You'll shake your head at the tiny chambers, secret passages, and stairways to nowhere. Details: Take the Winchester Boulevard exit from Interstate 280 South, or take Stevens Creek Boulevard from Interstate 880 to Winchester Boulevard; 525 South Winchester Boulevard, San Jose; (408) 247-2000; open daily with tours offered from 9 a.m. to 5 p.m. (9:30 a.m. to 4 p.m. November through February). Admission is $14. (1½ hours)

Paramount's Great America—Take the kids to the best amusement park in the bay and let them test their stomachs against the rides. Details: Take the Great America Parkway exit from either CA 101 or CA 237, Santa Clara; (408) 988-1776; summer hours are from 10 a.m. to 9 p.m., until 11 p.m. on Saturday (open weekends only in spring and fall, and closed during winter). Admission is $32. (½ day)

FITNESS AND RECREATION

The **Skyline to the Sea Trail** runs from the high ridges of Big Basin Redwoods State Park, down along West Waddell Creek to the Pacific. Take a long one-way hike, an overnight loop, or enjoy the marvelous groves downstream from park headquarters. Excellent 8-mile or 11-mile circuits access waterfalls and the best of the trees.

Another long, gentle trail follows a fire road up into the hills of the **Forest of Nisene Marks State Park**. Land for the park was donated by the Marks family in 1963 and features second-growth

redwoods. Take Aptos Creek Road to the north end of the town of
Aptos. Rock climbers will enjoy the outcrops in **Castle Rock State
Park**. Take CA 35 2½ miles south from the junction with CA 9 to
reach the trailheads.

Santa Cruz is a center for outdoor enthusiasts. Surfing is popular
at several spots around the upper Monterey Bay and Peninsula Coast.
Go Skate, 601 Beach Street, (408) 425-8578, is a good place to rent
surf gear, as well as in-line skates and other equipment. Mountain biking is popular in the hills above town, particularly in **Henry Cowell
Redwoods State Park**.

FOOD

In Palo Alto, the area around University Avenue between Alma and
Cowper is the place to browse. Architect Julia Morgan designed the
building that houses the excellent **MacArthur Park**, 520 Lagunita
Drive, (650) 321-9990, which features wonderful grilled dishes. Fine
French fare can be had for a price at **L'Amie Donia**, 530 Bryant
Street, (650) 323-7614. A good wine list, nice patios, and an unusual
zinc bar complement the great food. Stop in at the **Peninsula
Creamery Fountain & Grill**, 566 Emerson Street, (650) 323-3131,
for a thoroughly American foodfest at breakfast, lunch, or dinner.
Pollo's, 543 Emerson Street, (650) 473-0212, is a good place for fast,
cheap, and filling Mexican food.

Downtown San Jose has many good places within four or five
blocks of Plaza Park. The elegant **Les Saisons** in the Fairmont Hotel,
170 South Market Street, (408) 998-3950, is a lovely place to go for
continental cuisine if your suit isn't wrinkled and you have money to
burn. California cuisine with a good deal of international influence
characterizes the understated fine dining at **Eulipia**, 374 South First
Street, (408) 280-6161. For great Italian at more modest prices, head
to **Bella Mia** at 58 South First Street, (408) 280-1993. For good
Mexican food in a comfortable setting, **Casa Castillo** at 200 South
First Street, (408) 971-8132, is a good choice. Burgers and beer go
hand-in-hand at the **Tied House**, a brewpub at 65 North San Pedro
Street, (408) 295-2739.

Just north of Half Moon Bay in Princeton, enjoy outdoor dining
on the water at **The Shore Bird**, 390 Capistrano Road, (650) 728-
5541, a good steak and seafood place. **Pasta Moon** in Half Moon Bay
offers fantastic Italian food at mid-level prices. You'll find it in the Tin

Palace at 315 Main Street, (650) 726-5125. In Santa Cruz, browse Pacific and Front Streets for options. Cheap eats can be had in many places, notably the **Pontiac Grill**, 44 Front Street, (408) 427-2290, a diner that Elvis would have liked. The **Front Street Pub & Santa Cruz Brewing Company**, 516 Front Street, (408) 429-8838, is one of my favorites for big, tasty pub fare and good beer.

In Capitola, don't miss the **Shadowbrook Restaurant**, 1750 Wharf Road, (408) 475-1511. To reach the terraced restaurant from the parking lot, ride the funicular down past a waterfall. Get an outdoor table if the weather cooperates. Try **Mr. Toots Coffeehouse**, 221A Esplanade, (408) 475-3679, for a snack and coffee.

The **Faultline**, (408) 623-2117, in San Juan Bautista has a valley view and fine continental cuisine for a price. It's near the mission at 11 Franklin Street, reservations suggested. The **San Juan Bakery**, Third Street, (408) 623-4570, offers tasty sandwiches and out-of-this-world baked goods in the oldest bakery in the West.

LODGING

Chain motels and hotels litter the stretch from San Mateo through San Jose. Use the numbers listed under "Resources" in the Practical Tips chapter to locate many of them.

For plush in Palo Alto, the **Garden Court Hotel**, 520 Cowper Street, (650) 322-9000, fits the bill, and it's right in the center of things. Rooms start at $225. Nearby, the **Cardinal Hotel**, (650) 323-5101, is an aging gem. Rooms with shared bath are as low as $65, rooms with private bath, $100. South of campus in Los Altos Hills, the **Hidden Villa Hostel**, 26870 Moody Road, (415) 949-8648, has $10 beds.

The **De Anza Hotel**, 233 West Santa Clara Street, (800) 843-3700, is my top choice for a luxury stay in San Jose. Its quiet, classic elegance is a pleasure, as is the fine restaurant and cozy Hedley Club lounge. The best rate for rooms is $105, though you'll usually pay lots more. The **Best Western Inn**, 455 South Second Street, (408) 298-3500, is an economical option for downtown, with rooms from $70.

The restored **San Benito House**, 356 Main Street, (650) 726-3425, in the heart of Half Moon Bay, is a charming choice in this pleasant town. Rooms run from $55 (shared bath) to $105. Four miles north of Half Moon Bay in El Granada, the **Harbor View Inn**, 51 Avenue Alhambra, (650) 726-2329, is clean and reasonable with rooms

THE SOUTH BAY AND PENINSULA COAST

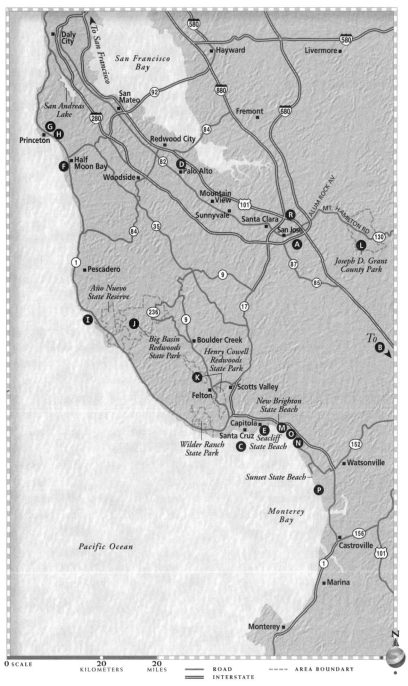

Food

- Ⓐ Bella Mia
- Ⓐ Casa Castillo
- Ⓐ Eulipia
- Ⓑ Faultline
- Ⓒ Front Street Pub & Santa Cruz Brewing Company
- Ⓓ L'Amie Donia
- Ⓐ Les Saisons
- Ⓓ MacArthur Park
- Ⓔ Mr. Toot's Coffeehouse
- Ⓕ Pasta Moon
- Ⓓ Peninsula Creamery Fountain & Grill
- Ⓓ Pollo's
- Ⓒ Pontiac Grill
- Ⓑ San Juan Bakery
- Ⓔ Shadowbrook Restaurant
- Ⓖ The Shore Bird
- Ⓐ Tied House

Lodging

- Ⓐ Best Western Inn
- Ⓓ Cardinal Hotel
- Ⓗ Cypress Inn on Miramar Beach
- Ⓒ Darling House
- Ⓐ De Anza Hotel

Lodging *(continued)*

- Ⓓ Garden Court Hotel
- Ⓖ Harbor View Inn
- Ⓓ Hidden Villa Hostel
- Ⓘ Pigeon Point Lighthouse Hostel
- Ⓑ Posada de San Juan
- Ⓕ San Benito House
- Ⓑ San Juan Inn
- Ⓒ Santa Cruz Hostel
- Ⓒ West Coast Santa Cruz Hotel

Camping

- Ⓙ Big Basin Redwoods State Park
- Ⓕ Half Moon Bay State Beach
- Ⓚ Henry Cowell Redwoods State Park
- Ⓛ Joseph D. Grant County Park
- Ⓜ New Brighton State Beach
- Ⓕ Pelican Point RV Park
- Ⓝ Santa Cruz KOA
- Ⓞ Seacliff State Beach
- Ⓟ Sunset State Beach
- Ⓠ Trailer Tel

Note: Items with the same letter are located in the same town or area.

for $65 to $90. Just south near Miramar, the **Cypress Inn on Miramar Beach**, 407 Mirada Road, (650) 726-6002, is on the water. Rooms range from $170 to $275 (includes breakfast, wine, and hors d'oeuvres) and all have a fireplace and ocean view. The **Pigeon Point Lighthouse Hostel** is a great place to stay. There's an outdoor hot tub and the location is amazing. Beds cost from $12 to $17, with private rooms going for $22 to $27. Reservations are essential in the summer. Special tickets and transportation to see the elephant seals are possible for hostel guests. It's at Pigeon Point, between Pescadero and Año Nuevo.

Chain motels are common around Santa Cruz, especially on or near CA 1. Check the numbers under "Resources" in the Practical Tips chapter. For a room on the Santa Cruz beach with a fine view, the newly refurbished **West Coast Santa Cruz Hotel**, 175 West Cliff Drive, (408) 426-4330, is a great choice. There's a pool, Jacuzzis, and restaurant. Rooms run from $110 to $250. A little farther out and a notch up the economic scale, the **Darling House**, 314 West Cliff Drive, (408) 458-1958, is a nice B&B with fabulous views. The Spanish-style house was built in 1910 as a summer home. Rooms range from $95 to $225. The **Santa Cruz Hostel**, 315 Main Street, (408) 423-8304, is within two blocks of the ocean. Beds are from $12 to $14.

In San Juan Bautista, the very nice **Posada de San Juan**, 310 Fourth Street, (408) 623-4030, has Spanish decor and rooms from $90 to $160. Rooms at the **San Juan Inn**, 410 Alameda Road at CA 156, (408) 623-4380, start at $55.

CAMPING

On CA 130 near San Jose, the road to Lick Observatory, sprawling **Joseph D. Grant County Park** has 22 first-come first-served camp-sites. Take the Alum Rock exit east from I-680 to Mt. Hamilton Road, (408) 358-3741. Just off U.S. 101, **Trailer Tel** has $30 RV sites. Take the Oakland Road exit and go north, (408) 453-3535.

Half Moon Bay State Beach has OK sites for $12. Take Kelly Avenue from town; call (650) 726-8820 for information, (800) 444-7275 for reservations. **Pelican Point RV Park** is at 1001 Miramontes Point Road, 2¼ miles south of Half Moon Bay, a 5-minute walk from the beach, (650) 726-9100.

There's good camping in **Big Basin Redwoods State Park**, including both walk-in and drive-in sites, as well as tent-cabins that are woodsy and peaceful. Sites are from $14 to $18. Take CA 9 to CA 236. Call (408) 338-6132 for information, (800) 444-7275 for reservations, and (800) 874-8368 for tent-cabin reservations. Just north of Santa Cruz on CA 9, **Henry Cowell Redwoods State Park** has nice sites from $14 to $18. Call (408) 438-2396 for information, (800) 444-7275 for reservations.

Along Monterey Bay, **New Brighton State Beach** east of Capitola, (408) 475-4850, and **Sunset State Beach** near Watsonville, (408) 724-1266, have tent sites for $15. **Seacliff State Beach**, (408) 688-3222, has $25 sites for self-contained camper units only. Call (800) 444-7275 for reservations for all three. The **Santa Cruz KOA**, (408) 722-0551, is 14 miles south of town. Take San Andreas Road west from CA 1. Sites are $32 and up.

NIGHTLIFE

In Palo Alto, **The Edge**, 260 California Avenue, (650) 324-3343, is the place for loud, young music. For a good game of pool, a beer, and Cajun food, visit the **Blue Chalk**, 630 Ramona Street, (650) 326-1020. The **Stanford Theatre** shows art films at 221 University Avenue, (650) 324-3700. A great place for coffee or beer is the **University Coffee Café** at 271 University Avenue, (650) 322-5301. Browse University Avenue for many other pleasant choices. **Stanford University** offers a fine performance schedule of music, dance, and theater. Call (650) 725-2787 for information.

San Jose's fine arts options are impressive. For specific performance schedules, call **Opera San Jose** at (408) 283-4880, the **San Jose Symphony** at (408) 279-5949, or the **San Jose Cleveland Ballet** at (408) 288-2800. For innovative, new theater productions, contact the **San Jose Repertory Theatre**, 1 North First Street, (408) 291-2255. More classic theater fare is produced by the **San Jose Stage Company**, 490 South First Street, (408) 283-7142. For musicals, call the **American Musical Theater of San Jose**, (408) 453-7108.

The area to browse in downtown San Jose is the general area east and north of Plaza Park, including First Street, Second Street, and San Pedro Street. The **Cactus Club** books local bands at 417 South First, (408) 280-0885. For a good pint of site-brewed beer, try the **Tied House**, 65 North San Pedro Street, (408) 295-2739. The three-story **Agenda**, 399 South First Street, (408) 287-3991, has live music nightly upstairs (jazz on the weekends) with deejay dancing in the basement.

In Santa Cruz, on Pacific Avenue and Front Street between Water and Laurel, you'll find many nightspots in this non-boardwalk heart of town, especially at the southern end of the zone. Browse the **Bookshop Santa Cruz** and enjoy an espresso within at **Georgiana's Café**, 1522 Pacific Avenue, (408) 427-9900. For house-brewed ales, stop at the **Front Street Pub**, 516 Front Street, (408) 429-8838. **Kuumbwa Jazz Center**, 320–2 Cedar Street, (408) 427-2227, features varied live music and dancing. The **Catalyst**, 1011 Pacific Avenue, (408) 423-1336, is a hopping, live music venue featuring occasional famous or soon-to-be famous bands.

5

THE MONTEREY PENINSULA

The Monterey Peninsula is a remarkable, squarish thumb of land that juts into the ocean at the southern end of Monterey Bay. The beautiful natural setting and concentration of attractions make it a very popular tourist destination.

The Spanish established a mission and presidio at Monterey in 1770 (though the mission was moved to Carmel a year later). The city became the capital of California in 1775, and a provincial capital for independent Mexico in 1821. After the Gold Rush, the city began to draw vacationers—a role interrupted by a 20-year stint as the "sardine capital of the world." Today, the face of Monterey reflects its colonial roots, its touristy present, and its Steinbeck-immortalized fishiness.

The Pebble Beach Land Company controls the southern two-thirds of the peninsula. Well-heeled residents can Lexus to any one of seven golf courses in about a dozen square miles. The estates and distractions of the well-to-do can be enjoyed via Seventeen-Mile Drive, a toll road through the property.

To the south, the town of Carmel-by-the-Sea is almost too nice a place to live. Long after the fading of the missions, Carmel was reborn as a resort town. It evolved, as so many places do, from artist's enclave to moneyed retreat. Despite a heavy burden of tourists, it is still a thoroughly charming place to live and visit.

Fortunately for those living in the easy, comfortable, and lovely town of Pacific Grove, few people bother to include it on a travel itinerary. I'm sure the residents don't mind at all. ◼

THE MONTEREY PENINSULA

Pacific Ocean

Monterey Bay

OCEAN VIEW BLVD

ASILOMAR AV

17 MILE DR

LIGHTHOUSE AV

17TH ST

CENTRAL AV

CANNERY ROW

Pacific Grove

F

C A

LIGHTHOUSE AV

SUNSET DR

FOREST AV

68

DAVID ST

SPANISH BAY RD

CONGRESS RD

E D

DEL MONTE AV

SLOAT RD

W R HOLMAN

VIA DEL REY DR

FREMONT ST

17 MILE DR

S F B MORSE RD

SKYLINE DR

HWY

Monterey

MUNRAS AV

LOPEZ RD

SUNRIDGE RD

MAR VISTA DR

Pebble Beach

17 MILE DR

1

G

SERRA AV

CARPENTER ST

CARMEL WY

4TH ST

N SAN ANTONIO AV

5TH ST

OCEAN AV

B

SCENIC RD

LINCOLN ST

JUNIPERO AV

Carmel Bay

Carmel

RIO RD

N

0 SCALE   1.5 KILOMETERS   1.5 MILES   ROAD   INTERSTATE

Sightseeing Highlights

Ⓐ Cannery Row

Ⓑ Carmel-by-the-Sea

Ⓒ Monterey Bay Aquarium

Ⓓ Monterey Fisherman's Wharf

Ⓔ Monterey State Historic Park

Ⓕ Pacific Grove

Ⓖ Seventeen-Mile Drive

A PERFECT DAY AROUND MONTEREY

You can do the whole peninsula in a day. Start in Monterey with an early morning walk on the historic plaza and Fisherman's Wharf. Arrive early at the Monterey Bay Aquarium (with your prepurchased ticket) for a three-hour visit. Drive along Ocean View Boulevard and Sunset Drive around Pacific Grove, stopping to see the monarchs if in season. Get on Seventeen-Mile Drive at the Pacific Grove Gate to see the golf courses, mansions, and Lone Cypress tree. You end up in Carmel in time for dinner and strolling on Ocean Avenue. Enjoy sunset from Carmel Beach.

SIGHTSEEING HIGHLIGHTS

★★★ **Monterey Bay Aquarium**—The Monterey Bay Aquarium is not a performance-oriented amusement attraction, but a premier marine life exhibit. It is devoted exclusively to the rich flora and fauna of Monterey Bay, presenting it with a devotion to ecological accuracy. This world-class attraction gives Cannery Row a shot of true class.

The aquarium features the Outer Bay—a new, million-gallon "indoor ocean" that is viewed through the largest window in the world. The kelp forest features a three-story view through 7-inch-thick acrylic. Telescopes enable viewing of sea otters lounging offshore, while microscopes permit an up-close look at plankton swimming in a dish. Kids can pet bat rays or touch starfish in a tidal pool exhibit.

The aquarium hosts more than 2 million visitors a year, so waits can be long to get tickets at the door. Consider buying in advance from the aquarium, from a BASS ticket outlet, or from any of the many local hotels and motels that sell tickets. Details: 886 Cannery Row, Monterey; (800) 756-3737; open daily from 10 a.m. to 6 p.m. (opens at 9 a.m., June 15 through Labor Day). Admission is $15. (2½ hours)

★★ **Carmel-by-the-Sea**—This wonderful town has a rich history. The **Mission San Carlos Borromeo del Rio Carmelo** was built above the Carmel River in 1771 to replace one established on a poorer site in Monterey a year earlier. Thanks to careful restoration begun in 1934, its size, layout, and buildings are close to the original. Junipero Serra, the main figure of the mission period, died here and is buried in the mission church. Details: ½ mile west of CA 1 on Rio Road, Carmel; (408) 624-3600; open 9:30 a.m. to 4:30 p.m. (opens at 10:30 a.m. Sunday). A $2 donation is suggested.

Carmel can be thought of as a living laboratory of community spirit. All residents must visit the post office because there is no mail delivery. There are no billboards, neon signs, mortuaries, or jails. Sidewalks are only found on a couple of main streets. Trees have the right to grow unimpeded unless the city council approves their demise.

Take Scenic Road south from downtown to Ocean View Avenue and Robinson Jeffers' **Tor House**. Jeffers ranks among the best American poets and is famous for works that evoke the spirit and mystery of the Big Sur and Monterey coasts. Tor House is a granite cottage named for the rugged knoll on which it is built. **Hawk Tower**, also on the grounds, was built by Jeffers himself as a retreat. You can take a look as you drive by above or below the property, or reserve one of the few tour slots available. Details: 26304 Ocean View Avenue, Carmel; call (408) 624-1813, or (408) 624-1840 on Friday and Saturday; six-person tours are scheduled hourly Friday and Saturday from 10 a.m. to 4 p.m. The fee is $5. (½ day)

★★ **Monterey State Historic Park**—The park preserves several homes and buildings from old Monterey, most of which can be toured. The main area is **Custom House Plaza**, next to Fisherman's Wharf. The **Custom House** (open daily from 10 a.m. to 5 p.m.) has flown the flags of Spain (1814–1822), Mexico (1822–1846), and the U.S., and is the oldest government building on the Pacific Coast. The 1847 **Pacific House** (call for hours) has served as a tavern, courthouse, newspaper office, church, and Army recreation hall. Nearby are California's **First Theater** (open Wednesday through Saturday from 1 to 5 p.m.), **First**

Brick House (open daily from 10 a.m. to 5 p.m.), the **Old Whaling Station Garden** (open daily from 10 a.m. to 5 p.m.), and more.

Other historic homes and sights are found along the streets above the plaza. The **Stevenson House**, where Robert Louis Stevenson is said to have written *Treasure Island*, features an outstanding Stevenson memorabilia collection. The **Cooper-Molera Adobe & Garden** offers a historic look at Monterey through the life of sea captain John Rogers Cooper and his descendants. Various walking tours depart hourly from the park headquarters of the Cooper-Molera Adobe. Special garden tours are offered. Information on all sights and tours is available at the park headquarters.

Pamphlets and books for the **Path of History**, a self-guided walking tour, are available at the headquarters and elsewhere. The route is about 2 miles long and can take the better part of a morning if you do a few house tours. Park details: Custom House Plaza, downtown Monterey waterfront; headquarters in Stanton Center at the southwest corner of the plaza on Oliver Street; (408) 649-7118; most sights are free, guided tours are $5. (2 hours)

Not actually a part of the park but on the plaza is the **Maritime Museum of Monterey**, featuring a fine maritime collection, including a display of ship models. Details: 20 Custom House Plaza; (408) 373-2469; open daily from 10 a.m. to 5 p.m. Admission is $5. (45 minutes)

★★ **Seventeen-Mile Drive**—Pebble Beach, essentially a huge gated community, will gladly take $6.50 per car at any one of four gates to allow you to drive through the area on this scenic toll road. The two main attractions are the fruits of wealth and the fruits of even more wealth. Stunning mansions litter Pebble Beach, particularly along the cliffs. You'll be hard-pressed not to feel like one of the Beverly Hillbillies if you don't have a fat wallet yourself.

The drive passes through or near all seven of the golf courses, including private Cypress Point and barely public Pebble Beach, both of which run right to the water's edge. Stop for a look at the world-famous **Lone Cypress**, the best-loved example of the Monterey cypress trees that thrive on the peninsula as nowhere else. If your vision of scenic perfection blends magnificent homes and perfect fairways with nature's surf-chiseled bluffs and gnarled trees, then this is your road. Details: The four gates are found two blocks north of Ocean Street in Carmel on North San Antonio Avenue; on CA 1, 1 mile north of Carmel; along CA 68 (Holman Highway) at the west end of the Monterey

Presidio; and in Pacific Grove off CA 68, ¼ mile east of Asilomar. Admission is $7 per car. (2 hours)

✱ **Monterey Fisherman's Wharf**—Adjacent to the plaza and Historic Park, the Monterey Fisherman's Wharf thrusts its shop-lined expanse into the sea. Tackier even than Cannery Row, its advantage is its location, surrounded by the waters of the bay with the current, active fishing wharf in plain sight (Municipal Wharf). Fishing, whale watching, and glass-bottom boat excursions depart here as well. Details: Park near Del Monte and Pacific Streets and walk to Custom House Plaza and the waterfront. (½ hour)

✱ **Pacific Grove**—This thoroughly underrated town is a great place to stay and relax on your Monterey Bay trip. The town occupies the northern point of the peninsula and rivals Santa Cruz as a place to view the wintering of monarch butterflies. From November through February monarchs can be viewed in the trees of the 3-acre **Monarch Habitat Sanctuary**, on Ridge Road off of Lighthouse Avenue. Sunset Drive and Ocean View Drive combine to provide a pleasant shoreline route.

Point Pinos Lighthouse is nestled among the fairways of the **Pacific Grove Municipal Golf Course**—a great choice for those who want to golf on the peninsula without taking out a second mortgage. Details: At the west end of Lighthouse Avenue, Pacific Grove; (408) 648-3116; the lighthouse is open Thursday through Sunday (and holidays) from 1 p.m. to 4 p.m. Admission is free.

The lighthouse is associated with the **Pacific Grove Museum of Natural History**, which features exhibits on native animals, plants, geology, and early cultures. This is a great place to learn about wintering monarch butterflies. Details: Corner of Forest Avenue and Central Avenue, Pacific Grove; (408) 648-3116; open Tuesday through Sunday from 10 a.m. to 5 p.m. Admission is free.

Asilomar State Beach, **Lighthouse Reservation Park**, **Hays Perkins Park**, **Lovers Point Park**, and **Shoreline Park** form a contiguous 3-mile strip of public land wrapping Point Pinos. The **Pacific Grove Marine Gardens Fish Preserve** takes the protection out from the shore. Nice walks and oceanside recreation are possible. (1 hour)

Cannery Row—This typical tourist row milks John Steinbeck for all he's worth. If not for the Monterey Bay Aquarium and a few bay exploration opportunities, Cannery Row would be a must-miss for all but souvenir and wax museum addicts. Having read that, you have to go and see it, don't you? I did. And, yes, I'd go back. There's something strangely enjoyable about browsing tacky shops in renovated cannery buildings and licking a frozen yogurt by the bust of an exploited author—and there are some very nice galleries and shops along the way. Details: Located on the waterfront ½ mile northwest of the Presidio (take Lighthouse Avenue, turn toward the bay on Prescott Avenue), Monterey. (1 hour)

FITNESS AND RECREATION

The **Monterey Bay Recreation Trail** runs from Lovers Point Park and Beach in Pacific Grove, along the waterfront through Monterey, and beyond into Seaside and Fort Ord. This is a good path for cycling, jogging, or strolling. From a Pacific Grove B&B, a 4-mile round-trip walk will take you to the aquarium, Cannery Row, the State Historic Park, and Fisherman's Wharf. Add another 1½ miles, and you can do the "Path of History" in Monterey.

For a good workout, visit the extensive **Monterey Sports Center** at 301 Franklin Street in downtown Monterey, (408) 646-3700. They have a gym, two pools, various fitness and weight rooms, and child care services. Hours are Monday through Friday from 6 a.m. to 9:30 p.m., Saturday from 8 a.m. to 5 p.m., and Sunday from 10 a.m. to 5 p.m. Admission is $5.50 per day.

Adventures by the Sea rents bikes, kayaks, and in-line skates. Kayak tours of the bay with all-day rental are $45. There are three locations: 299 Cannery Row, 201 Alvarado Mall (at the Maritime Museum), and at Lovers Point Beach in Pacific Grove. Call (408) 372-1807 for reservations and information. Diving equipment rental, tours, and classes are offered by the **Monterey Bay Dive Center**, 225 Cannery Row, (408) 656-0454; or 598 Foam Street, (408) 655-1818. For deep-sea fishing, try **Randy's Fishing Trips**, 66 Old Fisherman's Wharf, (408) 372-7440. Six-hour whale-watching trips by **Monterey Bay Whale Watch**, (408) 375-4658, are guided by marine biologists. Trips leave from Sam's Fishing on Fisherman's Wharf, and cost $40 to $45.

FOOD

Lighthouse Avenue is the main drag in Pacific Grove. Start your Pacific Grove morning with a great breakfast at the **Lighthouse Cafe**,

602 Lighthouse Avenue, (408) 372-7006. Elsewhere, **Gernot's Victoria House**, 649 Lighthouse Avenue, (408) 646-1477, is a splendid place to wine and dine. The setting is a huge mansion on the water at Lovers Point. The cuisine is European, and the prices are not far from earth. **The Fishwife** at Asilomar, 1996 H Sunset Drive, (408) 375-7107, is a great place for reasonably priced seafood, some of it with a Cajun twist. Just off Cannery Row, try the **Sardine Factory**, 701 Wave Street, (408) 373-3775, for good seafood at slightly inflated prices.

Fisherman's Wharf, Cannery Row, and downtown Monterey offer loads of restaurants. The top place is certainly **Fresh Cream**, in the Heritage Harbor complex, just across from Fisherman's Wharf, (408) 375-9798. Enjoy thoroughly French cuisine at its best as you take in the beautiful harbor view. Entrées start at $25. At the other end, **Stokes Adobe**, 500 Hartnell Street, (408) 373-1110, has good Mediterranean cuisine at a moderate price. Fisherman's Wharf boasts **Café Fina**, (408) 372-5200, where the pizza is good and the site-made pasta is even better.

In Carmel, Ocean Avenue and the surrounding side streets feature dozens of eateries. **Caffé Napoli** on Ocean above Monte Verde, (408) 625-4033, has good Italian dishes at reasonable prices. At Fifth Avenue and Junipero Street, you can sit next to a fire on the patio at the **General Store and Forge in the Forest**, (408) 624-2233. The food is basic and tasty. For a cup of pleasure, stop at **Morgan's Coffee & Tea in Carmel**, 125 Ocean Avenue, (408) 373-5601.

LODGING

The motel chains have dozens of outlets on the outskirts of Monterey and up the road in Seaside and Sand City, as well as clustered about the tourist centers. Use the numbers listed under "Resources" in the Practical Tips chapter to contact the one of your choice.

In Pacific Grove, consider a night at the **Asilomar Conference Center**, 800 Asilomar Boulevard, (408) 372-8016. Depending on availability, you can choose a smaller, rustic room in a building designed by architect Julia Morgan for $81, or a newer, larger room in a "deluxe" building for $92. Another $7 gets you a fireplace. There are a large heated pool, social hall, general store, cafeteria-style dining hall, lovely grounds, and a private trail to Asilomar State Beach. A full breakfast is included. The beautiful, Victorian **Green Gables Inn**, 104 Fifth Street, Pacific Grove, (408) 375-2095, built in 1888, is a classic and elegant B&B. Somehow, English antiques, a teddy bear, and splendid views of the bay seem a great combination here. With wine and hors d'oeuvres, rooms range from $110 to $225. Nearby, **The Martine Inn**, 255 Ocean View Boulevard, (408) 373-3388, is perhaps even more elegant than the Green Gables, though more spacious and less delicate. Perched right above Ocean View Boulevard, the views are unbeatable. A winter stay at the **Butterfly Grove Inn**, 1073 Lighthouse Avenue, (408) 373-4921, gives you a chance to view one of the few gathering spots for monarch butterflies—right on the property! Rooms run from about $50 to $95.

Right on Cannery Row in Monterey, the **Spindrift Inn**, 652 Cannery Row, (408) 646-8900 or (800) 841-1879, is a luxurious choice. Prices vary widely, with rooms starting at $150 in the winter and $225 on summer weekends. The **Old Monterey Inn**, 500 Martin Street, (408) 375-8284 or (800) 350-2344, is a classy B&B set amid the oaks and above the bustle of town. Rooms run from $180 to $240 and are worth it. A budget choice is the **Del Monte Beach Inn**, 1110 Del Monte Avenue, (408) 649-4410. Shared-bath rooms can be as low as $55, and it's close to the action. The venerable **Monterey Hotel**, 406 Alvarado Street, (408) 375-3184 or (800) 727-0960, in downtown has rooms ranging from $110 to $280 (fireplace suites). Breakfast and afternoon refreshments are included.

The historic **Pine Inn**, Ocean Avenue at Monte Verde, (408) 624-3851 or (800) 228-3851, is a landmark structure in the heart of Carmel. Rooms start at $85 and rise to $220 for a king suite. Close to the center, the **Adobe Inn**, Dolores Street and Eighth Avenue, (408) 624-3933, has a pool, sauna, and full-featured rooms with wood-burning fireplaces. Rooms range from $110 to $200. The **Best Western Town House Lodge**, Fifth Avenue and San Carlos Street, (408) 624-1261, is also close to the town center. It has good, basic rooms starting at $75. At the corner of Mission Street and Fourth Avenue, the **Carmel Wayfarer Inn**, (408) 624-2711, has rooms starting around $100.

CAMPING

Tent and RV sites are available at **Laguna Seca Recreation Area**, 9 miles east of Monterey on CA 218, (408) 758-3185. Right above Monterey, **Veterans Memorial Park**, (408) 646-3865, has 40 sites with no hookups. Take Jefferson Street west from Pacific Street. **Saddle**

THE MONTEREY PENINSULA

Food

A Café Fina

B Caffé Napoli

C The Fishwife

D Fresh Cream

E General Store and Forge in the Forest

F Gernot's Victoria House

G Lighthouse Cafe

H Morgan's Coffee & Tea in Carmel

I Sardine Factory

J Stokes Adobe

Lodging

K Adobe Inn

L Asilomar Conference Center

M Best Western Town House Lodge

N Butterfly Grove Inn

O Carmel Wayfarer Inn

P Del Monte Beach Inn

Q Green Gables Inn

R The Martine Inn

S Monterey Hotel

T Old Monterey Inn

U Pine Inn

V Spindrift Inn

Camping

W Laguna Seca Recreation Area

X Saddle Mountain Recreation Park

Y Veterans Memorial Park

Mountain Recreation Park, (408) 624-1617, a private facility, has tent and RV sites, a game room, and hiking trails. Take Carmel Valley Road east from CA 1 for 5 miles. Turn right on Schulte Road and continue on to 27625 Schulte.

NIGHTLIFE

The **Monterey Jazz Festival** brings together world-renowned musicians for a long weekend of splendid entertainment. If you'll be in the area in late September, try to fit it in. Events take place on several stages at the Monterey Fairgrounds. At other times, Cannery Row stays alive into the night. Try **Doc Rickett's Lab** at 95 Prescott Avenue, (408) 649-4241, for live music on weekends. At the corner of Prescott and Wave Street, **O'Kanes Irish Pub**, (408) 375-7564, is just that. On the top floor at 625 Cannery Row is **Planet Gemini**, (408) 373-1449, which offers live music on weekdays and comedy on the weekends.

6
BIG SUR

The coastline from Carmel south to San Simeon is an American treasure. Big Sur (meaning "big south") was named by early Monterey settlers in reference to the large rugged land down the coast—and rugged it is. From the 5,000-foot heights of the Santa Lucia mountains, the land drops steeply to the angry Pacific far below. Waves beat at the huge headlands, slowly eating away at the mountains' feet. Isolated sea stacks litter the shallows. Calmer coves, often invisible from the road above, host sea lions whose barking calls echo weirdly among the cliffs. Always, the roar of the gray-green Pacific fills the air.

In the lonely southern reaches, no human habitation interrupts the national forest lands that run to the sea. Further north, there are gentler stretches, private lands, state parks, and a few tiny towns and resorts. Throughout, the age-long battle of patient mountain versus eager ocean dominates all.

The Coast Highway provides the only access to this long, remote stretch. Completed in the 1930s and little-changed since then, the road is a marvel of engineering. Graceful arched bridges cross steep canyons, while across the faces of the headlands, the road climbs and winds, a tenacious snake clinging to survival. Plan on the better part of a day to cover the 80 miles from Carmel to San Simeon. The average speed on the road is around 35 mph—less on summer weekends when you're nine cars behind a trundling RV. This is no place to be in a hurry. Take your time and stop often. Big Sur, after all, is some of the best the planet has to offer. ◧

BIG SUR

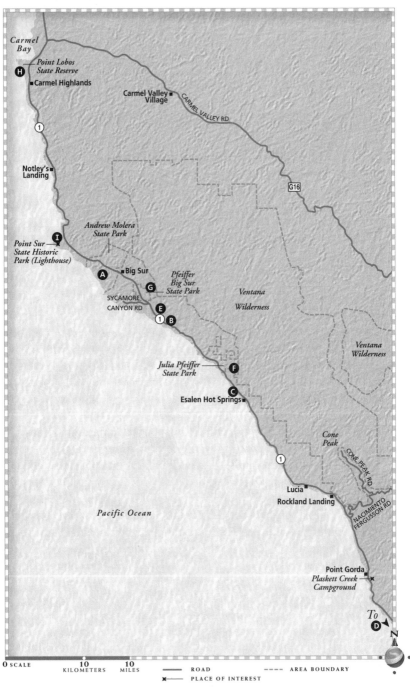

Carmel Bay

H
Point Lobos State Reserve
■ Carmel Highlands
Carmel Valley Village ■
CARMEL VALLEY RD

①

Notley's Landing ■

G16

Andrew Molera State Park

I
Point Sur — State Historic Park (Lighthouse)

A ■ Big Sur
Pfeiffer Big Sur State Park
G
SYCAMORE CANYON RD
E
① B
Ventana Wilderness

Ventana Wilderness

Julia Pfeiffer State Park — F
C
Esalen Hot Springs ■

Cone Peak
①
CONE PEAK RD
Lucia ■
Rockland Landing ■
NACIMIENTO FERGUSSON RD

Pacific Ocean

Point Gorda
Plaskett Creek Campground ✕

To
D

N

0 SCALE   10   10
KILOMETERS   MILES   ——— ROAD   - - - - AREA BOUNDARY
✕ — PLACE OF INTEREST

Sights

Ⓐ Andrew Molera State Park

Ⓑ Coast Gallery

Ⓒ Esalen Institute

Ⓓ Hearst Castle

Ⓔ Henry Miller Memorial Library

Ⓕ Julia Pfeiffer Burns State Park

Ⓖ Pfeiffer Big Sur State Park

Ⓗ Point Lobos State Reserve

Ⓘ Point Sur State Historic Park
and Light Station

A PERFECT DAY ON THE BIG SUR COAST

Enjoy the contrast between human opulence and natural spectacle. In the morning, tour the fabulous Hearst Castle and peer into the wealth and life of publishing magnate William Randolph Hearst. Drive north along the Big Sur Coast, stopping anywhere and everywhere. The Lucia Lodge is a good spot for lunch on the deck. Consider a tour up the Nacimiento Road and a hike to Cone Peak. Stop in at the Henry Miller Library or Coast Gallery to rest your eyes from the big vistas outside. An easy hike at Andrew Molera gives you sunset on the beach with just enough time to find campsite or car before nightfall.

SIGHTSEEING HIGHLIGHTS

★★★ **Hearst Castle**—With 165 rooms and 127 acres of gardens, pools, and patios, William Randolph Hearst's *La Cuesta Encantada*, The Enchanted Hill, is a glorious example of self-indulgence. Julia Morgan designed much of the castle, responding with plans to suit Hearst's ongoing purchases of art and architectural artifacts. The result is a glorious but almost bizarre blend of classic European styles. When Hearst died in 1951, it still wasn't finished—even after 30 years of construction. Since no one could afford to move in, the State of California took over the complex and added it to the State Park system.

You can choose from four different tours, each of which takes approximately 1¾ hours. Tour #1 is a good choice for your first visit. All tours leave by shuttle bus from the visitor center above CA 1. Details: The castle is in the hills overlooking San Simeon, 8 miles north of Cambria; call Destinet at (800) 444-4445, reservations are advised; the visitor center and ticket office are open from 8 a.m. to 5 p.m. Admission is $14. (2 hours)

★★★ **Point Lobos State Reserve**—At the south end of Carmel Bay, Point Lobos is a rugged promontory with numerous coves and headlands along a heavily eroded shoreline. The waters surrounding the point are also protected in a special underwater reserve. Wonderful short hikes lead to several great spots, including **Devil's Cauldron**, a churning pool with a high-tide blowhole. **Sea Lion Point** hosts California and Steller's sea lions. Diving and snorkeling are possible, but camping is not permitted. Details: (408) 624-4909; open from 9 a.m. to 4 p.m. Admission is $7 for day use. (1 hour)

★★ **Julia Pfeiffer Burns State Park**—This park encompasses a good stretch of spectacular coastline, though much of the 3,580 acres is above the road. At the north edge of the park, a fire road descends from a big road turnout to **Partington Cove** where the remains of a wooden bridge built in 1870 recall the cove's one-time use as a boat landing for bootleggers. At **McWay Canyon**, a trail leads from the parking area, under the highway, and down to the observation point for **McWay Falls**. This gorgeous waterfall drops 80 feet straight to the beach (best in spring). Two very special walk-in campsites on the headlands are available to those with reservations. Details: 15 miles south of the town of Big Sur on CA 1; call (408) 667-2315 for information. Entrance fee is $6 for day-use parking. (3 hours)

★★ **Point Sur State Historic Park and Light Station**—As you drive CA 1, you can't miss Point Sur, a volcanic hill attached to the coast with a gracefully curving sandbar. The lighthouse, built in 1899, sits 361 feet above the surf on the outer crest of the rock. Access is possible only at limited times—the land between the highway and lighthouse is private. Details: Call (408) 625-4419 for information and tour reservations. Wednesdays and weekends are the reported times for access, but they are not posted and there is no visitor facility. The tour is free. (1½ hours)

☆ **Andrew Molera State Park**—The Big Sur River meets the ocean after passing through the gentle valley and low hills of this pleasant, lightly used, 4,800-acre park. Several easy hiking and riding trails thread through the park, and beachcombing is easy south of the river mouth. The park features a nice walk-in campground with good, open sites. Details: 2 miles north of the town of Big Sur; (408) 627-2315. The **Ventana Wilderness Sanctuary** is open summers during morning hours for bird banding; (408) 624-1202. Admission is $4 for day use. (3 hours)

☆ **Henry Miller Memorial Library**—Henry Miller's writings and paintings are preserved at this small library. Miller was one of several artists who lived a rough-edged, bohemian existence for a time on the Big Sur Coast. Details: 3 miles south of Pfeiffer Big Sur State Park, ¼ mile south of Nepenthe Restaurant, on CA 1; (408) 667-2574; open daily from 11 a.m. to 5 p.m. in summer (weekends only in winter). Admission is $1. (½ hour)

☆ **Pfeiffer Big Sur State Park**—CA 1 loops inland, following the Big Sur River upstream through a forested valley, past the few businesses of the town of Big Sur, and into Pfeiffer Big Sur State Park. The 800-acre park is quite popular, featuring trails through stands of redwood, conifers, and oaks. A large campground and lodge accommodate visitors. There is access by trail to the **Ventana Wilderness** in Los Padres National Forest. Details: 3 miles south of the town of Big Sur; (408) 667-2315. Day-use parking is $6.

You can reach **Pfeiffer Beach** by turning down Sycamore Canyon Road at the southern edge of the park, just north of the Big Sur Ranger Station. The narrow, 2-mile road winds down to day-use parking and beach access. (3 hours)

Coast Gallery—This lovely Gallery appears at a bend in the road 3 miles south of Nepenthe. Artworks for sale include many by local artists. The café upstairs sells snacks and beverages. The building and grounds themselves are interesting. It's a great place to take a break from driving. Details: 3 miles south of Pfeiffer Big Sur State Park on CA 1; (408) 667-2301; open daily from 9 a.m. to 5 p.m. (½ hour)

Esalen Institute—At the mouth of Hot Springs Creek, 3 miles south of McWay Canyon, the Esalen Institute serves as a retreat for people seeking relaxation and enlightenment. All visits are by reservation only,

BIG SUR

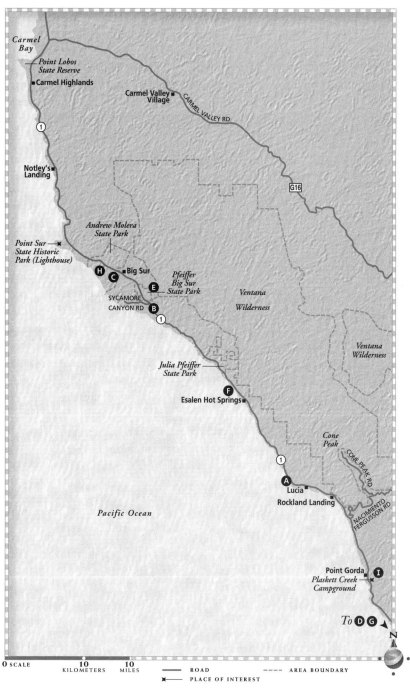

Carmel
Bay

Point Lobos
State Reserve

■ Carmel Highlands

Carmel Valley
Village

CARMEL VALLEY RD

① 1

Notley's
Landing ■

G16

Andrew Molera
State Park

Point Sur ✕
State Historic
Park (Lighthouse)

H C ■ Big Sur

Pfeiffer
Big Sur
State Park

SYCAMORE
CANYON RD B

① 1

E

Ventana

Wilderness

Julia Pfeiffer
State Park

F

Esalen Hot Springs ■

Ventana
Wilderness

Cone
Peak

CONE PEAK RD.

① 1

A

Lucia
Rockland Landing

NACIMIENTO
FERGUSSON RD

Pacific Ocean

Point Gorda ■ I

Plaskett Creek
Campground

To D G ▶

N

0 SCALE   10   10
        KILOMETERS   MILES   ————— ROAD   - - - - AREA BOUNDARY
                              ✕—— PLACE OF INTEREST

Food

A Lucia Lodge

B Nepenthe

C Ripplewood Café

C Village Pub

D Whalewatcher Café

Lodging

E Big Sur Lodge

B Deetjen's Big Sur Inn

F Esalen Institute

A Lucia Lodge

G Ragged Point Inn

B Ventana Big Sur Country Inn Resort

Camping

H Andrew Molera State Park Campground

C Big Sur Campground and Cabins

E Pfeiffer Big Sur State Park Campground

I Plaskett Creek Campground

B Ventana Big Sur Campground

Note: Items with the same letter are located in the same town or area.

and most involve participation in group seminars and activities. The institute's accommodations are open to individuals on a space-available basis. (Currently, hot tubs are available to guests only.) Details: 4 miles south of Julia Pfeiffer Burns State Park; call (408) 667-3047 for information and reservations. (overnight)

FITNESS AND RECREATION

Coastal trails in the state parks and Los Padres National Forest provide numerous options for hiking, biking, and riding, though paths can be steep. **Andrew Molera State Park** is the best for easy loops of 2 to 5 miles. **Molera Horseback Tours**, (408) 625-5486 or (800) 942-5486, operates from a building at the park headquarters. Their offerings include one- to 2½-hour trips. Fees range from $25 to $55.

The **Ventana Wilderness** has a good network of trails. The terrain is steep and dry, and most loop possibilities are better done as an overnight. Consult the rangers and maps at the ranger station just south of Pfeiffer Big Sur State Park, or call (408) 385-5434.

FOOD

For a drink and a hearty, budget bite with the locals, try the **Village Pub**, (408) 667-2355, in the Village Shops at the River Inn near the town of Big Sur. Also in the Big Sur town area, the **Ripplewood Café**, (408) 667-2242, offers good, basic breakfast and lunch fare.

A long drive leads down to the splendid **Nepenthe**, (408) 667-2345, a bar and restaurant by the sea. The dining is fine, but so too is gazing over the waves from the terrace. Nepenthe is 3 miles south of Pfeiffer Big Sur State Park.

In Lucia, the **Lucia Lodge**, (408) 667-2391, is a marvelous place for a meal. It offers the only outdoor dining over the water anywhere on the Big Sur coast. Morning coffee as the fog begins to break is magical. Above San Simeon in the tiny town of Gorda, the **Whalewatcher Café**, (805) 927-3918, offers California cuisine by the sea and wonderful homemade desserts.

LODGING

In Pfeiffer Big Sur State Park, the **Big Sur Lodge**, (408) 667-3100 or (800) 424-4787, has basic rooms, the Trail Head Café, and a heated pool. Rates are from $90 for a basic room in the winter to $180 for a fireplace and kitchen unit in the summer.

For money-is-no-object, romantic, private, luxury lounging with a loved one, the **Ventana Big Sur Country Inn Resort**, (408) 667-2331 or (800) 628-6500, is the place for you. Rooms start at $200 and climb to a cool $1,000. It's above the road near Nepenthe.

Deetjen's Big Sur Inn, (408) 667-2377, was started by Norwegian Helmuth Deetjen. Over the years he created a marvelous, rustic inn with single-wall construction, hand-hewn doors, and wood-burning stoves. There are no phones or TVs, and rooms range from $70 to $150. It's just north of the Coast Gallery near Nepenthe.

You can stay at the **Esalen Institute**, (408) 667-3000, when beds aren't needed for seminar participants. Beds are sold as "room and board," featuring three full meals and use of grounds, baths, and massage services. A bunk is $85 per person, a double room is $125 per person.

The **Lucia Lodge**, (408) 667-2391, in Lucia, is an oasis on the lonely southern stretches of CA 1. Rooms and cabins range from $95 to $165. Dinner or breakfast on the restaurant deck is sheer pleasure.

Near Hearst Castle and San Simeon, the **Ragged Point Inn**, (805) 927-4502, is on a bluff above the sea. A nature trail leads to a seasonal, 300-foot waterfall. Rooms range from $90 to $150—ask for a cliffside room.

CAMPING

Walk-in sites at the **Andrew Molera State Park Campground** are only $3. Call (408) 667-2315 for information.

To reach the happy jumble of **Big Sur Campground and Cabins** in Big Sur, (408) 667-2322, you have to cross the Big Sur River on a narrow bridge just off the highway. There are tent sites for $25 and RV sites for $30. Down the road, the **Pfeiffer Big Sur State Park Campground** has good sites for $15 to $18. Call (408) 667-2315 for information, (800) 444-7275 for reservations.

The **Ventana Big Sur Campground**, near Nepenthe, (408) 667-2688, is the nice but poor cousin to the resort in the hills above. The 60 good and fair sites are strung through a narrow valley and cost $25 each.

In the south, **Plaskett Creek Campground** is in the National Forest.

Scenic Route: Nacimiento Road

Five miles south of the tiny town of **Lucia**, on the Big Sur Coast, the
Nacimiento Fergusson Road climbs in great, winding switchbacks up
to the crest of the **Santa Lucia Mountains**, 3,000 feet above the
ocean. At the ridgeline, the road continues inland to **Fort Hunter
Leggett**, but you can turn right or left to wind along the crest where
you can enjoy occasional views. By turning left, winding Cone Peak
Road will bring you to the parking area at the base of **Cone Peak**. A
2-mile hike takes you up to the lookout to stand on the highest coastal
peak in the Santa Lucias, 5,155 feet in elevation.

Free camping is available at any of several pullouts along the
ridgecrest. Two official campgrounds can be reached by continuing 6
or 8 miles past the ridgecrest on the Nacimiento Road. Another is
located a few miles from the ridge junction on the **Coast Ridge Road**.

A loop up from Lucia and back with a hike to Cone Peak will
take at least four hours. A simple driving loop with a short stint south
along the ridgecrest can be done in 1½ hours. The closest services
are in Lucia. RV's not recommended ◼

NACIMIENTO ROAD

7

WINE COUNTRY

The nation's finest wines are produced in several valleys north of San Francisco known collectively as the "Wine Country." It's delightful to explore the region, visiting vineyards for a taste or a tour, enjoying fine dining as the sun sets, and soaking in hot mineral waters in the evenings. Budget lodging and camping are available in several areas, as are historic sites, recreation options, and family activities.

The greatest concentration of vineyards is in the northern half of the famous and heavily visited Napa Valley. Take CA 29, north of the town of Napa, to find wineries like Robert Mondavi, Sutter Home, Beringer, and Christian Brothers. Across the river, the less traveled Silverado Trail provides access to wineries on the valley's east side. The town of Calistoga sits at the head of the valley, home to several resorts that channel the area's hot springs into pools, tubs, and mud baths.

West of Napa, the Sonoma Valley features wineries, resorts, and the wonderful, historic town of Sonoma, the birthplace of the short-lived Bear Flag Republic. The pace here is slower, and the wineries often less crowded. Other northern wine growing areas are found in or near the Russian River Valley and scattered through the Coast Range south of San Francisco, the Central Valley, and the Sierra foothills.

A nice alternative to the Napa-Sonoma region is the peaceful Anderson Valley. North of Cloverdale, CA 128 leaves the Russian River basin, climbs over a divide, and drops into the Anderson Valley on its way to the Mendocino Coast. Several charming wineries line the way between Boonville and Navarro. ∎

WINE COUNTRY

Mt. St. Helena

To **A**

Lake
Berryessa

C
Calistoga

B

ST. HELENA RD
SPRING MOUNTAIN RD
SILVERADO TRAIL
L
St. Helena

To **D** **J**
K
CALISTOGA ST
RUTHERFORD CROSS RD

F
Spring
Lake
ADOBE CANYON RD
YOUNTVILLE CROSS RD
G

101

12
E
ARNOLD DR
LONDON RANCH RD
29

121

M Sonoma

Napa

ADOBE RD

I

Petaluma
LAKEVILLE HWY
116
CARNEROS HWY
121

121
12

101
37
Napa River

MARINE WORLD PKWY
H
29
80
Novato
San Pablo Bay
Vallejo

N

0 SCALE   10   10   ——— ROAD   ✕—— PLACE OF INTEREST
KILOMETERS   MILES
═══ INTERSTATE

Sights

- **Ⓐ** Anderson Valley
- **Ⓑ** Bale Grist Mill State Historic Park
- **Ⓒ** Calistoga
- **Ⓓ** Healdsburg
- **Ⓔ** Jack London State Historic Park
- **Ⓕ** Luther Burbank Home and Gardens
- **Ⓖ** Napa Valley
- **Ⓗ** New Marine World Theme Park

- **Ⓘ** Petaluma Adobe State Historic Park
- **Ⓙ** Real Goods Solar Living Center
- **Ⓚ** Russian River
- **Ⓛ** St. Helena
- **Ⓛ** Silverado Museum
- **Ⓜ** Sonoma and the Sonoma Valley
- **Ⓜ** Sonoma State Historic Park
- **Ⓜ** Sonoma Traintown Railroad

Note: Items with the same letter are located in the same town or area.

A PERFECT DAY IN WINE COUNTRY

Start in Sonoma with breakfast on the square. Visit the mission, M. G. Vallejo's mansion, and Buena Vista Winery and Vineyards—the first in California. Take CA 12 to the cutoff for Glen Ellen. Visit the tiny center of this historic town before visiting Jack London State Historic Park. Follow winding Trinity Road east over the ridge and down into the Napa Valley. Visit a winery or two and the waterwheel-powered Bale Grist Mill. After registering at your spa resort in Calistoga, soak in a hot tub as you muster the courage for a balloon trip in the morning.

SIGHTSEEING HIGHLIGHTS

☆☆ **Sonoma and the Sonoma Valley**—Nowhere else in Wine Country can you enjoy such a perfect blend of regional history, charming surroundings, good food, pleasant strolling, and, of course, fine wine. The Sonoma Plaza is the heart of town. Here you'll find the interesting City Hall, with its four identical facades, and the Bear Flag Monument, honoring Sonoma's brief stint as the capital of an independent California. Stop in at the Vasquez House just off the square for tea, cookies, and a look at the historic library collection. Details: Located on El Paseo Plaza, First Street East; (707) 938-0150; open

Wednesday through Sunday from 1:30 to 4:30 p.m. Admission is free. (½ hour)

The Sonoma Valley Historical Society's **Depot Park Museum** features regional heritage exhibits. Details: First Street West one block north of the plaza; (707) 938-1762; open Wednesday through Sunday from 1 to 4:30 p.m. Donations accepted. (½ hour)

Sonoma is a great place to put together a picnic. Stop at the **Artisan's Bakery** at Seventh and Napa Streets for some bread, visit the **Vella Cheese Company** at 315 Second Street East for cheese, team them up with that bottle you bought while wine tasting, and find a pleasant place to dine. (½ day)

Like the Napa Valley, two main roads pass through the Sonoma Valley. CA 12 is the busy route that connects the town of Sonoma with Santa Rosa to the north and the Bay Area to the south. On the western side of the valley, Arnold Drive is the equivalent of the Silverado Trail, offering a quieter route from Sonoma to Glen Ellen.

★★ **Wine Tasting**—It would simply be unfair to recommend any particular wineries for visiting. The joy of wine tasting is in the sense of exploration, spontaneity, and discovery that accompanies your search for the one that's just right. Perhaps it's a name remembered from a good bottle you enjoyed on a special occasion. Maybe you spot some inviting buildings on a sunny hillside. It could be the artfulness of a roadside sign or the colorful landscaping around a gate that leads you to turn up a drive. Whatever it is, your Wine Country tour will be more enjoyable because you responded to inspiration rather than targeted a famous name.

Pick up a map, brochure, or winery guide so you can choose your driving route wisely. Bookshops, convenience stores, tourist offices, and the wineries themselves offer such resources. Pay special attention to tasting hours and to whether or not tours are offered. Ask the opinions of local folks, using words like "charming," "small," and "friendly" in your inquiries. Take a chance—leave Robert Mondavi to the masses.

Roads where you will pass by several good wineries include CA 29 and the Silverado Trail between Napa and Calistoga, the Westside Road from Guerneville to Healdsburg, CA 128 from Geyserville south to the higher hills, Dry Creek Road from Healdsburg to Lake Sonoma, U.S. 101 from Hopland to Redwood Valley, and CA 128 between Yorkville and Navarro. Sonoma Valley wineries are more dispersed, as are those for other areas. (½ day)

A number of wineries host concerts or festivals throughout the summer. Free visitor guides and newspapers that list these events are available throughout the area.

Note: The police throughout Wine Country know full well that wine tasting is the same thing as wine drinking. DUI laws in California are no picnic. Decide wisely.

Despite the preceding words, you might still want a suggestion or two. The following are attractive choices:

In Napa Valley:
Beringer Brothers—This large winery, the oldest continuously operated in the valley, is worth a visit for a look at the splendid Rhine House, built in 1883. Details: 2000 Main Street, St. Helena (on CA 29); (707) 963-4812; open daily with tours every half hour. There is a free tour with tasting; special premium wines taste for $2 to $6. (1 hour)

The Hess Collection—In the hills between Sonoma and Napa, this fine winery has a museum-quality art gallery. Details: 4411 Redwood Road (from CA 29 north of Napa); (707) 255-1144; open daily from 10 a.m. to 4 p.m. Admission to the gallery is free; the tasting is $3. (1½ hours)

Nichelini Winery—Head into the quiet hills for a relaxing visit to the oldest continuously family-run winery in the county. Details: Highway 128 (10 miles east of CA 29); (707) 963-3312; open weekends from 10 a.m. to 6 p.m. or by appointment. (1 hour)

Robert Mondavi Winery—This extensive winery features excellent tours of a large wine-making operation. Details: 7801 St. Helena Highway (CA 29), Oakville; (800) MONDAVI, ext. 2001 for information and tour reservations; open daily from 9 a.m. to 5 p.m. (9:30 a.m. to 4:30 p.m. November through April). A complimentary one-hour tour includes a free tasting; Premium wine tastings are $3 to $10. (1½ hours)

In Sonoma Valley:
Buena Vista Winery—This is California's oldest premium winery, dating back to 1857. Enjoy the lovely, wooded grounds and complimentary tasting in the original press room. Call to reserve a lovely picnic spot. Details: 18000 Old Winery Road, from East Napa Street, Sonoma; (800) 926-1266; open daily from 10:30 a.m. to 5 p.m. Self-guided tours are offered. Small fee for tasting vintage wines. (1 hour)

Gundlach-Bundschu Winery—Founded in 1858 and revitalized in the 1970s, this easygoing winery has a quiet hills setting, small lake, and nice picnic spots. Details: 2000 Denmark Street, from Eighth Street East, Sonoma; (707) 938-5277; open daily from 11 a.m. to 4:30 p.m. Complimentary wine tasting, cave tours on summer weekends. (1 hour)

In The Russian River Region:
Hop Kiln Winery—This backroad winery, a National Historic Landmark, is housed in a restored hop kiln with three large chimneys, once used in the drying of hops. Details: 6050 Westside Road, from Healdsburg; (707) 433-6491; open daily from 10 a.m. to 5 p.m. A self-guided tour is offered, along with a free tasting. (1 hour)

Johnson's of Alexander Valley—In the Alexander Valley along the Russian River, this small winery features a 1924 theater pipe organ in the tasting room. Details: 8333 Highway 128, Healdsburg, north of Calistoga; (707) 433-2319; open daily from 10 a.m. to 5 p.m. Free tasting. (1 hour)

Korbel Champagne Cellars—This stately and popular winery, dating to the 1880s, sits among lovely gardens and redwood trees. Details: 13250 River Road, east of Guerneville; (707) 824-7000; open daily from 9 a.m. to 5 p.m., hourly tours are given from 10 a.m. to 3 p.m. Complimentary tasting. (1 hour)

In Anderson Valley:
Husch Vineyards—Husch was the first winery in the Anderson Valley and is still a great place for a taste and a visit. Details: 4400 Highway 128, between Philo and Navarro; (707) 895-3216; open from 10 a.m. to 6 p.m. (until 5 p.m. in winter), tours by appointment. Complimentary tasting room. (1 hour)

Lazy Creek Vineyards—You won't find a more easygoing, friendly, family winery than this one. Call for an appointment and meet Hans and Theresia—or just drop in! You'll be welcome. Details: 4610 Highway 128 (H-mile-long driveway); (707) 895-3623. (1 hour)

Pepperwood Springs Vineyards—Enjoy Pinot Noir, Chardonnay, or Sauvignon Blanc and a fabulous view at this small winery, 2 miles northwest of mile-marker 17.5 on CA 128. Details: 1200 Holmes Road, just beyond Husch Vineyards; (707) 895-2920. Call for current hours. (1 hour)

✦ **Bale Grist Mill State Historic Park**—The **Old Bale Mill** was built in 1846 and has been restored to full operating condition. You can buy stone-ground flour made at the mill for $2 a bag and enjoy pleasant minutes watching the water tumble over the 36-foot wooden waterwheel. Details: 5 miles north of St. Helena on CA 29; (707) 963-2236; open daily from 10 a.m. to 5 p.m. Admission is $2. (1 hour)

✦ **Calistoga**—Newspaper mogul and big dreamer Sam Brannan founded this pleasant town in 1859, blending the words "California" with "Saratoga" to create the town name. Brannan spent a fortune building a glorious resort for weary and wealthy San Franciscans. Not enough of them showed up, however, and he lost everything. Today Lincoln Avenue is a pleasant street for strolling and dining between rejuvenation sessions at one of the many spas. Check out the **Calistoga Depot**, the second oldest train depot in the state.

While here, you might also visit the **Old Faithful Geyser**—that's right, there's another one. Eruptions average 60 to 100 feet in height. Details: 1299 Tubbs Lane (between CA 29 and CA 128), Calistoga; (707) 942-6463; open daily from 9 a.m. to 6 p.m. (until 5 p.m. in winter). Admission is $6. (½ hour)

Just west of town at the **Petrified Forest**, a ¼-mile trail leads past 10 varied examples of petrified trees. Details: 4100 Petrified Forest Road, Calistoga, (707) 942-6667; open daily from 10 a.m. to 5 p.m. Admission is $4. (½ hour)

In town, the **Sharpsteen Museum** features the historical dioramas of Ben Sharpsteen, one of Walt Disney Studio's original animators, as well as numerous other heritage exhibits. Next door is the restored and relocated **Brannan Cottage**, a remnant of Sam Brannan's ill-fated Calistoga Resort. Details: The museum is at 1311 Washington Street, Calistoga; (707) 942-5911; open daily from 10 a.m. to 4 p.m. (noon to 4 p.m. November through March). Admission is free. (1 hour)

✦ **Jack London State Historic Park**—In the hills above Glen Ellen, Jack London lived the last years of his life in a small cottage with his wife, Charmian. He had commissioned the construction of the magnificent **Wolf House** nearby, but it mysteriously burned a month before completion in 1913. He intended to rebuild it, but he died in 1916 at age 40. An easy 1¼ mile loop hike through woodsy parkland takes you to the Wolf House ruins and the Londons' graves. A museum of his memorabilia and park headquarters are in **Happy Walls**, the home built by Charmian after London's death. Details: Take London Ranch Road from Arnold Drive in Glen Ellen; (707) 938-5216; open from 9:30 a.m. to 7 p.m. (until 5 p.m. in winter), Happy Walls hours are 10 a.m. to 5 p.m. daily. Day-use parking is $6. (2 hours)

★ **Petaluma Adobe State Historic Park**—This living history park features a large, balconied, adobe structure that served as the central building for General M. G. Vallejo's 66,000-acre ranch. The hacienda sits on a hill, overlooking the Petaluma River Valley. On weekends, costumed park volunteers reenact farm routines from the 1850s. Details: 3325 Adobe Road, 5 miles north of CA 116; (707) 762-4871; open daily from 10 a.m. to 5 p.m. Admission is $2 (same ticket is good for Sonoma State Historic Park). (1 hour)

★ **Sonoma State Historic Park**—Remnants and reconstructions of several historic structures are preserved on the north side of Sonoma's central plaza. Little is left of the original **Mission San Francisco Solano de Sonoma**, except one wing, the 1840 mission chapel, and the courtyard which can be visited. Other adobe and historic structures include soldiers' barracks, nineteenth-century hotels and residences, and **La Casa Grande**, General M. G. Vallejo's first home.

A ½ mile west of the square on West Spain Street is the entrance to **Lachryma Montis**, the Vallejo Home, built between 1851 and 1852. General Vallejo and his wife lived here for more than 35 years. Many of the current furnishings belonged to the Vallejos, and the gardens have been restored to their original beauty. Details: Sonoma Plaza, Sonoma; (707) 938-1519; open daily from 10 a.m. to 5 p.m. Admission to the home and park is $2 (same ticket is good for Petaluma Adobe State Historic Park). (2 hours)

★ **Sonoma Traintown Railroad**—A mile south of the town square in Sonoma, Traintown features 10 acres of miniature settings and is accessed by a scaled-down passenger train. Built in the 1950s by rail buff Stanley Franks, the facility is lovingly maintained. There's a petting zoo for the kids, but you won't be alone if you come childless. Details: 1 mile south of downtown Sonoma on CA 12, Sonoma; (707) 938-3912; open daily June through September from 10 a.m. to 5 p.m. (open only Friday through Sunday, October through May). The ride is $3.50, $2.50 for kids, and takes about 20 minutes. (1 hour)

☆ **New Marine World Theme Park** (formerly Marine World Africa U.S.A.)—This popular family attraction has been refurbished and expanded. Fifteen new rides complement the animal shows, which include killer whales, dolphins, tigers, elephants, birds, and more. In the **Shark Experience**, you walk through a large shark aquarium in an acrylic tunnel. Enter **Butterfly World** to interact with hundreds of free-flying butterflies. Check out the appropriately named **Tiger Island Splash Attack**. Details: Take CA 37 West from Interstate 80, Vallejo; (707) 643-6722; open daily from 10 a.m. to 10 p.m. in the summer (until 8 p.m. in spring and fall). Admission is $29, $20 for kids. (½ day)

Healdsburg—This is a pleasant village for strolling, dining, and relaxing. The shady town square is surrounded by well-kept shops and cafés. Healdsburg Avenue, the town's main street, parallels the freeway to the east. The **Healdsburg Museum** features regional heritage items. Details: 221 Matheson Street, Healdsburg; (707) 431-3325; open Tuesday through Sunday from 11 a.m. to 4 p.m. Admission is free. (45 minutes)

Luther Burbank Home and Gardens—A renowned horticulturist, Luther Burbank introduced over 800 new varieties of plants, including 200 varieties of fruit. The home where he lived from 1884 to 1906 and the gardens where he did much of his work are open to the public. Details: The gardens are on Santa Rosa Avenue across from Julliard Park in Santa Rosa. The main entrance is on Tupper Street. Call (707) 524-5445 for information; gardens open daily from 8 a.m. to 5 p.m. House tours are offered Wednesday through Sunday April through October, every half hour from 10 a.m. to 3:30 p.m. Admission and tours are free. (1 hour)

St. Helena—This town is certainly worth a stop, with the disadvantage being that CA 29 and the town's Main Street are one and the same. North of town you'll easily spot the old Christian Brothers Winery that is now the **Culinary Institute of America**. Details: 2555 Main Street; (707) 967-1100; "kitchen viewing" tour offered daily at 10:30 a.m., 1:30 p.m., or 3:30 p.m. Tours are $2 weekdays, $5 weekends (including live cooking demonstration). (½ hour)

For some valley heritage, visit the **Napa Valley Museum**. Details: 473 Main Street, St. Helena; (707) 944-0500; open Wednesday through Monday from 10 a.m. to 5 p.m. Admission is $3.50. (45 minutes)

Real Goods Solar Living Center—Just south of Hopland, Real Goods is both a store and an ongoing experiment featuring the latest goods and technologies for environmentally friendly design and construction. Explore the crafted grounds, examine the architecture, and browse the shelves to orient your thinking toward a sustainable future. Details: U.S. 101 at the south edge of Hopland; (707) 744-2100; open daily from 11 a.m. to 7 p.m., 10 a.m. to 6 p.m. in winter. (½ hour)

Silverado Museum—Located next to the public library in St. Helena, the Silverado Museum is devoted to the life and works of Robert Louis Stevenson. Some 8,000 items are in the collection, including original letters and manuscripts, first editions, artwork, and the last words he ever penned. Details: 1490 Library Lane, St. Helena; (707) 963-3757; open Tuesday through Sunday from noon to 4 p.m. Donations accepted. (½ hour)

FITNESS AND RECREATION

From the trailhead in **Robert Louis Stevenson State Park**, you can hike to the top of 4,344-foot Mount St. Helena, the tallest in the region. The 10-mile round-trip hike takes the better part of a day and is best in the spring or fall when temperatures are moderate. The views from the summit are spectacular. Be sure to carry plenty of water. The park is 6 miles north of Calistoga on CA 29.

Several outfits offer hot-air balloon rides. **Napa Valley Balloons, Inc.**, (707) 944-0228 or (800) 253-2224, offers daily flights departing from the **Napa Valley Grill** in Yountville. One-hour trips are $175 and leave at sunrise. Plan on a three- to five-hour morning due to preparation and shuttling time.

Cycling is great on area backroads. **Saint Helena Cyclery**, 1156 Main Street, St. Helena, (707) 963-7736, rents decent bikes for $7 an hour or $25 a day. The **Good Time Bicycle Company**, located 1½ miles north of Sonoma Plaza at 18503 Highway 12, (707) 938-0453, has rentals for $5 per hour or $25 per day. Guided trips are also offered.

Scenic biplane and glider flights from the Sonoma Valley Airport are offered by **Aeroschellville**, 23982 Arnold Drive (CA 121), (707) 938-2444. They have several vintage military planes in their fleet. The 15- to 40-minute flights range from $80 to $195. Try the "Kamikaze" flight for some aerial acrobatics. **Calistoga Gliders**, (707) 942-5000, offers glider and biplane rides from the **Calistoga Gliderport**, right in town. Flights of 20 to 30 minutes range from $80 to $180.

The **Sonoma Cattle Company**, (707) 996-8566, offers rides through **Jack London State Historic Park**, **Sugarloaf Ridge State Park**, or **Bothe-Napa Valley State Park**. Scheduled rides range from $40 to $55, private rides are $45 per hour.

Canoeing and tubing on the Russian River are popular activities. At **Johnson's Beach** in central Guerneville, you can rent an innertube for $3 a day, (707) 864-2045.

South of the Healdsburg town center, at 20 Healdsburg Avenue, **W. C. "Bob" Trowbridge** offers canoe and kayak trip packages. Half-day trips are $30, overnight trips start at $50, (707) 433-7247 or (800) 640-1386.

FOOD

In the town of Napa, stroll down First Street and along the brick walks of the pedestrian mall for a good selection of eateries. **Downtown Joe's**, at 902 Main Street, (707) 258-2337, is a popular brewpub and restaurant serving breakfast, lunch, and dinner. It's next to the Riverfront Park.

For an elegant and unusual meal, take a lunch or dinner trip on the **Napa Valley Wine Train**, (707) 253-2111 or (800) 427-4124. The train makes two three-hour round-trips daily from Napa to St. Helena and back. The lunch train runs daily at 11:30 a.m. on weekdays and 12:30 p.m. on weekends, and costs $63. The dinner train runs Wednesday through Friday at 6:30 p.m., and on weekends at 5:30 p.m., and costs $70. Prices include a gourmet meal, but not wine.

In Yountville, **Domaine Chandon**, 1 California Drive, (707) 944-2892, at the winery of the same name, offers fine French-California cuisine in elegant surroundings. Sit on the patio if weather permits. **The French Laundry**, 6640 Washington, (707) 944-2380, has pricey but wonderful California cuisine.

In Rutherford, **Auberge du Soleil**, 1050 Charter Oak Avenue (from CA 29), (707) 963-1211, is the place to rub elbows with the platinum-card set while enjoying exquisite California-French entrées and stellar views from the patio. Right on the highway, the **Rutherford Grill**, (707) 963-1792, is deservedly popular. Stylish American fare anchors the menu—notice the chickens rotating deliciously on spits behind the glass.

The raves for **Tra Vigne**, 1050 Charter Oak (off CA 29), (707)

WINE COUNTRY

Mt. St. Helena

M

29

Lake
Berryessa

To C O
R

128

D

Calistoga

128

Q

N

ST. HELENA RD

SPRING MOUNTAIN RD

SILVERADO TRAIL

128

H

St. Helena

To B J
P

CALISTOGA ST

A

RUTHERFORD
CROSS RD

S

Spring
Lake

ADOBE CANYON RD

T

F

YOUNTVILLE
CROSS RD

I

12

29

101

L

121

ARNOLD DR

E

LONDON RANCH RD

G

K

Sonoma

Napa

ADOBE RD

121

Petaluma

CARNEROS HWY

LAKEVILLE HWY

116

121

12

Napa River

101

37

MARINE WORLD PKWY

29

80

Novato

San Pablo Bay

Vallejo

N

0 SCALE   10   10
           KILOMETERS   MILES   ━━━━ ROAD   ✕━━━ PLACE OF INTEREST
                                        ══════ INTERSTATE

Food

- **A** Auberge du Soleil
- **B** Bear Republic Brewing Co.
- **C** Boonville Hotel
- **D** Bosko's
- **E** Calabazas Creek Café
- **D** Calistoga Inn
- **F** Domaine Chandon
- **G** Downtown Joe's
- **F** The French Laundry
- **H** Greystone
- **I** La Gare
- **J** Mendocino Brewing Company
- **K** Murphy's Irish Pub
- **L** Napa Valley Wine Train
- **K** Plaza Hill House at the Feed Store
- **A** Rutherford Grill
- **B** Southside Saloon and Dining Hall
- **H** Tra Vigne

Lodging

- **C** Boonville Hotel
- **F** Burgundy House
- **D** Calistoga Inn
- **H** El Bonita Motel
- **M** Harbin Hot Springs
- **N** Hilltop House
- **H** Hotel St. Helena
- **D** Nance's

Lodging (continued)

- **O** Philo Pottery Inn
- **A** Rancho Caymus
- **D** Roman Spa
- **K** Sonoma Hotel
- **H** Thatcher Inn
- **P** Vichy Springs Resort

Camping

- **Q** Bothe-Napa Valley State Park
- **R** Cloverdale Alexander Valley KOA
- **O** Hendy Woods State Park
- **O** Indian Creek County Park
- **P** Napa County Fair Campground
- **S** Spring Lake Regional Park
- **T** Sugarloaf Ridge State Park

Note: Items with the same letter are located in the same town or area.

963-4444, in St. Helena keep coming. Choose between a full-scale Italian meal in the grand, high-ceilinged dining room or lighter fare in the wonderful, walled courtyard patio. It serves lunch and dinner daily, and breakfast on weekends, at prices in the ballpark for average travelers. Expectations are high at the **Greystone**, 2555 Main Street (north of St. Helena), (707) 967-1010. It shares space in the magnificent old Christian Brothers Winery with the Culinary Institute of America. There are also several good places right on Main Street in town.

The **Calistoga Inn**, 1250 Lincoln Avenue, (707) 942-4101, on the Napa River in Calistoga is a wonderful place to enjoy fine patio dining and a home-brewed beer. Hearty, reasonably priced Italian cuisine can be enjoyed for lunch or dinner at **Bosko's**, 1364 Lincoln Avenue, (707) 942-9088.

There are more than 20 restaurants around the Sonoma Plaza and many more nearby. You won't do better than the **Plaza Hill House at the Feed Store**, 529 First Street West, (707) 939-7147, for breakfast or lunch. **Murphy's Irish Pub**, 464 First Street East, (707) 935-0660, offers fish and chips or Irish stew to go with a pint, and traditional live music Thursday through Sunday.

In the tiny historic end of Glen Ellen, enjoy a lunch or dinner on

© Robert Holmes/California Dept. Tourism

Napa Valley Wine Train

the streamside deck at the **Calabazas Creek Café**, 13740 Arnold Drive, (707) 996-4401.

West of U.S. 101 in Santa Rosa is Historic Railroad Square, featuring shops and restaurants in a couple of blocks of renovated buildings. **La Gare**, 208 Wilson Street, (707) 528-4355, is a delightful and romantic French restaurant.

The new **Bear Republic Brewing Co.**, 345 Healdsburg Avenue, (707) 433-2337, in Healdsburg has good site-brewed ales and fine pub grub. The brewpub is spacious and light, and it faces the small park across the street from the plaza. On the plaza you'll find the **Southside Saloon and Dining Hall**, 106 Matheson Street, (707) 433-4466, serving up moderately priced eclectic fare.

Lots of U.S. 101 travelers stop in Hopland for a bite and a pint at the **Mendocino Brewing Company**, 13351 U.S. 101, (707) 744-1361. The beer garden is a simple pleasure.

In Boonville, the **Boonville Hotel**, CA 128 in Boonville, (707) 895-2210, has California cuisine that strays wonderfully in several directions. Entrées run from $12 to $20.

LODGING

The cities of Vallejo, Napa, Petaluma, Santa Rosa, and Ukiah all have budget and moderate chain motel outlets. Use the numbers listed under "Resources" in the Practical Tips chapter to contact them. Elsewhere, accommodations tend to be more expensive.

In Yountville, the **Burgundy House**, 6711 Washington Street, (707) 944-0889, is a charming, French country–style B&B built in the 1890s. The six guest rooms start at $150.

Next to the Rutherford Grill, **Rancho Caymus**, 1140 Rutherford Road, (707) 963-1777 or (800) 845-1777, offers spacious comfort. This hacienda-style inn has beamed ceilings, individually designed rooms and suites, stained glass, fireplaces, and all the amenities. Rooms are from $145 (a bargain) to $295.

Dating back to 1881, the downtown **Hotel St. Helena**, 1309 Main Street, (707) 963-4388, is a lovely choice with gracious hosts, complimentary breakfast, garden patio, wine bar, and an air of history. Rooms range from $77 to $195. At 195 Main Street, the **El Bonita Motel**, (707) 963-3216, has rooms from $90 to $220.

Calistoga has several spa resorts featuring mud baths, massages, and mineral pools. None of them really stand out as accommodations, but each has its strengths. **Nance's**, 1614 Lincoln Avenue, (707) 942-6211, has the lowest spa and lodging rates, $55 to $90. The **Roman Spa,** 1300 Washington Street, (707) 942-4441, is more intimate and decorated, and has nice pools for $66 to $135 (includes in-room whirlpool spa). For a non-spa stay, try the charming and historic **Calistoga Inn**, right on the Napa River at 1250 Lincoln Avenue, (707) 942-4101. All rooms are shared-bath and are priced from $50 to $65. There's a wonderful restaurant with a riverside patio. A tiny brewery offers lagers and ales on the premises.

A great, cheap spa option out of town is **Harbin Hot Springs**, about 23 miles north of Calistoga. You can stay in a dorm for $30 to $45. Private accommodations run from $50 to $185. There's a vegetarian restaurant and a clothing-optional pool. Bring your own linens or sleeping bags. Take CA 29 to Middletown and then to Harbin Springs Road, (707) 987-2477.

On the top of the ridge separating the Napa and Sonoma Valleys, you'll find **Hilltop House**, 9550 St. Helena Road (take Spring Mountain Road north of St. Helena), (707) 944-0880, with rooms from $135 to $175. Sip wine on the deck as you enjoy the incredible views, or soak in the hot tub under the stars.

Right on the square in Sonoma, the charming vintage **Sonoma Hotel**, 110 West Spain Street, (707) 996-2996 or (800) 468-6016, has private- and shared-bath rooms from $75 to $125.

The **Thatcher Inn**, located on the highway in the center of Hopland, (707) 744-1890 or (800) 266-1891, was built in 1890. The splendid library is a great place to sit and read by the fire. Rooms cost from $110 to $180.

In the Anderson Valley, Boonville offers the **Boonville Hotel**, CA 128 and Lambert Lane in central Boonville, (707) 895-2210, a tasteful and spacious B&B with gardens and a fine restaurant. Rooms run from $75 to $200. At the south end of Philo, the **Philo Pottery Inn**, 8550 CA 128, (707) 895-3069, is a wonderfully rustic B&B. The main building was built in 1888 and was once used as a stagecoach stop. Rooms range from $85 to $100.

In Ukiah, consider a night at the **Vichy Springs Resort**, 2605 Vichy Springs Road, (707) 462-9515. The warm, bubbling mineral springs, named after the almost identical waters of Vichy in France, have been used for centuries. A stay at this B&B inn includes soaking and relaxing on the quiet, sprawling grounds. Rooms are $135 and cabins are $195.

CAMPING

Just south of Calistoga on CA 29, **Bothe-Napa Valley State Park**, has 50 very nice sites for $15 to $16 stretching up along Ritchey Creek. There's an interesting Native American Garden by the park headquarters, 3801 St. Helena Highway North, (707) 942-4575. Reservations are advised. In Calistoga, RVs might want to park at the **Napa County Fair Campground**, (707) 942-5111. Sites are $18. The fairgrounds are on Oak Street, a few blocks north of downtown.

In the upper Sonoma valley, **Sugarloaf Ridge State Park** has very nice sites surrounding a meadow for $14 to $16. Trail rides are available and hiking trails lead to the summits of Red Mountain and Mount Hood. Take Adobe Canyon Road from CA 12 north of Kenwood. Call (707) 833-5712 for information or (800) 444-7275 for reservations.

Near Santa Rosa, **Spring Lake Regional Park**, (707) 539-8082, has $14 sites on a small reservoir. Take Montgomery Drive from CA 12 to Summerfield Drive.

The **Cloverdale Alexander Valley KOA**, (707) 894-3337 or (800) 368-4558, is well off the highway on the east side of the Russian River, not far from Cloverdale. Take the Asti exit and follow the signs for a few miles. Tent sites are $23, RV sites $28, "Kamping Kabins" $38.

Just east of Philo in the Anderson Valley, **Indian Creek County Park** has a few nice but primitive tent sites for $10. West of Philo, **Hendy Woods State Park**, (707) 937-5804, has sites for $14 to $16.

8

THE NORTH COAST: SONOMA AND MENDOCINO

The southern half of California's North Coast extends from Bodega Bay to the town of Rockport above Fort Bragg. Though the stretch is beaded with points of interest, the chief attraction is the magnificent coast itself. The Coast Highway, CA 1, snakes along the brink of the continent, hugging treacherous bluffs one minute and winding through gentle pastures the next. Always, it is the stunning junction of land and sea that draws the eye. You could easily spend a week on the North Coast alternating between headland hikes, forest forays, cliff climbs, whale watches, and beach basks.

Several towns along the coast got their starts as mill and port towns, preparing raw logs and rough lumber, then shipping it by sailing vessel to booming San Francisco. Today, the redwoods are all but gone, though the hills have a new beauty. Where once there were mills and saloons, you'll now find romantic inns, fine restaurants, and art galleries.

Visitors who cannot drive the entire Coast Highway can choose more limited explorations in two popular areas. Bodega Bay and the lower Russian River Valley are close to the Bay Area and are brimming with parks, attractions, and accommodations. Further north, the area around Mendocino and Fort Bragg is similarly blessed. Mendocino can be reached from San Francisco in as little as three hours via U.S. 101 and CA 128 through Anderson Valley. Traveling up CA 1 and back down U.S. 101 makes a good three-day loop. ◣

THE NORTH COAST

Westport

F

C

Ft. Bragg
Noyo
Q

N

101

H
K

Mendocino

Little River
P

Albion

20

Big River

Willits

Mendocino Co.
Lake Co.

I

Pacific Ocean

Elk

Navarro

1
G

Navarro River

J
Manchester

Point Arena

MOUNTAIN VIEW RD

Ukiah

20

Boonville

253

Anchor Bay

128

Nice

E
Gualala

Hopland

101

Lakeport

Clear
Lake

Lucerne

175

Mendocino Co.
Sonoma Co.

Sea Ranch

Cloverdale

Russian River

29

Clearlake

STEWARTS POINT/SKAGGS SPRING RD

Lake
Sonoma

M

D

Healdsburg

Lake Co.
Napa Co.

Jenner
Duncan
Mills
Guerneville

128

Ocean View

O

L

Salmon Creek

B
Bodega Bay

A
Bodega

116

Sebastopol

Calistoga

Bodega Harbor

Santa Rosa

Bodega
Bay

12
St. Helena

0 SCALE

20
KILOMETERS

20
MILES

——— ROAD

╌╌╌ AREA BOUNDARY

┝╍┿╍┥ RAILROAD

N

Sights

Ⓐ Bodega

Ⓑ Bodega Head

Ⓒ Fort Bragg

Ⓓ Fort Ross State Historic Park

Ⓔ Gualala

Ⓕ MacKerricher State Park

Ⓖ Manchester State Park

Ⓗ Mendocino

Ⓒ Mendocino Coast Botanical Gardens

Ⓘ Navarro River Redwoods State Park

Ⓙ Point Arena Lighthouse

Ⓚ Russian Gulch State Park

Ⓛ Russian River Valley

Ⓜ Salt Point State Park

Ⓝ Skunk Train

Ⓞ Sonoma Coast State Beaches

Ⓟ Van Damme State Park

Ⓠ Whale Watching

Note: Items with the same letter are located in the same town or area.

A PERFECT DAY ON THE NORTH COAST

The town of Mendocino makes a great base of operations. In the cool of the morning, enjoy the recreational pursuit of your choice: hiking in Van Damme State Park, cycling in Jackson State Forest, or canoeing up Big River, for example. Drive to Fort Bragg and have lunch down at the wharf on the Noyo River. In the afternoon stroll along the sculpted paths of the Mendocino Coast Botanical Gardens to the ocean. Return to Mendocino for late afternoon shopping, gallery browsing, and aimless strolling. After a tasty dinner, walk out onto the headlands for sunset and evening views of the historic town.

SIGHTSEEING HIGHLIGHTS

★★★ **Mendocino**—If you approach the town of Mendocino from the south, stop at the viewpoint south of the Big River bridge for a picture-postcard view. Perched in historical splendor on protected bluffs, Mendocino began as a logging and milling town in the 1800s. When the wood was gone, it languished in obscurity until discovered first by artists, then by money and tourism. Despite the pressures, it has held its charm remarkably well and remains the top destination on the North Coast.

The town's finest feature is **Mendocino Headlands State Park**. On both sides of the mouth of Big River, the park protects open headlands with wonderful views of town and coast. The look of historic Mendocino perched on a grassy shelf high above the waves is classic. You can literally step off Main Street and onto the bluffs.

The **Ford House Visitor Center** features Mendocino heritage displays including a scale model of the historic town. Details: 735 Main Street, Mendocino; (707) 937-5397; open daily from 10 a.m. to 5 p.m. (11 a.m. to 4 p.m. in winter). A $1 donation is requested. (45 minutes)

At the Kelly House Museum, built in 1861, you'll discover more heritage items and a library with a history and genealogy collection. Details: 45007 Albion Street, Mendocino; (707) 937-5791; open daily from 1 to 4 p.m. in summer (Friday through Monday in winter). Admission is $2. (1 hour)

The **Mendocino Art Center Showcase** on Main Street features works by local artists. The center also has galleries and offers classes that attract students from across the country. Enjoy a play put on by the Mendocino Theater Company at the **Mendocino Art Center**. Details: 45200 Little Lake Street, Mendocino; (707) 937-5818, (707) 937-4477 for theater information. (1 hour)

For great information on what's happening around town, check out the notices posted on the fence next to the **Corners of the Mouth Natural Foods Grocery** after you stock up on healthy stuff.

★★★ **Mendocino Coast Botanical Gardens**—Established by retired nursery man Ernest Schoefer in 1961, the gardens are at the south end of Fort Bragg on 47 acres, stretching from CA 1 to the Pacific. While visually stunning during blooming cycles from April to October, the garden is a wonderful place for easy walks and relaxation year-round. Whale watching from the bluffs is best in December and March. Details: 18220 North CA 1, Fort Bragg; (707) 964-4352; open daily from 9 a.m. to 5 p.m. (until 4 p.m. in winter). Admission is $6. (1–3 hours)

★★ **Bodega Head**—For fine views of bay, coast, and open ocean, Bodega Head can't be beat. Whale watching is an option during the gray whale migration (best in and around December and March), and harbor seals can be seen and heard. Trails lead up and down the coast from the day-use parking areas.

To the north, the **Bodega Marine Reserve** and **Bodega Marine Laboratory**, extensions of the University of California at Davis, are off-limits to hiking. The lab can only be visited on docent-led tours. Details: The entrance is along Bay Flats Road, Bodega Head; (707) 875-2211; tours are given Fridays from 2 to 4 p.m., call for details. A $2 donation is suggested. (2½ hours)

★★ **Point Arena Lighthouse**—Built in 1908 to replace a predecessor damaged in the 1906 earthquake, the Point Arena Lighthouse is one of California's tallest at 115 feet. A good museum, great coastal views, and the chance to climb to the top make the lighthouse an excellent stop. Details: Just north of Point Arena, turn left onto Lighthouse Road for the five-minute drive to the point; (707) 882-2777; open daily from 11 a.m. to 3:30 p.m. (opens at 10 a.m. weekends), winter hours are 11 a.m. to 2:30 p.m. Admission is $2.50. (1½ hours)

★★ **Salt Point State Park**—With over 5,600 acres to explore, Salt Point is a great recreational resource. Miles of trails are available to hikers and horseback riders, providing access to headlands, sandy coves, and forested slopes. The associated **Gerstle Cove Reserve** preserves tidal pools and shallows rich in marine life. At the north end of the park, narrow Kruse Ranch Road winds up into the **Kruse Rhododendron State Preserve**. Here, the steep, forested hills feature a lush undergrowth of rhododendron that produces a magnificent display of pink blossoms in April and May. There are trailheads and turnouts along the road. Details: 20 miles north of Jenner on CA 1; (707) 847-3221. Day-use parking is $5. (½ day)

★★ **Whale Watching**—Every year, gray whales swim close by the coast of California on their annual migrations, passing southward in December and January, then northward from February through April. During peak season, watchers enjoy a high rate of success in sighting the passing behemoths from headland vantage points. Special whale-watching boat excursions leave from the larger coastal towns. Proper timing, binoculars, and a little patience are all that's required. Details: Noyo Harbor in Fort Bragg is the best base for trips. Reserve your $20 spot with one of the boats listed below in "Fitness and Recreation." (2 hours)

★ **Fort Ross State Historic Park**—In 1812 Russian traders seeking otter pelts established Fort Ross as a base of operations. Thirty years later, the region's otter population was decimated and the site was abandoned. Today you can visit an accurate reconstruction of the settlement and enjoy the library and historical exhibits in the visitor center. There are also several good hiking trails on the coast and in the hills above the highway. Details: 12 miles north of Jenner on CA 1; (707) 847-3286; open daily from 10 a.m. to 4:30 p.m. Day-use parking is $6. (1 hour)

★ **Manchester State Park**—CA 1 cuts away from the coast to get around this sprawling beach. The San Andreas Fault, which runs along the North Coast above Bolinas, exits the continent here once and for all. If you want miles of sand, wind, waves, driftwood, and shorebirds, you'll love it here. Details: Access is via Kinney Road, ½ mile north of Manchester; (707) 937-5804. There's a $5 day-use fee in some areas. (3 hours)

★ **MacKerricher State Park**—Located north of Fort Bragg, the 8 miles of wide beach backed by dunes make this park one of the sandiest stretches on the North Coast. Near the campground is a small lake

© Paul Otteson

Northern California Coast

with a perimeter trail. An old logging haul road runs the length of the park behind the beach, providing a great route for cycling, walking, or jogging. Harbor seals are common visitors and migrating whales can be seen from November through March. Details: 3 miles north of Fort Bragg on CA 1; (707) 937-5804. No fee. (3 hours)

✴ **Navarro River Redwoods State Park**—Turn up CA 128 south of Mendocino to pass through a lush corridor of second-growth red-woods, now preserved from the chainsaw because of their proximity to the fragile riverine environment—and their proximity to the eyes of drivers who prefer forest to clear-cuts. There are several spots to stop along the way to enjoy both river and trees. If you are zooming to or from the Anderson Valley, this is a great place to slow down. Details: CA 128, south of Mendocino; (707) 937-5804. No fee. (1 hour)

✴ **Russian Gulch State Park**—Just north of Mendocino, a mile of protected coast features the **Punch Bowl**, a churning inlet in a col-lapsed sea cave that has a "boiling cauldron" look. A lovely waterfall is one possible hiking destination on the miles of trails through the inland portion of the park. Details: Located 2 miles north of Mendocino on CA 1; (707) 937-5804. Day-use parking is $5. (2 hours)

✴ **Russian River Valley**—Highway 116 follows the final miles of the Russian River from the town of **Guerneville** to the coast at **Jenner**. The entire region, including the towns of **Forestville**, **Occidental**, **Monte Rio**, and **Cazadero**, is a resort area that is replete with vacation homes, riverside inns, fishing lodges, and other attractions.

Duncans Mills is a tiny, "historic" town, with shops largely owned by one family. It's a bit too cute to be believable, though the museum and rail cars may be worth a look. **Monte Rio** offers a public beach, mini-golf, and a small amusement park. Cross the river on the Bohemian Highway to reach the town center. **Bohemian Grove**, retreat of the rich and powerful, sits in the hills east of Monte Rio, but it is closed to the public.

Located just north of Guerneville, on the Armstrong Woods Road, is **Armstrong Redwoods State Reserve**. The park preserves the largest grove of old-growth redwoods in Sonoma County and offers several short hikes. Adjacent to the park on the north is **Austin Creek State Recreation Area**, offering 20 miles of hiking in a rugged terrain of open forest and rolling hills. Details: Armstrong Woods Road, Guerneville; (707) 869-2015; open daily from 8 a.m. until one hour after sunset. Day-use parking for both areas is $5, though you're encouraged to use the limited free parking just outside the entrance. (1½ hours)

✭ **Skunk Train**—Named after the foul fuel smells of yesteryear, the historic Skunk Train runs through redwood country along the Noyo River between Fort Bragg and Willits. Details: The station is east of CA 1 at 100 Laurel Street, Fort Bragg; (707) 964-6371; in summer round-trip train excursions leave Fort Bragg at 9:30 a.m. and 2 p.m. The schedule is a bit complex so call ahead. Half-day trips are $25 and full-day trips are $35. (½ day–all day)

✭ **Sonoma Coast State Beaches**—From Bodega Bay north to Stewart's Point, much of the Sonoma County coastline is preserved in the **Sonoma Coast State Beaches**, **Fort Ross State Historic Park**, and **Salt Point State Park**. Choose any of the coastal access points for picnicking and beachcombing. Details: (707) 875-3483. Day-use parking fee is $5 at certain areas. (1 hour–½ day)

✭ **Van Damme State Park**—This park is a favorite of joggers and cyclists who enjoy the 3-mile paved road along Little River. An easily accessible beach attracts abalone divers, and there's a golf course. An unusual "pygmy forest" is easily reached by a wheelchair-accessible trail. Details: 3 miles south of Mendocino; (707) 937-5804. Day-use parking fee is $5. (2 hours)

Bodega—One mile east of the Coast Highway, the small town of Bodega (not Bodega Bay) offers a few art and antique shops, along with a chance for a meal and supplies. Historic **Santa Teresa's Catholic Church**, a National Historical Landmark, sits on the south slope above the road. Of greatest interest, perhaps, is the **Potter School**, now a private residence. On a side road behind Santa Teresa's, the Potter School catches the eye with its mildly odd appearance and interesting architectural highlights. No wonder Alfred Hitchcock used it in his film *The Birds*. (1 hour)

Fort Bragg—Easy to overlook as Mendocino's ugly relative, Fort Bragg has two areas worth exploring. The somewhat scruffy Wharf area along the mouth of the Noyo River is often only glimpsed by people as they zoom over the Noyo River Bridge, but it offers great eating, boat trips, and loads of character. Drop down from the east side of CA 1 at the north end of the bridge. In the historic downtown area around North Main (CA 1) and Redwood, there are pleasant shops and cafés, several of which are located in restored historic buildings. (1 hour)

Gualala—This pleasant town lies north of Sea Ranch at the mouth of the Gualala River. A hundred years ago the town was one of several up and down the coast that milled redwood and hauled it offshore to waiting schooners. Today it's a slightly overgrown hamlet of 500 or so that serves tourists and Sea Ranch residents. (½ hour)

FITNESS AND RECREATION

Tame and easy fun for the kids can be had at **Hagemann Ranch Trout Farm**, (707) 876-3217, just east of CA 1 between Bodega and Bodega Bay—watch for the sign. For $2 and up, you can catch lunch while the young ones hunt for frogs. Pole rental is available, and picnicking is permitted. It's open 9 a.m. to 6 p.m. Thursday through Monday, June through September.

In Bodega Bay, **Wil's Fishing Adventures** on East Shore Road, (707) 875-2323, offers daily ocean fishing excursions for around $50. The **Bodega Harbour Golf Links**, (707) 875-3538, offers beautiful ocean views on a "Scottish-style" course. Green fees are $35 to $80. Take Heron Drive, just south of Bodega Bay. Beach and headlands hiking is possible from many access points along the Sonoma Coast.

Located in the Armstrong Redwoods State Reserve, **Armstrong Woods Pack Station**, (707) 887-2939, offers private and scheduled trail rides through the reserve and Austin Creek State Recreation Area that range from two hours to three days in length. Rides start at $35. With outlets in Fort Bragg and Van Damme State Park, **Lost Coast Adventures**, 19275 South Harbor Drive, Fort Bragg, (707) 937-2434, offers sea kayaking and diving tours, as well as gear rental.

Catch-a-Canoe and Bicycles 2, (707) 937-0273, is a great place to rent canoes or kayaks for a paddle on Big River. They also rent mountain bikes and recommend routes on the thousand miles of bikeable roads in **Jackson State Forest**. Turn south on Comptche-Ukiah Road just south of the Big River Bridge below Mendocino, then left down the hill.

THE NORTH COAST

Westport

101

Ft. Bragg Ⓗ
Noyo Ⓒ
Ⓣ
Mendocino Ⓔ
Little River Ⓙ
Ⓘ Ⓤ
Albion

20

Big River

Willits

Mendocino Co.
Lake Co.

Pacific Ocean

Elk

Navarro

1

Nasarro River

Manchester
Ⓢ
MOUNTAIN VIEW RD
Point Arena Ⓕ

Ukiah

20

Boonville

253

128

Anchor Bay
Ⓖ
Gualala

Hopland

101

Lakeport

Clear
Lake

Nice

Lucerne

175

Mendocino Co.
Sonoma Co.

Sea Ranch

Cloverdale

Lake
Sonoma

29

Clearlake

STEWARTS POINT/SKAGGS SPRING RD

Russian River

Ⓡ
Ⓛ

Ⓝ Healdsburg
Ⓠ
Ⓓ
Duncan
Mills Guerneville

Lake Co.
Napa Co.

Jenner

Ⓐ

128

Ocean View

Ⓞ

Ⓚ
Salmon Creek
Bodega Bay
Ⓑ Bodega
Bodega Harbor

116

Sebastopol

Santa Rosa

Calistoga

Bodega
Bay

Ⓟ

Ⓜ

12 St. Helena

N

0 SCALE   20   20
        KILOMETERS   MILES   ——— ROAD   ┝━┥ RAILROAD
                                  - - - AREA BOUNDARY

Food

- **A** Applewood Restaurant
- **B** Breakers Café
- **C** Carine's Fish Grotto
- **D** Coffee Bazaar
- **D** Last Great Hiding Place
- **B** Lucas Wharf Restaurant and Bar
- **E** McCallum House
- **E** Mendocino Bakery and Café
- **C** North Coast Brewing Company Tap Room and Grill
- **F** Pangaea Café
- **B** Sandpiper Dockside Café and Restaurant
- **G** St. Orres Restaurant
- **H** The Restaurant

Lodging

- **I** Andiron Lodge
- **A** Applewood Inn
- **B** Bodega Harbor Inn
- **J** Brewery Gulch Inn
- **K** Chanslor Guest Ranch
- **E** Coast Guard House
- **C** Coast Motel
- **G** Gualala Hotel
- **B** Inn at the Tides
- **E** McCallum House
- **E** Mendocino Hotel
- **L** Salt Point Lodge

Lodging *(continued)*

- **G** St. Orres
- **L** Stillwater Cove Ranch
- **L** Timber Cove Inn
- **M** Valley Ford Hotel

Camping

- **N** Austin Creek State Recreation Area
- **K** Bodega Dunes
- **O** Casini Family Campground
- **P** Doran Regional Park
- **Q** Faerie Ring Campground
- **R** Gerstle Cove
- **G** Gualala Point Regional Park Campground
- **C** MacKerricher State Park
- **S** Manchester State Park
- **R** Ocean Cove Camping
- **T** Russian Gulch State Park
- **U** Van Damme State Park
- **R** Woodside

Note: Items with the same letter are located in the same town or area.

From the wharf, along the north shore of the Noyo River in Fort Bragg, several companies offer charter and scheduled ocean fishing and whale-watching trips. Try the **Noyo Bell**, (707) 964-3104; the **Tally Ho II**, (707) 964-2079; or **Trek II/Cavalier**, (707) 964-4550. Turn east at the north end of the Noyo River Bridge.

FOOD

Bodega Bay has the **Lucas Wharf Restaurant and Bar**, 595 CA 1, (707) 875-3522, which offers good seafood at tourist prices. The **Sandpiper Dockside Café and Restaurant**, 1410 Bay Flat Road, (707) 875-2278, is where you might go for moderately priced breakfasts if you lived here, as well as for salad and sandwich lunches and a wide dinner menu. The **Breakers Café**, 1400 CA 1, (707) 875-2513, is darn good and more reasonable than the rest. How about Belgian waffles with hot spiced peaches and whipped cream for $6? They serve lunch and dinner too.

I like the **Coffee Bazaar**, 14045 Armstrong Woods Road, (707) 869-9706, in downtown Guerneville for happy ambiance to go with coffee and pastries or lunch. Go 3/4 mile east of downtown Guerneville on Main Street to reach the **Last Great Hiding Place**, 15025 River Road, (707) 887-9506, for a tasty meal on the deck overlooking the water. It's open for breakfast, lunch, and dinner, and good sandwich plates run from $6 to $9. A must for fine dining is the **Applewood Restaurant**, (707) 869-9093, in the inn with the same name. It's on Highway 116 across the bridge from downtown Guerneville. Prix fixe dinners are served Tuesday through Saturday.

The **St. Orres Restaurant**, 36601 CA 1 (2 miles north of Gualala), (707) 884-3335, at the St. Orres Inn is one of the finest places to dine on the North Coast—doubly nice if you have a room at the inn to walk back to after dinner. The North Coast–style, French country cuisine features amazing wild game recipes. Reserve in advance (even if you're an inn guest).

In Point Arena, try the **Pangaea Café**, 250 Main Street, (707) 882-3001. Tasty entrées run from $13 to $18.

Mendocino has enough options to keep you busy for a few days. A stop at the **Mendocino Bakery and Café**, 10485 Lansing Street, (707) 937-0836, seems like the right thing to do. It's friendly, reasonable, and just plain pleasant. For fancy fare, the historic **McCallum House**, 45020 Albion Street, (707) 937-5763, blends traditional and California cuisines with great success. Entrées run from $15 to $20.

In Fort Bragg, try **The Restaurant**, 418 Main Street, (707) 964-9800, for excellent seafood dishes in an artistic setting. From the north end of the bridge over the Noyo River in Fort Bragg, head east and down to the wharf for a huge and tasty seafood dinner at **Carine's Fish Grotto**, (707) 964-2429. Bessie Carine herself may guide you through the feast. The **North Coast Brewing Company Tap Room and Grill**, 444 Main Street, (707) 964-3400, has great microbrews and better-than-pub grub-food.

LODGING

The North Coast has lots of romantic getaway inns and B&Bs, most hoping that you leave the kids at home. If you're particularly interested in this type of lodging, consult a B&B or country inn guide like those noted under "Recommended Reading" in the Practical Tips chapter. Chain motels are rare, but there are a few in Fort Bragg. Options that have particular charm, character, or historic interest are listed below, as are budget and family-friendly choices. One thing that all North Coast lodging and camping options have in common is that they are booked solid on summer weekends. Make reservations if need be.

In Valley Ford, the **Valley Ford Hotel**, 14415 CA 1, (707) 876-3600 or (800) 696-6679, built in 1864, offers charming rooms starting around $80 in a ranch country setting. At dinner, served Friday through Sunday, a locally renowned Basque White Bean Soup is featured.

A good budget option in Bodega Bay is the **Bodega Harbor Inn**, 1345 Bodega Avenue (one block above CA 1), (707) 875-3594, with motel rooms from $60 to $82. The **Inn at the Tides**, 800 CA 1, (707) 875-2751 or (800) 541-7788, offers several buildings that climb the hills above the harbor, separated by landscaped walks and lawns. There's plenty of luxury here at $125 to $220 per room.

North of Bodega Bay on CA 1 is the family-oriented **Chanslor Guest Ranch**, 2660 CA 1, (707) 875-2721, offering lodging, guided horseback rides, hiking, fishing, and more on a 700-acre spread. There's even a petting zoo for the kids. Rooms start at $65.

The lower Russian River Valley has many lodging options. Elegant but friendly, the **Applewood Inn**, 13555 Highway 116 (1 mile south of Guerneville), (707) 869-9093 or (800) 555-8509, is one of the area's finest. Built in 1922 as a private home, the inn has nine rooms with woodsy or vineyard views. A full breakfast is served to inn guests only. It's pricey, but worth it.

Once a school for boys, **Stillwater Cove Ranch**, 22555 CA 1, (707) 847-3227, is a unique and inexpensive option located just south of Salt Point State Park. Peacocks strut through the rustic grounds of this working farm, shrieking whenever the mood takes them. Other animals will delight the kids. There are cottages and a small bunkhouse for groups up to eight. Rooms are $40 to $80.

Just 17 miles north of Jenner, the **Salt Point Lodge**, 23255 CA 1, (800) 956-3437, offers family-friendly accommodations for $50 to $107. Set above the highway just south of Salt Point Park, there are gardens and a small playground. The **Timber Cove Inn**, 21780 CA 1 (north of Fort Ross State Historical Park), (707) 847-3231 or (800) 987-8319, is worth a stay for its lofty lobby, Japanese pond, and knoll-top obelisk. What makes it truly outstanding is its location on a ragged coastal headland with exclusive trails. Rooms start at $110, but climb quickly toward $390.

For a taste of history, try the **Gualala Hotel**, (707) 884-3441, in central Gualala. Built in 1903, it features shared-bath rooms for only $45. Private-bath, ocean-view rooms are $55 to $65. The "logging bar" retains all the charm that made Jack London a frequent visitor. One of the best known inns on the coast, **St. Orres**, 36601 CA 1 (2 miles north of Gualala), (707) 884-3303, is styled like a Russian dacha with onion-shaped domes. Rooms are reasonable, ranging from $60 (shared bath) to $225 (cottage). Breakfast is included.

Just south of central Point Arena, Port Road follows Point Arena Creek to the ocean. There you'll find the **Coast Guard House**, 695 Arena Cove, Point Arena, (707) 882-2442. Long used by the Coast Guard as a base for life-saving operations, it is now a friendly and historic B&B. Schooner the dog greets you when you arrive. Rooms run from $115 to $175.

The **Andiron Lodge**, (707) 937-1543, in Albion has no-frills, family-friendly cottages above the road with rooms from $45 to $60 and cabins (sleep four) from $100 to $135.

In the fields east of the highway, Ann and her dog Ben keep the wonderful **Brewery Gulch Inn** (my favorite), 9350 CA 1, south of Mendocino, (707) 937-4752, a small B&B in an 1860s farmhouse. The charming gardens and grounds will make you sigh. Rooms are a bargain from $85 to $135. The inn is scheduled to move into a splendid new structure built of ancient redwood, cut decades ago and recently salvaged from the bottom of Big River.

The **Mendocino Hotel**, 45080 Main Street, (707) 937-0511 or

(800) 548-0513, built in 1878, sits right on Main Street overlooking the headlands and Mendocino Bay. Shared-bath rooms start at $85 and range to suites for $250. The classy, Victorian **McCallum House**, 45020 Albion Street, (707) 937-0289, has a variety of rooms from $100 to $190.

Fort Bragg has a real "motel row" at the south end of town. You might even find a vacancy sign still out on a Saturday afternoon in July. The **Coast Motel**, 18661 CA 1, a mile south of the river, (707) 964-2852, is OK and one of the cheapest in the region with rooms starting at about $40.

CAMPING

The top camping choices on the North Coast are the beautiful California State Park campgrounds. Always in prime locations, state park sites are usually well designed and maintained, in addition to being spacious and relatively private. Most have coin showers. About half the parks can accommodate trailers or motor homes over 30 feet, though only a handful have hookups. All the campgrounds have clearly marked entrances along the Coast Highway. Call (800) 444-7275 to make reservations or to get a brochure describing all park facilities. The parks with developed campgrounds are listed below, from south to north.

- **Bodega Dunes** at Sonoma Coast State Beaches, just north of Bodega Bay—$12 to $16, (707) 875-3483.
- **Gerstle Cove** at Salt Point State Park—$12 to $16, (707) 847-3221.
- **Woodside** at Salt Point State Park—$12 to $16 (walk-ins $10 to $14), (707) 847-3221.
- **Manchester State Park**, 5 miles north of Point Arena—$7 to $9 (hike-ins $2), primitive sites, no reservations, (707) 937-5804.
- **Van Damme State Park**, 3 miles south of Mendocino—$12 to $16 (some sites for self-contained vehicles on the water, regular camping above the highway), (707) 937-5804.
- **Russian Gulch State Park**, just north of Mendocino—$12 to $16, (707) 937-5804.
- **MacKerricher State Park**, north of Fort Bragg—$12 to $16, (707) 937-5804.

In Bodega Bay, **Doran Regional Park** has pretty good sites on the open, sandy spit that separates Bodega Bay from Bodega Harbor.

There's a good beach and hiking trails. Take Doran Beach Road where CA 1 meets the coast south of town.

A few miles from the coast on Highway 116, **Casini Family Campground**, (800) 451-8400, has 225 sites on a 120-acre spread with a long river frontage. Sites range from spacious, private tent sites to RV pull-throughs with hookups. There are a store and recreation hall, canoe rental, fishing, a duck pond, playgrounds, river beaches, and Saturday night hayrides. It's a great family choice and costs from $19 to $25.

There are 24 sites at Bull Frog Pond in **Austin Creek State Recreation Area**, (707) 869-2015, at the end of the Armstrong Woods Road north of Guerneville. Sites are $12. **Faerie Ring Campground**, (707) 869-2746, has 44 sites in a lovely setting, 1½ miles north of Guerneville on the Armstrong Woods Road. The campground features several "faerie rings," that is, circles of redwood trees that sometimes sprout up around the site of the dead "mother" tree. Tents can actually be placed within the rings at a couple of sites, tent sites are $20, RVs are $25.

At $12 per vehicle with no charges for extra people, **Ocean Cove Camping**, 23125 CA 1, (707) 847-3422, is a good budget option. More than 100 sites are scattered across low hills, including several at bluff's edge on the ocean. The campground is active with families, fisher folk, and abalone divers (in season).

Gualala Point Regional Park Campground, (707) 785-2377, has very nice sites in the redwoods along the Gualala River. Access to the river mouth is across the road. The entrance is south of the river, and sites cost $15.

9

THE REDWOOD PARKS

North of Mendocino, CA 1 ends and U.S. 101 becomes the sole coastal route. A freeway most of the way, it follows the course of the Eel River to Eureka, then continues up the coast to Oregon. U.S. 101 passes through a region known as the "Redwood Empire." As you look out at the thick carpet of green that drapes the hills, you're seeing American decks and fences, and resources for export.

The largest remaining groves of ancient redwoods in the world are protected in parklands along U.S. 101. Humboldt Redwoods State Park lies south of Eureka, while the jointly administered Redwood National and State Parks are to the north. If your travels will take you as far north as Mendocino, driving an extra 110 miles to see the largest of all old-growth groves in Humboldt Redwoods is worth it. For the loveliest groves, you'll have to make your way to the northern parks where a healthy remnant of past splendor still grows almost to the ocean's edge.

California's fabled "Lost Coast" is the only significant stretch of the state without a shoreline highway. It lies west of U.S. 101, between Rockport to the south and Ferndale to the north. Access to the coast-line here is time-consuming, but the rewards are many. The Lost Coast may no longer be lost, but it's still reluctant to be found.

Other attractions exist on the upper North Coast, and almost all are a stone's throw from U.S. 101. You'll notice a shift from the "California lifestyle" to one that is distinctly Pacific Northwestern. Everything from attitudes to art reflects the difference. ◼

THE REDWOOD PARKS

Smith River

199 Patrick
     Creek

Crescent City ■
E

Happy Camp ■

Smith River
National
Recreation
Area

Redwood
National
Park

96

3

Klamath ■ M

K
■ Orick

Redwood
National
Park

Pacific
Ocean

J
■ Trinidad
N

Willow Creek ■

299

Arcata ■ A

3

F
Eureka ■

299

101

Weaverville ■

Ferndale ■ 211
          G

299

Scotia ■ L

36

3

■ Mad River

B

36

MATTOLE RD

I

Humboldt
Redwoods
State Park

■ Miranda

H
■ Garberville
■ Benbow

D
C
■ Leggett

N

0 SCALE   25   25
      KILOMETERS MILES   ——— ROAD   ---- AREA BOUNDARY

Sights

- **A** Arcata
- **B** Avenue of the Giants
- **C** Chandelier Tree
- **D** Confusion Hill
- **E** Crescent City
- **F** Eureka
- **G** Ferndale
- **H** Garberville
- **I** Humboldt Redwoods State Park and Rockefeller Forest
- **J** Patrick's Point State Park
- **K** Redwood National and State Parks
- **L** Scotia
- **M** Trees of Mystery
- **N** Trinidad

A PERFECT DAY IN THE REDWOODS

Leave your campsite early at Gold Bluffs Beach to be the first one to the Fern Canyon Trailhead. Relish a hike through the canyon and onward to the mist-shrouded, primeval groves. Drive south to Patrick's Point State Park for a short headlands walk, a picnic lunch, and some beachcombing on aptly named Agate Beach. If you're in a people mood, pick a sight or two from the list in Trinidad, Arcata, and Eureka. Your hotel room awaits in Ferndale, or perhaps it's a campsite at the mouth of the Mattole River near Petrolia. You'll fall asleep convinced you need another day for the upper North Coast.

THE REDWOOD EMPIRE

Less than four percent of the old-growth trees from the western coastal forests still stand, and the redwoods have been as hard hit as any. Where are the remaining trees? Over 90 percent of those that are left are protected, most in parks, yet even park boundaries are deceiving. Most of the land in the North Coast's dedicated redwood parks was logged in this century. When you look at the parks on your map, less than a third of what you see has virgin forest. The rest of the old growth—and that of virtually all the sprawling private timberlands of the Redwood Empire—is gone.

The battle lines have been drawn, but there really is no compromise. Either you cut them, or you don't. Enjoy the splendor of the remaining groves. The massive yet graceful California redwoods are all the more amazing for their rarity.

SIGHTSEEING HIGHLIGHTS

★★★ **Humboldt Redwoods State Park and Rockefeller Forest**—About 50 miles south of Eureka, Humboldt Redwoods preserves more than 17,000 acres of old growth, including the 10,000-acre **Rockefeller Forest**, which is the largest contiguous tract of virgin redwoods in the world.

Bull Creek runs through the heart of the forest, paralleling the Mattole Road about ½ mile to the south. The **Bull Creek Trail** is easily accessible from the road at **Bull Creek Flats**, where the creek meets the Eel River, and also 4 miles upstream at the sites of **Giant Tree** and recently fallen **Flat Iron Tree**. Loop hikes of varying length can be designed using the trail map in the park brochure. Plan on more time than the mileage indicates. You will find yourself drawn to a quiet spot among the great sentinels for some moments of quiet reverence. To reach the forest from U.S. 101 or the Avenue of the Giants, take the Mattole Road west into the park interior.

In the southern end of the park, a particularly nice segment of the Avenue of the Giants runs between the freeway and the river. Lovely riverside groves offer good short walks undisturbed by road noise. Details: Located on CA 101, north of Leggett; (707) 946-2409. (½–all day)

★★★ **Redwood National and State Parks**—Between Eureka and Crescent City, an almost continuous band of jointly managed federal and state land preserves the finest remaining examples of several old-growth redwood ecosystems: **Redwood National Park**, **Prairie Creek Redwoods State Park**, **Del Norte Redwoods State Park**, and **Jedediah Smith Redwoods State Park**. Together with the **Smith River National Recreation Area**, they offer the traveler numerous recreational opportunities.

In the main body of Redwood National Park, only about 20 percent of the trees are old growth, but two areas deserve special note. There is a pleasant, 1-mile loop trail through the impressive **Lady Bird Johnson Grove**. Take Bald Hills Road (no trailers or large RVs) 2½ miles to the parking area. For the trailhead of the 8½-mile path along Redwood Creek to the **Tall Trees Grove**, take a right to the picnic area just after you turn onto Bald Hills Road. The easier route to see the grove is to obtain one of 50 free daily car permits to drive down the access road. Permits and tours are arranged at the Redwood Information Center a mile south of Orick—get there early in July and August.

One of the nicest parks is Prairie Creek Redwoods, practically the only place where ancient redwoods grow down almost to the Pacific. Old Highway 101, now **Newton B. Drury Scenic Parkway**, provides a lightly traveled pathway through a very large stand of old growth along Prairie Creek. Several trails head deep into the groves and to the ocean. The short **Cal-Barrel Road** (no trailers or large RVs) offers a vehicular dip into solitude. Winding, 8-mile **Davison Road** (no trailers or large RVs) leads to the low dunes of **Gold Bluffs Beach**. Roosevelt elk browse between the base of the bluffs and the dunes. The road ends at the trailhead for mystical **Fern Canyon** where tiny waterfalls drip down the 70-foot, fern-covered canyon walls. Connecting trails lead to the old-growth stands, as well as up and down the coast.

Howland Hills Road in **Jedediah Smith State Park** is a great route through a fine old-growth forest. Take Elk Valley Road from the south end of Crescent City. It connects to U.S. 199. There is no fee to drive through the redwood parks, though a $5 per day fee is charged for Gold Bluffs Beach and Fern Canyon. Call (707) 822-7611, ext. 5265 for information. (all day)

✮✮ **Avenue of the Giants**—Whether you're approaching Humboldt Redwoods State Park from the north or south, leave U.S. 101 and drive the 30-mile long Avenue of the Giants, a segment of the old Highway 101 that passes through several fine redwood groves. Stop at one of many turnouts for a dip in the pleasant waters of the Eel River. Watch for egrets wading in the shallows. Enjoy the groves as you go, but save your hiking time for the Rockefeller Forest.

The central segment of the Avenue of the Giants is the best, passing through a continuous corridor of public land between the freeway and the Eel River. Enjoy the tunnel of green and the river vistas on your way to the junction with Mattole Road and access to the park interior. Watch for exit signs on U.S. 101 between Leggett and Scotia. (1½ hours)

✮✮ **Patrick's Point State Park**—This small and wonderful coastal park features a 2-mile headlands hike with interesting rock formations, some fine tidal pools, a replica of a Yurok Indian village to explore, and good whale watching in season. Ocean-polished agates can indeed be found along **Agate Beach**. Hike to **Wedding Rock** for that rugged coast feel. There are three nice campgrounds. Details: Located 5 miles north of Trinidad on U.S. 101; (707) 677-3570; open daily from dawn to dusk. As with most California state parks, there is a day-use fee of $5. (3 hours)

✵ **Crescent City**—In the early morning of March 28, 1964, the most powerful earthquake ever recorded in North America struck in Alaska, devastating parts of Anchorage and several smaller communities. Several hours later, four tsunamis, each progressively larger, struck Crescent City. Half of this town of 9,000 was washed away. Fourteen people were killed or never found. It doesn't take too sharp an eye to find evidence of the disaster in the current layout and architectural variation of the town.

For photographic insights into this event, as well as good displays on many aspects of the region's heritage, visit the **Del Norte Historical Society Museum**. Details: 577 H Street, Crescent City; (707) 464-3922; open 10 a.m. to 4 p.m., Monday through Saturday May to September. Admission is $2. (45 minutes)

The **Battery Point Lighthouse** can be reached across a walkway at low tide. It has been converted into a museum, and tours are available. Details: Located at the end of A Street on Battery Point Island; (707) 464-3089; tours given Wednesday through Sunday from 10 a.m. to 4 p.m., April through September. Admission is $2. (½ hour)

✵ **Eureka**—As the state's largest port city north of San Francisco, Eureka is the site of commercial activity and the unattractive industrial sprawl that goes along with it. U.S. 101 splits into Fourth Street and Fifth Street as it passes through downtown. Head down to Second and Third, between C Street and M Street, to reach the almost successful Victorian renaissance **Old Town**. While there, don't miss a look at the **Carson Mansion** at Second and M Streets, one of the most ornate Victorian structures to be found anywhere. You can't go inside unless you manage to be invited as a guest of "Ingomar," the resident men's club. (½ day)

The **Humboldt Bay Maritime Museum** features loads of regional and marine heritage exhibits and memorabilia. Details: 1410 Second Street, behind the new library, Eureka; (707) 444-9440; open daily from 11 a.m. to 4 p.m. Admission is free. (45 minutes)

Consider a visit to the **Clarke Memorial Museum** for a look at American Indian history and regional heritage artifacts. Details: 240 E Street, Eureka; (707) 443-1947; open Tuesday through Saturday from noon to 4 p.m. Donations accepted. (45 minutes)

Try a guided, 1½-hour cruise on the *Madaket* to see the sights on Humboldt Bay. The *Madaket* is the oldest boat in continuous service on the Pacific Coast. Details: Located where C Street meets Humboldt Bay below 1st Street; (707) 445-1910 for schedule and reservations; tours are available from May through October. Admission is $9.50. (1½ hours)

Fort Humboldt State Historic Park preserves the site of Fort Humboldt, which served as a base to suppress Indian activity in the area. There is a good museum of logging and Native American history, as well as an excellent outdoor exhibit on logging history. Details: At the south end of Eureka, turn east on Highland Avenue, then left into the park; (707) 445-6567; open daily from 9 a.m. to 5 p.m. Admission is free. (1 hour)

Several diversions offer themselves to travelers in the vicinity of Eureka and Arcata. Bird-watching is good in the estuarine and sheltered inlet environments of the **Eel River Wildlife Area** and **Humboldt Bay National Wildlife Refuge** south of Eureka, or the **Mad River Slough and Dunes** north of Arcata. Enjoy the sands at **Samoa Dunes Recreation Area** as you watch the boat traffic flow in and out of Humboldt Bay. If you're here in the spring, walk the short loop path through the stunning blooms at the small **Azalea State Reserve**, 1 mile east of U.S. 101 on CA 200, the southernmost McKinleyville exit. (1 to 3 hours)

✸ **Arcata**—Take the CA 255, Samoa Boulevard exit west from U.S. 101 to reach the home of **Humboldt State University**. Arcata provides a somewhat liberal counterpoint to Eureka's conservative, resource-harvest economics. The **Arcata Plaza**, a large square at G Street and Ninth Street, is the heart of the town and worth a look. The Chamber of Commerce, two blocks from the plaza, provides information and walking-tour maps. Details: 1062 G Street; (707) 822-3619; open Monday through Friday from 10 a.m. to 4 p.m., Saturday from 9 a.m. to 3 p.m.

The people of Arcata own 600 acres of second-growth redwood in the **Arcata Community Forest**. Ten miles of roads and paths are open for hiking and biking. The **Historic Logging Trail** features displays on historic logging practices. A forest management plan allows for the harvesting of trees while protecting watershed and habitat. Revenue from timber sales supports park and recreation projects in the community. Access is through Redwood Park at the east end of 14th Street. At the bottom of I Street, the **Arcata Marsh** is a good spot for bird-watching. Details: Located at 600 South G Street; (707) 826-2359; open daily from 1 to 5 p.m. (2 hours)

★ **Ferndale**—The town of Ferndale, 5 miles west of the Fernbridge exit on U.S. 101, anchors a large dairy farming region. So many Victorian buildings of historic importance clutter the town center that all of Main Street was dedicated as a historic landmark. It's worth a look, though the current commercial emphasis on tourism has made it easier to find frozen yogurt than bulk beans and hardtack. Details: Take the Fernbridge exit from U.S. 101 and follow CA 211 for 5 miles. (1½ hours)

★ **Garberville**—Much of California's "sinsemilla" marijuana is grown in Humboldt County. As the area's main town, Garberville has become renowned as the home of a hidden culture of pot growth and distribution. Two decades ago the town was alive with the trappings of the marijuana subculture. Today, growers have become very savvy indeed. It's fun to guess who might be in the business, and who might work for the D.E.A. Drive through town for a bite and a peek. Details: Located on U.S. 101 between Leggett and Humboldt Redwoods State Park. (1½ hours)

★ **Scotia**—Stop several miles north of the Humboldt Redwoods in the town of Scotia to see the **Pacific Lumber Company Mill**—the largest sawmill in the world. Scotia is the last of the once common "company towns," owned in its entirety by Pacific Lumber. Mill workers and their families rent the uniformly designed and flawlessly maintained redwood homes at low rates. The company provides some of the best wages, benefits, and pensions in the industry. Of course, Pacific Lumber also owns the Headwaters Forest—the last large privately held reserve of ancient redwoods—and they've been unwilling to allow preservation of the groves for anything less than a vast fortune. Details: The mill entrance is on Scotia's one main street so you can't get lost; (707) 764-2222; free, self-guided tours of the mill last about an hour. Get a permit at the museum across Main Street from the company headquarters (skip the museum unless you're into company history). Show up at the entrance gate to begin the tour between 8 a.m. and 10:30 a.m., or between 11:30 a.m. and 1:30 p.m. The mill shuts down completely from 10:30 a.m. to noon, and at 2:30 p.m. for the day. (1½ hours)

☆ **Trinidad**—This is one of the more pleasant and relaxing towns on the upper North Coast. A lovely beach curves away to the south along Trinidad Bay. Enjoy a bite at the wharf or a walk around **Trinidad Head**. The small headland is connected by a short, narrow neck of land to the broader shelf where the town is located. A loop trail goes around the head, though the trailhead is awkward at the beginning where a block of private land forces a detour. Trinidad Head Lighthouse is closed to visitors.

The Yurok Indian village of Tsurai existed for hundreds of years on the shores of Trinidad Harbor, below the present day location of the **Trinidad Memorial Lighthouse**—a scaled-down mockup of the real thing on Edwards Street at Trinity Street. Drive down to **Trinidad State Beach** for some beachcombing. Details: Located 12 miles north of Arcata from the Trinidad exit off U.S. 101. (1 hour)

Chandelier Tree—If you want to drive through a living redwood tree, here's your chance. Details: Follow the "Drive-Thru Tree" road signs near Leggett; (707) 925-6363. The cost is $3 per vehicle (6'8"-limit on vehicle height). (½ hour)

Confusion Hill—Your kids will swear that gravity doesn't work here. You might have your doubts too. It's a hokey attraction, but . . . you never know! Details: It's 9 miles north of Leggett on U.S. 101; (707) 925-6456; open daily from 10 a.m. to 5 p.m. Admission is $3. (½ hour)

Trees of Mystery—Just north of Klamath and Requa on U.S. 101, you'll pass Trees of Mystery, an attraction more famous, perhaps, for its bumper stickers than for anything else. Featured are a gift shop, the **"End of the Trail" Indian Museum**, a nature walk with mildly interesting redwood sights, and giant statues of Paul Bunyan and Babe the Blue Ox. Details: Just north of Klamath and Requa on U.S. 101; (707) 482-2251; open daily from 8 a.m. until dusk. Admission is $6.50, museum and statues free. (1 hour)

FITNESS AND RECREATION

There are more than a hundred miles of trails in **Humboldt Redwoods State Park**, many of which are open to cyclists (no single-track). The 5-mile **Bull Creek Flats Trail** follows Bull Creek and accesses the larger trees. It's an easy walk, though the logical return loop runs close to the Mattole Road on the north side of the creek. Loops and overnights that climb to the ridges are possible, including a good 12-mile bike loop to **Grasshopper Peak** and **Fire Lookout**.

The 24-mile **Lost Coast Trail** is good for a three-day or hard two-day backpack. Hike south from the mouth of the Mattole River (Lighthouse Road from the Mattole Road, south of the bridge into Petrolia) so that the often strong wind is likely to be at your back. The trail ends in Shelter Cove. For a great 7-mile loop, hike as far as the abandoned **Punta Gorda Lighthouse**, then return via the bluffs by following the old lighthouse access road that climbs up near the tiny cluster of cabins north of the light. Watch out for poison oak!

In **Redwood National Park**, the moderately easy, 8½-mile **Redwood Creek Trail** runs from the **Tall Trees Grove** to a picnic area near the base of Bald Creek Road. Loops are awkward but possible. A park shuttle can get you to Tall Trees for a one-way, downhill walk. A ½ mile north of the Bald Creek Road junction, on U.S. 101, are a picnic area and trailhead for the **Coastal Trail**. A great two-day hike will take you through old growth and down to **Gold Bluffs Beach** in **Prairie Creek Redwoods State Park** for the night. In the morning, head up through **Fern Canyon** and back to the road for a hitch to your car. Great day-hike loops are possible from Fern Canyon.

There's a bikeable segment of the **Coastal Trail** through old growth in **Del Norte Redwoods State Park**. Look for the trailhead on the west side of U.S. 101, about 2 miles north of the overlook, near the park's south end. A beautiful loop circles the **Mill Creek Campground** and access road to the north. **Jedediah Smith Redwoods State Park** has great old-growth walks from trailheads on U.S. 199 and the narrow Howland Hill Road. **Smith River National Recreation Area** has good opportunities for fishing, canoeing, rafting, and kayaking.

FOOD

You'll shake your head and wonder what the marvelous **Benbow Inn**, 445 Lake Benbow Drive (take the Benbow exit from U.S. 101), (707)

923-2124, is doing in the middle of nowhere, but you'll be glad it's here. It's a fine-dining oasis in the wilderness (closed in winter).

The **Woodrose Café**, 911 Redwood Drive, (707) 923-3191, in Garberville is the place to go for a fine breakfast or lunch. Sandwiches and pasta plates are in the $5 to $7 range.

Don't miss the **Samoa Cookhouse** in Eureka, (707) 442-1659. Delicious, all-you-can-eat American fare breakfasts, lunches, and dinners are served up family-style at long tables. It's on the way to Samoa Dunes across the CA 255 bridge. Enjoy moderately priced seafood meals in a historic setting at the **Sea Grill**, 316 E Street, (707) 443-7187. Splurge on the unbelievable breakfast buffet at the **Hotel Carter**, 301 L Street, (707) 444-8062.

In Arcata, fine dining with a fresh face is available at the excellent and always crowded **Folie Douce**, 1551 G Street, (707) 822-1042. The **Humboldt Brewing Company**, 956 Tenth Street, (707) 826-2739, is the pub grub brewpub in town. The beers are very tasty. A fine bohemian oasis on the hard-working upper North Coast is the **Café Mokka Coffeehouse**, on the corner of Fifth Street and J Streets, (707) 822-2228. It's also the home of Finnish Country Sauna & Tubs, so you can enjoy a soak as you sip. They have live folk music on the weekends.

At the harbor in Trinidad, the **Seascape Restaurant**, (707) 677-3862, offers OK seafood in a great location. Better fare is available at the **Larrupin' Café** at 1658 Patrick's Point Drive, north of town, (707) 677-0230.

Try the **Harbor View Grotto**, 150 Starfish Way, (707) 464-3815, in Crescent City for great seafood with a view, all reasonably priced. It's south of downtown at the docks.

LODGING

On the Avenue of the Giants 12 miles north of Garberville, you'll find the **Miranda Gardens Resort**, 6766 Avenue of the Giants, (707) 943-3011, in a redwood grove. Kids love the walk-through tree, pool, and play facilities. Rooms go from $65 to $175.

Take the Benbow exit from U.S. 101 to reach the **Benbow Inn**, 445 Lake Benbow Drive, (707) 923-2124, a grand edifice that seems splendidly out of place. This historical landmark has rooms for $125 to $295.

In the Pacific Lumber company town of Scotia, the **Scotia Inn**, Main Street and Mill Street, (707) 764-5683, offers quite an illusion to the visitor. It appears to be quite large, but only 12 of the many rooms

THE REDWOOD PARKS

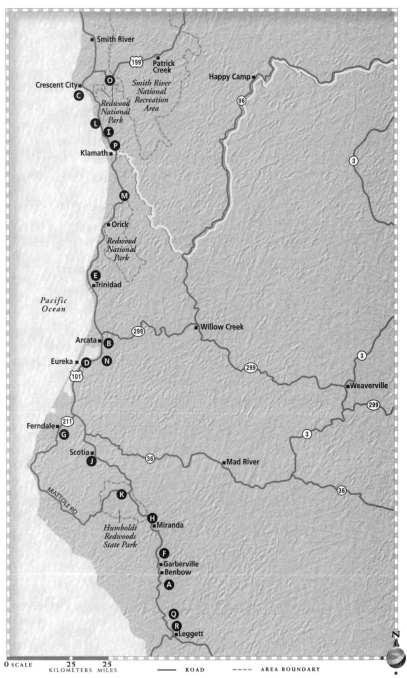

Smith River

Patrick Creek

199

Happy Camp

Crescent City

O

C

Smith River National Recreation Area

Redwood National Park

96

L

I

P

Klamath

3

M

Orick

Redwood National Park

E

Trinidad

Pacific Ocean

Willow Creek

Arcata

299

B

3

Eureka

D

N

299

101

Weaverville

Ferndale

211

G

299

Scotia

J

36

Mad River

3

K

36

H

Miranda

Humboldt Redwoods State Park

F

Garberville

Benbow

A

Q

R

Leggett

N

0 SCALE   25   25   ——— ROAD   - - - - AREA BOUNDARY
KILOMETERS MILES

Food

- **A** Benbow Inn
- **B** Café Mokka Coffeehouse
- **B** Folie Douce
- **C** Harbor View Grotto
- **D** Hotel Carter
- **B** Humboldt Brewing Company
- **E** Larrupin' Café
- **D** Samoa Cookhouse
- **D** Sea Grill
- **E** Seascape Restaurant
- **F** Woodrose Café

Lodging

- **A** Benbow Inn
- **C** Crescent Beach Motel
- **D** Downtowner Motel
- **D** Eureka Inn
- **G** Francis Creek Inn
- **G** Gingerbread Mansion
- **B** Hotel Arcata
- **H** Miranda Gardens Resort
- **I** Redwood National Park Hostel
- **J** Scotia Inn

Camping

- **K** Albee Creek Campground
- **A** Benbow Lake State Recreation Area
- **L** Del Norte Redwoods State Park
- **M** Elk Prairie Campground
- **N** Eureka KOA
- **M** Gold Bluffs Beach Campground
- **K** Humboldt Redwoods State Park
- **O** Jedediah Smith State Park
- **P** Mystic Forest RV Park
- **E** Patrick's Point State Park
- **Q** Richardson Grove State Park
- **R** Standish-Hickey State Recreation Area

Note: Items with the same letter are located in the same town or area.

are open. Other wings and floors are collecting dust. Still, the available rooms, lobby, and restaurant are excellent. Rooms run from $65 (a bargain) to $175.

A stay at the ornate, Victorian **Gingerbread Mansion**, 400 Berding Street, (707) 786-4000, in Ferndale is a special treat. Rooms run from $140 to $350. More reasonable is the **Francis Creek Inn**, 577 Main Street, (707) 786-9611, with nice rooms and a morning Danish for $55.

Most of the chain motels are represented in Eureka, right along U.S. 101. Use the numbers listed under "Resources" in the Practical Tips chapter to contact them. In the center of town, the **Eureka Inn**, 518 Seventh Street, (707) 442-6441 or (800) 862-4906, is a fine, English Tudor–style, historic landmark hotel with a player grand piano gracing the elegant lobby. Rooms start at a surprisingly low $110 and range upward to $200. The inn is famous for its Christmas displays. A nice budget choice is the **Eureka Inn Annex/Downtowner Motel**, 424 Eighth Street, (707) 443-5061. Rooms are $50, and a pool and sauna are available.

Several chain outlets are available on the outskirts of Arcata. In town, the **Hotel Arcata**, 708 Ninth Street, (707) 826-0217 or (800) 344-1221, a historical landmark on the square, is dignified in a humble way. Rooms run from $63 to $110.

Near the south end of Del Norte Redwoods, the **Redwood National Park Hostel**, 14480 U.S. 101 (entrance on Wilson Creek Road), (707) 482-8265, has beds for $12 to $14, and they're often booked in advance. There are curfews and checkout rules.

Crescent City is also blessed with chain motels and wannabes. The **Crescent Beach Motel**, 1455 U.S. 101 South, (707) 464-5436, is on the beach along U.S. 101 south of town. Rooms are $50 to $60.

CAMPING

Standish-Hickey State Recreation Area, (707) 925-6482 for information, (800) 444-7275 for reservations, has nice sites for $14 to $16. The park features great Eel River access and hiking trails to small redwood groves.

Further north, **Richardson Grove State Park**, (707) 247-3318 for information, (800) 444-7275 for reservations, has two campgrounds with $14 to $16 sites. This 1,300-acre park offers fishing and swimming in the Eel, as well as grove walks.

Benbow Lake State Recreation Area, (707) 247-3318 for information, (800) 444-7275 for reservations, has waterside and other open sites for $14 to $16. Take the Benbow exit from U.S. 101. A nine-hole golf course is nearby.

There are four campgrounds in **Humboldt Redwoods State Park**, each with sites for $14 to $16. They're all good, but the **Albee Creek Campground** is the most remote, (707) 946-2409 for information, (800) 444-7275 for reservations.

Between Eureka and Arcata, the **Eureka KOA**, 4050 North U.S. 101, (707) 822-4243 or (800) 562-5754, has typical sites for $20 to $30.

Several private campgrounds and RV parks are located on Patrick's Point Road between Trinidad and Patrick's Point. All are bearable except "Big D." **Patrick's Point State Park**, 5 miles north of Trinidad on U.S. 101, (707) 677-3570 for information, (800) 444-7275 for reservations, has two campgrounds with great sites for $14 to $16.

There are many RV parks at the mouth of the Klamath River. One of the better ones is **Mystic Forest RV Park**, 15875 U.S. 101, (707) 482-4901. Several nice, $14 tent sites are isolated from the rest. RV sites are $16.

Only **Elk Prairie Campground** in Prairie Creek Redwoods State Park takes reservations. The wonderful **Gold Bluffs Beach Campground**, (707) 445-6547, has first-come, first-served primitive sites, but it is closed to trailers and large RVs. **Del Norte Redwoods State Park**, (707) 464-9533, has sites for $14 to $16, as does **Jedediah Smith State Park** on U.S. 199, (707) 464-9533. Call (800) 444-7275 for reservations at all three parks.

Scenic Route: The Mattole Road

A wonderful 80-mile detour from U.S. 101 connects the **Humboldt Redwoods** with the historic town of **Ferndale**, via the fabled Lost Coast. Follow the Mattole Road as it climbs through **Rockefeller Forest**. Enjoy the views of the Mattole Valley as you wind down to the riverside village of **Honeydew**.

Continue about 12 miles along the **Mattole Valley**. At the Lighthouse Road turnoff, just before the bridge into **Petrolia**, turn left to reach the mouth of the Mattole at the northern end of **King Range National Conservation Area**. Primitive camping is permitted. If time allows, hike the windy **Lost Coast Trail** for 3 miles south along the shore to the abandoned **Punta Gorda Lighthouse**. For spectacular views, return via the old road that climbs up onto the headlands just north of the lighthouse. Allow four hours for the hike—and watch out for poison oak!

Return to the Mattole Road and cross the river to Petrolia, named during the days when the valley produced oil. Continue to **Cape Mendocino Lighthouse**, enjoying the views before winding inland to the **Eel River** delta and Ferndale. ◪

THE MATTOLE ROAD

10
VOLCANOES

The Cascade Range extends from southern British Columbia, through Washington and Oregon, and a hundred miles into Northern California. Throughout the range, volcanic peaks rise thousands of feet above what is otherwise a generally low system of mountains. California hosts two such volcanoes: Mount Shasta in the north and Mount Lassen at the range's southern tip.

Mount Shasta is a splendid, glacier-capped cone, visible for miles. At 14,162 feet, it is the second tallest volcano in the lower 48, only 250 feet shorter than Mount Rainier. A national forest wilderness protects its upper reaches while Mount Shasta Ski Park is high on a southern spur. Interstate 5 passes by to the west, crossing from the Upper Sacramento River Valley and over into the broad basin of Shasta Valley. The towns of Mount Shasta and Weed are on either side of the divide that separates the Central Valley from the Klamath River watershed.

Located 75 miles southeast of Shasta, Mount Lassen is very different from its perfect neighbor. In 1915 the mountain blew its top, much as Mount St. Helens did in 1980. Now the broken peak reaches a mere 10,457 feet in elevation. After the eruption, the area was made into a national park.

At the head of the Central Valley, the city of Redding hosts a superb recreational area. Whiskeytown, Shasta, and Trinity Lakes offer boating, fishing, swimming, and camping. To the west, the peaks and valleys of Trinity Alps draw backpackers from throughout the region. Castle Crags south of Shasta is a favorite for rock climbers. ◼

VOLCANOES

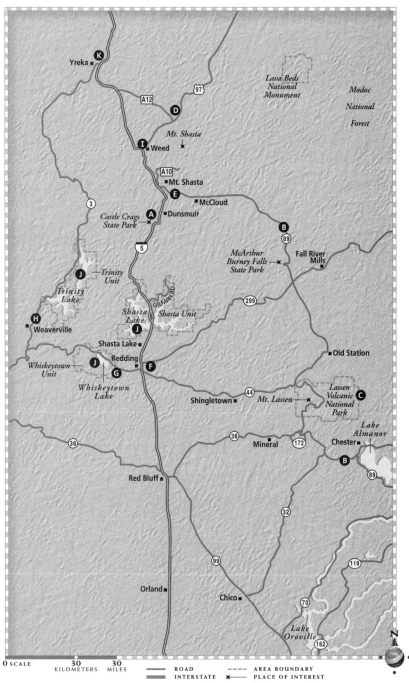

Yreka ■ **K**

97

A12

D

Lava Beds
National
Monument

Modoc

National

Forest

Mt. Shasta
✕

I ■ Weed

A10

■ Mt. Shasta

3

E ■ McCloud

Castle Crags
State Park

A ■ Dunsmuir

B

89

McArthur
Burney Falls — ✕
State Park

Fall River
Mills ■

5

J — Trinity
Unit

299

Trinity
Lake

GILMAN RD

H ■
Weaverville

Shasta
Lake

Shasta Unit

Shasta Lake ■

J

J ■ Redding

Old Station ■

Whiskeytown —
Unit

G

F

Whiskeytown
Lake

44

Lassen
Volcanic
National
Park

C

Shingletown ■

Mt. Lassen — ✕

Lake
Almanor

36

36

Mineral ■

172

Chester ■

B

89

Red Bluff ■

32

99

119

Orland ■

Chico ■

70

Lake
Oroville

162

N
▲

Sights

Ⓐ Castle Crags State Park

Ⓑ Highway 89 South

Ⓒ Lassen Volcanic National Park

Ⓓ Living Memorial Sculpture Garden

Ⓔ Mount Shasta (the town)

Ⓕ Redding

Ⓖ Shasta State Historic Park

Ⓗ Weaverville

Ⓘ Weed

Ⓙ Whiskeytown-Shasta-Trinity National Recreation Area

Ⓚ Yreka

A PERFECT DAY FROM SHASTA TO LASSEN

Enter Lassen Volcanic National Park from the south, stopping for a look and a sniff at the Sulfur Works. Near the pass, park at the trailhead and ascend 2,000 feet to Lassen's summit. Bask in the stunning panorama and explore the high ridge. After your descent, enjoy a picnic lunch at King's Creek or Lupine. Cruise north on CA 89, seeing Mount Shasta loom ever larger in your view. From the town of Mount Shasta, take the Everitt Memorial Highway (A10) to Panther Meadows, high on Shasta's southern slopes. From here, prepare for your summit attempt, camp, or retreat to town for a hot shower and a cool drink.

SIGHTSEEING HIGHLIGHTS

★★★ **Lassen Volcanic National Park**—After several months of volcanic activity, Mount Lassen exploded in 1915, showering the region with ash and devastating several square miles of land in the blast zone. Lassen's summit was shortened, and it's roughly conical shape was made much rougher. Today Lassen is something of a wonderland. Dwarfed trees grow in the recovering **Devastated Area**. Sulfurous mudpots and steaming springs bubble up in thermal areas. Pristine lakes share the forest with cinder cones. Relatively few visitors come here, both because it's off the beaten track and because CA 89, the main park road, can be closed by snow well into the summer.

Much of Lassen Volcanic National Park is designated as wilderness. Miles of trails criss-cross the forest, though access to the fragile soils and loose gravel around the peak is limited. A good, moderately difficult trail climbs 2,000 vertical feet to the summit, affording a 360-degree panorama that can't be beat. Access is from the parking area close to the summit of the road. Another trail descends from near Lake Helen down to the thermal features of **Bumpus Hell**. If you can't do the hike, the **Sulfur Works** near the road has many similar features. The **Summit Lake Campgrounds** are the nicest, though they're often closed until midsummer. Check out the early photos and other exhibits at the **Loomis Museum** near the north entrance. Details: Park information is available at (530) 595-4444. (all day)

★★ **Castle Crags State Park**—The park and adjacent **Castle Crags Wilderness** protect splendid granite cliffs and pinnacles. Climbers and hikers alike enjoy formations that resemble those of Yosemite. The **Pacific Crest Trail** passes through on its way from Mexico to Canada. Take the Castle Crags exit to reach a viewpoint and trailheads. Other views are had from the north. Details: For park information, call (530) 235-2684. Day-use parking is $5. (1½ hours)

★★ **Living Memorial Sculpture Garden**—Next to U.S. 97, 13 miles east of Weed, is a remarkable collection of sculpture dedicated to "all the veterans of all conflicts that the United States has been involved in." Created by Vietnam veteran Dennis Smith, sculptures such as *Coming Home*, *The Peaceful Warrior*, and *The Refugees* offer windows into core issues of war and peace. Spread across an acre or so of land, the garden features open vistas of Mount Shasta. Careful placement of sculptures, paths, and viewing benches enhances the perspective of relationships between various themes. The Living Memorial Sculpture Garden is a "must see" for anyone driving U.S. 97 with a half hour to spare. Look for the large turnout and entrance about 1 mile east of the junction of U.S. 97 and A12. (1 hour)

★ **Highway 89 South**—As you travel south between Mount Lassen and the Lake Tahoe region, the Sierra Nevada grow ever taller. The road winds through forested valleys and over easy passes, running through small towns oriented toward logging, ranching, and vacationing.

Watch for debris from passing logging trucks as you drive past lovely **Lake Almanor** and over into the Indian Creek Valley. CA 70 from Paxton leads down through the sometimes spectacular **Feather River Canyon**. For a good loop after a day exploring Lassen Volcanic National Park, drop down CA 32 into **Chico** to spend the night, then return to the high country through the Feather River Canyon in the morning.

The town of **Quincy** is the county seat for Plumas County and the site for the **Plumas County Museum**. Buck's Lake Road (County 119) heads south from town, providing access to the lovely **Buck's Lake**, **Pacific Crest Trail**, and **Buck's Lake Wilderness**. The lake has two small resorts. Canoes can be rented allowing access to the north and east shore wilderness.

Further south, the area around **Graeagle** has vacation rentals, golf courses, and the **Plumas Eureka State Park**. The historic mining village of **Johnsville** and a ski basin are within the park. From Graeagle, the Gold Lake Forest Highway (N.F. 24) climbs into the beautiful **Lakes Basin**, then heads down to join CA 49. Staying south on CA 89 from Graeagle, the road drops into the wide **Sierra Valley** and the swampy headwaters of the Feather River. (½ day)

✫ **Mount Shasta** (the town)—Nestled below its volcanic namesake, this pleasant town offers a respite from the freeway race. The exits funnel you right onto Mount Shasta Boulevard, the only street of consequence. You can visit the headwater springs of the Sacramento River in Mount Shasta's **City Park**, north of downtown on Nixon Road.

The **Everitt Memorial Highway** heads east from town and climbs to **Panther Meadows**, almost 8,000 feet up on Mount Shasta's southern flank. This drive is your best way to get close to the mountain by car. Take any Mount Shasta exit from Interstate 5. (2 hours–all day)

✫ **Weaverville**—At the base of the Trinity Alps, on CA 299, little Weaverville owes its charm, as do so many other towns, to its Gold Rush history. Unlike many others, however, that charm has aged well, without the pressures of the tourist masses. All of Weaverville is listed on the National Register of Historic Places. Stop at **Joss House State Historic Park** to see the oldest Chinese temple in California. Details: 508 Main Street, Weaverville; (530) 623-5284; open Thursday through Monday from 10 a.m. to 5 p.m. (open only on Saturdays in winter), tours given hourly until 4 p.m. Admission is $2. (1 hour)

✷ **Weed**—Abner Weed moved his lumber mill onto the low slopes of Mount Shasta so that the highland winds would dry his lumber faster. Thus, Weed was born. It's not much today, but visit the **Weed Historic Lumbertown Museum** where Sam and Elmer will give you the lowdown—and they know their stuff! Details: 303 Gilman Avenue; (530) 938-5050. Open daily, Memorial Day through September, 10 a.m. to 5 p.m. Admission is cheap. (1 hour)

✷ **Whiskeytown-Shasta-Trinity National Recreation Area**— Boating, fishing, and lakeside fun are the primary activities along the miles of shoreline these three lakes offer. All of them were created to increase and control the flow of water for Central Valley irrigation.

In the U.S., only Washington's Grand Coulee Dam is more massive than **Shasta Dam**. The impressive spillway of the Shasta Dam is the world's highest at 487 feet. Details: Take Shasta Dam Boulevard (CA 151) from Interstate 5 (stop at the viewpoint on the way); (530) 275-4463; free tours are available at the visitor center. Visitor center open daily from 7:30 a.m. to 5 p.m.; one-hour tours depart hourly from 9 a.m. to 4 p.m. Call for off-season hours.

Typical lake recreation opportunities abound around **Shasta Lake**. The lake also features the **Shasta Caverns**. Details: Take the O'Brien exit from Interstate 5 to Shasta Cavern Road; a boat and bus take you to the caverns; (530) 238-2341; tours leave every half hour daily, from 9 a.m. to 4 p.m. Memorial Day through Labor Day, 9 a.m. to 3 p.m. in shoulder season, and at 10 a.m., noon, and 2 p.m. in winter. Admission is $14. (2½ hours)

Whiskeytown Lake is easily accessed from Redding on CA 299. You can enjoy recreational gold panning in this unit of the park, but not the others. Details: Located 10 miles west of Redding on CA 299; (530) 246-1225; visitor center open daily from 9 a.m. to 5 p.m. Memorial Day through Labor Day (10 a.m. to 4 p.m. at other times). Get a $1 panning permit at the visitor center at the southeast end of the lake; $5 day-use parking.

Trinity Lake is a thousand feet higher in elevation than the other two, and it's also more remote. Lake recreation of all sorts can be enjoyed here. Details: Take Dam Boulevard from Lewiston or CA 3 north from Weaverville. (½–all day)

✷ **Yreka**—If you can, enter (or exit) Yreka via CA 283 to the north of town. You'll enjoy the climb from the Klamath River through the steep canyon of Yreka Creek. It gives some added perspective to the perky, busy town. Check out the fake gold nuggets in the lobby of the 1857 **Siskyou County Courthouse**, 311 Fourth Street. Visit the collected historic buildings of the **Siskyou County Museum**, as well as the heritage exhibits inside. Details: 910 S. Main Street, Yreka; (530) 842-3836; open Tuesday through Saturday from 9 a.m. to 5 p.m. Admission is $2. (1 hour)

The "Blue Goose" steam train of the **Yreka Western Railroad** takes passengers on three-hour, round-trip excursions from Yreka to the historic cattle and railroad town of Montague. The train passes wood processing plants and a large sawmill. Views of Mount Shasta and a crossing of the Shasta River are featured. Check out the amazing model train in the depot. Details: Yreka Depot, east of Interstate 5 in central Yreka; (530) 842-4146; trains depart at 10 a.m. Wednesday through Saturday in the summer; weekend trips continue through Halloween. Tickets are $10. (3½ hours)

Redding—Poor Redding is one of those towns where they decided to build an enclosed center city mall to revitalize the area and the idea failed. Now downtown is ugly and without character, while the suburbs offer what suburbs always do: strip malls, real malls, and houses.

It's another story on the banks of the Sacramento River. Lovely **Caldwell Park** hosts two good museums. The **Redding Museum of Art and History** has Indian art, local historical art and artifacts, and changing exhibits. Nearby, Northern California natural history is on display at the **Carter House Natural Science Museum**. Details: Quartz Hill Road, in the park, across the river north of downtown Redding; (530) 243-8801 for art museum information, (530) 243-5457 for the science museum; both are open Tuesday through Sunday from 10 a.m. to 5 p.m. Admission to both museums and to the Paul Bunyan Forest Camp is $2. (1 hour)

Turtle Bay Museum and Arboretum on the River is the new umbrella name for the museums above, for a riverside arboretum currently being developed, and for the **Paul Bunyan Forest Camp**. The camp is a forest museum with great hands-on outdoor activities for kids. Details: 800 Auditorium Drive, from CA 44/299 west of Redding; (530) 243-8890; open Tuesday through Sunday from 10 a.m. to 5 p.m. Admission is $2 (good for all three museums). (1 hour)

Shasta State Historic Park—If you travel CA 299, you can't miss the historic buildings of this park along either side of the road, 6 miles west of Redding. The sites, ruins, and restorations are interesting to examine as you get a feel for the layout of this once bustling mining town. Details: Located 6 miles west of Redding on CA 299; (530) 243-8194; open Wednesday through Sunday from 10 a.m. to 5 p.m. Most of the park is free to see, except the museum, where admission is $2. (45 minutes)

FITNESS AND RECREATION

Great hikes and climbs are found in the region's fine parks and wilderness areas. The summit climb in **Lassen Volcanic National Park** is my top choice for stellar views. Trail access to the flanks of **Mount Shasta** is available at Panther Meadows, accessible from the town of Mount Shasta via the Everitt Memorial Highway. Take the **Castle Crags State Park** access road from I-5 to enter the 25-mile trail system and the park's granite spires. Several good walks are found in **Lava Beds National Monument**.

Segments of the **Pacific Crest Trail** offer backpackers great longer treks. The route keeps almost entirely to public lands throughout the region, passing through **Bucks Lake Wilderness** near Quincy, a volcanic plateau in **Lassen Volcanic National Park**, **Castle Crags Wilderness**, and the magnificent **Trinity Alps Wilderness**. Those in the know find solitude, good fishing, and great hikes in the **South Warner Wilderness** east of Alturas.

River running is an excellent choice in the rugged region north of Redding. Easy and moderate runs are found on the **Upper Sacramento River**, **Trinity River**, and **Klamath River**. The **Salmon River** offers Class V runs for experts. Living Waters Recreation, based in the town of Mount Shasta, offers a variety of raft and inflatable kayak trips on these and other rivers, (800) 994-RAFT.

FOOD

In Chester, stop at the **Chester Saloon and Italian Restaurant**, 159 Main Street, (530) 258-2887, for a plate of culinary goodness from the old country. To raise the stakes a notch, try the wonderfully architected **Timber House Restaurant**, 501 Main Street (CA 36 and First Street), (530) 258-2729, for a splendid meal in a memorable setting.

For steaks in Redding, hit **Jack's Grill**, south of the hideous downtown mall at 1743 California Street, (530) 241-9705.

In Weaverville, try **Noelle's Garden Cafe**, 233 Center Street, (530) 623-2058, for fresh gourmet soups, salads, espresso, and baked goods. **La Grange Cafe** at 315 North Main Street, (530) 623-5325, features "traditional, creative cuisine."

Dunsmuir boasts the **Railroad Park Restaurant and Lounge**, 100 Railroad Park Road, (530) 235-4611, where you can pay a bit more for the ambiance of dining in historic rail cars.

The town of Mount Shasta has several good places, most on or near Mount Shasta Boulevard. Enjoy the beer garden and German menu at **Willy's Bavarian Kitchen**, 107 Chestnut Street, (530) 926-3636.

Grandma's House, next to the freeway at 123 East Center Street in Yreka, (530) 842-5300, has just what you'd expect on the menu.

LODGING

The **Chester Manor Motel**, 306 Main Street, Chester, (530) 258-2441, is a comfortable place with lots of space and rooms from $48 to $75. At the east end of Chester on CA 36, the **Bidwell House** overlooks the lake at 1 Main Street, (530) 258-3338. It's a lovely bed-and-breakfast with a fascinating history and rooms from $70 to $160.

Twelve miles west of CA 89 on CA 299 is the town of Fall River and the **Fall River Hotel**, 24860 Main Street, (530) 336-5550. Built in 1936, the hotel combines well-kept history with rural charm. Shared-bath rooms are $45, private-bath rooms start at $50.

Redding has many chain motels, including **Best Western**, **Comfort Inn**, **Red Lion**, **Super 8**, and **Motel 6**. Use the numbers listed under "Resources" in the Practical Tips chapter to contact them. For something more charming, try the **Tiffany House**, 1510 Barbara Road (from Benton Drive), (530) 244-3225, a Victorian B&B with a pool and a great view. The three rooms range from $80 to $130.

The **Weaverville Hotel**, 201 Main Street (CA 299), (530) 623-3121, is historic, well-kept, and cheap, and has rooms from $35.

The town of Mount Shasta has the **Mount Shasta Ranch Bed and Breakfast**, west of Interstate 5 at 1008 W.A. Barr Road, (530) 926-3870. It's an easy and comfortable place, and there's a great fireplace in the main lodge. Rooms range from $40 to $95. There are several budget and moderate choices along Mount Shasta Boulevard.

VOLCANOES

Yreka ■ **B**

Lava Beds
National
Monument

Modoc

National

Forest

97

A12

Mt. Shasta
✕

H ■ Weed

A10 **P**

F ■ Mt. Shasta

K

■ McCloud

3

*Castle Crags
State Park* ✕ **I**
■ Dunsmuir
E

89

*McArthur
Burney Falls
State Park* ✕ **J**

*Fall River
Mills* ■ **G**

5

R — *Trinity
Unit*

*Trinity
Lake*

GILMAN RD.

*Shasta
Lake*
Q

Shasta Unit

299

D ●
■ Weaverville

■ Shasta Lake

■ Old Station

*Whiskeytown
Unit* **S** ●
● Redding

O

C

M

*Whiskeytown
Lake*

*Lassen
Volcanic
National
Park*

44

Shingletown ■ **N** *Mt. Lassen* ✕

*Lake
Almanor*

36

L

172
Chester ■ **A**

36
■ Mineral

89

■ Red Bluff

32

99

■ Orland

Chico ■

70

119

*Lake
Oroville*

162

N

0 SCALE
30
KILOMETERS
30
MILES
— ROAD
----- AREA BOUNDARY
═══ INTERSTATE
✕ PLACE OF INTEREST

Food

- Ⓐ Chester Saloon and Italian Restaurant
- Ⓑ Grandma's House
- Ⓒ Jack's Grill
- Ⓓ La Grange Cafe
- Ⓓ Noelle's Garden Cafe
- Ⓔ Railroad Park Restaurant and Lounge
- Ⓐ Timber House Restaurant
- Ⓕ Willy's Bavarian Kitchen

Lodging

- Ⓐ Bidwell House
- Ⓐ Chester Manor Motel
- Ⓖ Fall River Hotel
- Ⓗ Grand Manor
- Ⓑ Klamath Motor Lodge
- Ⓕ Mount Shasta Ranch Bed and Breakfast
- Ⓔ Railroad Park Resort

Lodging (continued)

- Ⓗ Sis-Q-Inn Motel
- Ⓒ Tiffany House
- Ⓑ Wayside Inn
- Ⓓ Weaverville Hotel

Camping

- Ⓘ Castle Crags State Park
- Ⓙ McArthur-Burney Falls Memorial State Park
- Ⓚ McCloud
- Ⓛ Mineral
- Ⓜ Mount Lassen National Park
- Ⓝ Mount Lassen–Shingletown KOA
- Ⓞ Old Station
- Ⓟ Panther Meadows
- Ⓠ Shasta Lake
- Ⓡ Trinity Lake
- Ⓢ Whiskeytown Lake

Note: Items with the same letter are located in the same town or area.

In Dunsmuir, you can stay in a caboose at the **Railroad Park Resort**, 100 Railroad Park Road (from Interstate 5), (530) 235-4440 or (800) 974-7245. Cabins and cabooses are $70.

The **Grand Manor**, 1844 Shastina Drive, (530) 938-1982, in Weed is a nice motel with rooms from $65 to $80. A bit cheaper, the **Sis-Q-Inn Motel**, 1825 Shastina Drive, (530) 938-4194, has good basic rooms for about $50.

Yreka has several chain motels. Use the phone numbers listed under "Resources" in the Practical Tips chapter to contact them. There are budget options at the north and south end of town, paralleling the freeway, including the **Klamath Motor Lodge**, 1111 South

Main Street, (530) 842-2751, with rooms for $40 to $50; and the **Wayside Inn**, 1235 South Main Street, (530) 842-4412, which has rooms for $45 to $60.

CAMPING

Many national forest and national recreation area campgrounds are found in the region. South of Mount Lassen, three campgrounds are located near **Mineral**, on CA 89 and CA 172. North of Mount Lassen, six campgrounds are along CA 89 near **Old Station**. Three campgrounds are along an 18-mile stretch of CA 89, east of **McCloud.** There are two national forest campgrounds on Everitt Memorial Highway above the town of Mount Shasta, including **Panther Meadows** at the end of the road.

Just off of CA 3 along the west shore of **Trinity Lake** are several national recreation area and national forest campgrounds. **Whiskeytown Lake** has a campground at the end of Kennedy Memorial Drive and one at the lake's west end on CA 299. The campgrounds for **Shasta Lake** are accessible from Interstate 5. **Castle Crags State Park** has sites for $14 to $16 during the summer. Take the Castle Crags/Castella exit from Interstate 5. Call (530) 235-2684 for information, (800) 444-7275 for reservations. The campground at the lovely **McArthur-Burney Falls Memorial State Park** has $14 to $16 sites. The park is on CA 89, 5 miles north of the CA 299 junction. Call (530) 335-2777 for information, (800) 444-7275 for reservations. The **Mount Lassen–Shingletown KOA**, 7749 KOA Road (off CA 44), Shingletown, (530) 474-3133 or (800) KOA-3403, has RV and tent sites from $18 to $25.

Scenic Route: The Lava Loop

Few travelers ever venture onto the **Modoc Plateau**, which spreads across the sparsely populated northeastern corner of California. East of **Mount Shasta**, this is a land of broad forested uplands, low buttes and hills, tight canyons, and lonely roads. As you drive from **Shasta** to **Lassen**, you will see both subtle and vivid signs of the volcanic activity that shaped the area. Open the car windows, set the cruise control, sit back, and just say, "Aaahhh."

From **Weed**, take U.S. 97 northeast. Stop at the **Living Memorial Sculpture Garden** (see preceding chapter), then drive over **Mount Hebron Summit** and down through **Butte Valley**, enjoying the sudden flatness of the irrigated plain as you continue to the state line. Turning east on Stateline Road (CA 161), enter the **Lower Klamath National Wildlife Refuge**. Turn south onto CA 139, then right 8 miles later onto Great Northern Road, and then south along the edge of **Tule Lake National Wildlife Refuge**.

These two refuges are vital stopovers for millions of migrating water birds. Viewing is possible from the main roads through the refuges and via several perimeter roads. Migrating populations peak

THE LAVA LOOP

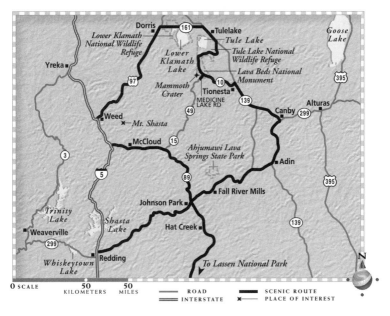

March through April and September through October. Many species come and go well into the summer, some remaining to nest and raise young. From December through February, up to a thousand bald eagles winter in the region.

The road soon enters **Lava Beds National Monument**. Most of the monument is covered with smooth pahoehoe ("pa-hoy-hoy") lava, overlain by thicker flows of aa ("ah-ah") lava. Volcanic cones and craters dot the area. Stop and hike in to **Captain Jack's Stronghold**. In this lava maze in 1872, Modoc Indian "Captain Jack" and 160 members of his tribe held off the U.S. Army for more than six months. Visit **Schonchin Butte**, taking the short hike to the top for a marvelous view of the monument. Borrow a helmet and flashlight from the visitor center and explore one of the lava tube caves along **Cave Loop Road**. To see where much of the pahoehoe originated, drive to **Mammoth Crater**, 3 miles south of the visitor center. If it's time to camp, continue 12 miles to **Medicine Lake**, a water-filled volcanic crater.

Head southeast out of Lava Beds National Monument and back to CA 139. Stop at the store in **Tionesta** and ask about its history as a saloon and brothel catering to lumberjacks. Continue to CA 299 in Canby, or save a dozen miles by turning south on **Lookout Hackamore Road**.

Take CA 299 west, more or less following the Pit River Valley. If it's late, stop in **Fall River** at the old **Fall River Lodge**, (530) 336-5550. You'll find a homemade quilt on every bed, rooms as low as $45, and a fine restaurant. Two miles past town, stop at the viewpoint for a look into the **Pit River Canyon**. At the junction of CA 89 and CA 299, you can opt to return north to Mount Shasta or continue west to **Redding**. Otherwise turn south toward **Lassen Volcanic National Park** and the scenic route through the Sierra. Remember, CA 89 through the park may not open until late May or June. ◼

11
SACRAMENTO AND
THE CENTRAL VALLEY

In 1839, German-born John Augustus Sutter arrived in California. The Mexican government granted him 76 square miles of land at the confluence of the American and Sacramento Rivers, the site of present day Sacramento. He called it "New Helvetia" and built Sutter's Fort to secure his ownership. When the Gold Rush came along, entrepreneur Sam Brannan and others saw their chance and started businesses, many related to the transport capacity of the Sacramento River. Sutter's son named the town that, in 1850, became the capital of the brand new state of California.

Today, Sacramento has a population of about 395,000. The sprawling exurban communities spreading along the major arteries into the Sierra foothills bring the metropolitan population to about 1.5 million. The region is one of the fastest growing in the state, and the resulting "Los Angelization" is an unfortunate byproduct. Unless you have loads of time or a compelling interest in the attractions, I don't recommend putting it on your itinerary. If you decide to spend some hours in "Sacto," head for the heart of downtown. The main sights are within a 1-square-mile area from Capitol Park to the Sacramento River. A good walking loop takes in the capitol, Governor's Mansion State Historic Park, Old Sacramento, the Wells Fargo History Museum, Crocker Art Museum, and the Leland Stanford Mansion. ◪

SACRAMENTO

Sights

- Ⓐ California State Capitol
- Ⓑ California State Railroad Museum
- Ⓒ Chico
- Ⓓ Crocker Art Museum
- Ⓔ Fresno
- Ⓕ Governor's Mansion State Historic Park
- Ⓖ Hershey Chocolate Factory
- Ⓗ Leland Stanford Mansion
- Ⓘ Old Sacramento and Old Sacramento State Historic Park
- Ⓙ Red Bluff
- Ⓚ Sacramento National Wildlife Refuge
- Ⓛ State Indian Museum
- Ⓜ Stockton
- Ⓞ Sutter's Fort State Historic Park
- Ⓝ Towe Ford Museum

Note: Items with the same letter are located in the same place.

A PERFECT DAY IN SACRAMENTO

Do your walkabout before the heat sets in. Start with a 10 a.m. visit to Sutter's Fort State Historic Park for a taste of local roots. Park near the capitol, then take a look at the workplace of those who govern 30 million Californians. Walk the K Street pedestrian mall toward the river, then cross under the freeway to Old Sacramento. Spend the afternoon moving slowly, exploring museums. Loop over to the Crocker Museum for an hour of browsing before closing. Now smile and head for your reserved room or campsite in the Sierra or on the coast.

THE CENTRAL VALLEY

A 400-mile swath of pancake-flat basin and barely-rolling lowlands covers close to 20,000 square miles in the heart of California. Once an inland sea, this great "Central Valley" now hosts mile upon mile of irrigated farmland, surrounded by pastures that blend into the foothills. The rivers of the Sierras and northern mountains are plugged with scores of dams, enabling the waters to be fed through thousands of miles of aqueducts and canals. Little is left of the natural environment—the sea of grass that once hosted huge populations of elk and antelope, predators, and birds has given way to enormous farms and sprawling subdivisions.

The Central Valley is devoted to agricultural production and has relatively little interest to the tourist. **Oroville** offers access to the recreational opportunities on the Oroville Reservoir. **Marysville** features a historic center and the Bok Kai Chinese Temple. Several other towns in the valley have something to offer, but they tend to show up near the bottom of most sightseeing checklists. With the unbearable heat that can afflict the valley in the summer, air conditioning and a fast freeway to the mountains or coast may seem like your best friends.

If you have a little extra time for the flatlands, focus your attention on the delta region where the Sacramento and San Juaquin Rivers converge before draining into the San Francisco Bay. CA 160 and CA 4 makes a great alternate route from Sacramento to the Bay Area. CA 4 runs atop the levies that hold back the Sacramento River. Slow down for a look around the historic Chinese community of **Locke** with its narrow lanes. Explore the backroads that access wildlife refuges and connect the many islands.

SIGHTSEEING HIGHLIGHTS

★★ **California State Capitol**—Built between 1860 and 1874 and recently restored to glory, the capitol building is a classic structure with a dome that reaches 210 feet above the base. There's a nice rotunda, historic exhibits, statues, and murals. Details: The capitol sits at the west end of **Capitol Park** facing the mall and river. The park is bounded by L, N, Tenth, and 15th Streets, Sacramento; (916) 324-0333; free guided tours are given daily, on the hour, from 9 a.m. to 4 p.m. Get your tour ticket in room B-27 in the capitol basement. (1½ hours)

✻✻ **Old Sacramento and Old Sacramento State Historic Park**—
The restored riverside district of Old Sacramento includes the four
blocks of Front Street and Second Street north of Capitol Avenue.
Among the buildings that hold the tourist shops and restaurants are
several dating back to Gold Rush days.

At the north end of the district, the Old Sacramento State
Historic Park has two fine museums. The excellent **California State
Railroad Museum** has a wonderful collection of 21 historic cars and
locomotives, as well as exhibits, films, and dioramas related to rail history. It's a must for rail buffs and the nostalgic. The reconstructed
Central Pacific Passenger Station across the street can be visited on
the same ticket. Rides on the historic **Sacramento Southern Railroad**
are offered on weekends and holidays from April through September.
Details: Second and I Streets, Sacramento; (916) 445-6645; open daily
from 10 a.m. to 5 p.m. Admission is $6, train rides are $6. (1½ hours)

Next to the Railroad Museum is the **Discovery Museum**, featuring history, science, and technology. Exhibits, several of which are
interactive, include a million-dollar gold display from the mother lode
and an operating newspaper print shop from the city's early days.
Several hands-on exhibits will interest the kids. Details: 101 I Street,
Sacramento; (916) 264-7057; open daily from 10 a.m. to 5 p.m.
Admission is $4 for adults, $2 for kids. (1½ hours)

✻ **Chico**—This pleasant college town is worth a stop on your way to
or from Mount Lassen. CA 99 splits into Main Street and Broadway,
opposing one-ways that pass through the heart of town. The **Chico
Museum** has regional heritage displays, including Ishi Indian and
Chinese Temple exhibits. Details: Second Street and Salem Street,
Chico; (916) 891-4336; open Wednesday through Sunday from noon
to 4 p.m. (½ hour)

CA 99 unites into the Esplanade to cross north over Big Chico
Creek. The **Bidwell Mansion State Historic Park** preserves the home
of town founder General John Bidwell on grounds at the edge of the
California State University campus. Details: 525 The Esplanade; (916)
895-6144; tours start from the visitor center, weekdays from noon to 4
p.m., weekends from 10 a.m. to 4 p.m. Admission is $3. (1 hour)

The **Sierra Nevada Brewery** offers tours of its building. Details:
1075 East 20th Street, Chico; (916) 893-3520; tours Tuesday through
Friday at 2:30 p.m., Saturday between noon and 3 p.m. Admission is
free. (1 hour)

✷ **Crocker Art Museum**—A good collection of modern California artists is featured in the one-time home of Edwin and Margaret Crocker. The house itself is one of Sacramento's most elaborate Victorians and is worth seeing on its own. You can count on there being a high-caliber touring exhibit on hand. Details: 216 O Street, Sacramento; (916) 264-5423; open Tuesday through Sunday from 10 a.m. to 5 p.m. (until 9 p.m. on Thursday). Admission is $4.50. (1½ hours)

✷ **Governor's Mansion State Historic Park**—Sacramento's first governor's mansion was built in 1877. Memorabilia and furnishings from past governors are displayed along with historic period pieces. Details: 16th and H Streets, Sacramento; (916) 323-3047; tours are given daily, on the hour, from 10 a.m. to 5 p.m. Admission is $3, more on days with living history activities. (1 hour)

✷ **Red Bluff**—Where the flat Central Valley breaks upward into the hills, the pleasant town of Red Bluff sits on the Sacramento River. It's an easy on and off from Interstate 5. Drive or walk the **Victorian Homes Tour** to see lovely homes, dated by historical plaques, in the blocks near Main Street. Details: The Chamber of Commerce has tour information at 100 Main Street, Red Bluff; (916) 527-6220.

The **Kelly-Griggs House Museum** offers the chance for an inside look at a lovely Victorian. Details: 311 Washington Street, Red Bluff; (916) 527-1129; open Thursday through Sunday from 1 to 4 p.m. Admission is free, but donations are accepted. (½ hour)

The **William B. Ide Adobe State Historic Park**, a small living history park on the Sacramento River, features the 1850 adobe home of Mr. Ide and family. Ide was the first and only president of the short-lived California Republic, established after the Bear Flag Revolt of 1846. Details: 2 miles north of Red Bluff on Adobe Road, right on the Sacramento River; (916) 529-8599; open daily from 8 a.m. to dusk. Admission is free, but parking is $3. (½ hour)

✷ **Sacramento National Wildlife Refuge**—No state in the lower 48 boasts a greater seasonal concentration of waterfowl than California. Snow geese, sandhill cranes, ducks, egrets, herons, swans, pheasant, hawks, and eagles can all be seen at this large refuge 80 miles north of Sacramento on Interstate 5. A self-guided auto tour through the refuge is a good 1½-hour detour from the speeding freeway. Details: Take the

Norman Road exit from Interstate 5; (916) 934-2801; open daily from dawn to dusk. Admission is $3 per car. (1–3 hours)

✴ **Sutter's Fort State Historic Park**—Originally built in 1839, Sutter's adobe fort has been restored to its original appearance and qualifies as the oldest restored fort in the West. The summer's living history exhibits and activities are of particular interest. Visitors may take a self-guided audio tour. Details: L Street at 27th, Sacramento; (916) 324-0539; open daily from 10 a.m. to 5 p.m. Admission is $3, higher in summer on living history days. (1 hour)

Next to the fort on the large commons is the **State Indian Museum** with native history exhibits. Details: 2618 K Street, Sacramento; (916) 324-0539; open daily from 10 a.m. to 5 p.m. Admission is $3. (1 hour)

✴ **Towe Ford Museum**—This is a must-see attraction for car buffs. Over 150 vintage Fords in pristine condition are on display. Every model from 1903 to 1953 is represented, as are many newer models. Don't be surprised if you see people drooling. Details: Located between Interstate 5 and the Sacramento River on Front Street at V Street. Take Front Street south from Capitol Mall, Sacramento; (916) 442-6802; open daily from 10 a.m. to 6 p.m. Admission is $5. (1 hour)

Fresno—This sprawling city on Highway 99 never seems to end. If you find downtown (take the downtown exits at Fresno Street or Stanislaus Street), you can visit the very nice **Fresno Art Museum**, which hosts good rotating exhibits and a fair permanent collection with interesting highlights. Details: 2233 North First Street, Fresno; (209) 485-4810; open Tuesday through Friday from 10 a.m. to 5 p.m., weekends from noon to 5 p.m. Admission is $2 (free on Tuesday). (1 hour)

The kids will like the hands-on exhibits and lasers at the **Fresno Metropolitan Museum**. Excellent traveling exhibits complement regular offerings. Details: 1515 Van Ness Avenue, Fresno; (209) 441-1444; open Tuesday through Sunday from 11 a.m. to 5 p.m. Admission is $4. (1½ hours)

Hershey Chocolate Factory—Located off CA 120 in Oakdale (conveniently on the way to Yosemite), this West Coast chocolate factory still offers genuine plant tours, unlike its Pennsylvania counterpart.

After the tour you get a free chocolate bar and the chance to buy lots more. Details: 120 South Sierra Avenue, Oakdale; (209) 848-8126; open Monday through Friday from 8:30 a.m. to 3 p.m. Admission is free. (1 hour)

Leland Stanford Mansion—Stanford was one of the "big four" railroad magnates who dominated state politics in the mid- and late 1800s. The mansion, built in 1859, is undergoing a gradual restoration. Details: Located on the corner of Eighth and N Streets, Sacramento; (916) 324-0575. Tours are offered most Tuesdays and Thursdays at 12:15 p.m., and most Saturdays at 12:15 and 1:30 p.m.; call to confirm. Admission is $3. (1 hour)

Stockton—The **Haggin Museum** has a wonderful collection of Native American artifacts, regional history items, and paintings. Free musical and arts events are offered throughout the summer months. It is the best of the few reasons to visit Stockton. Details: Museum is at 1201 North Pershing Avenue, Stockton; (209) 462-4116; open Tuesday through Sunday from 1:30 to 5 p.m. Admission is free. (1 hour)

FITNESS AND RECREATION

The 22½-mile **Jedediah Smith National Recreation Trail** follows the course of the American River through the sinuous American River Parkway park. The parkway stretches eastward from the point where the American flows into the Sacramento. It's a good path for jogging and cycling.

At 1600 Exposition Boulevard, just east of Business Interstate 80 and north of the American River, **WaterWorld USA**, (916) 924-0556, features water slides, a wading pool, a play area, and the new "Shark Attack." It's open daily from 10:30 a.m. to 6 p.m. (until 4 p.m. from Labor Day through Memorial Day), and admission is $17.

FOOD

You'll probably find something you like as you browse the K Street Pedestrian Mall, Downtown Plaza, and Old Sacramento. The **River City Brewing Company**, 545 Downtown Plaza #1115, (916) 447-2739, has a good mixed grill and selection of microbrew beer in the mall. Also in the mall is **Morton's of Chicago**, 521 L Street,

(916) 442-5091, serving steaks and more for a price. In Old Sacramento, **California Fats**, 1015 Front Street, (916) 441-7966, has terrific seafood, pizzas, and more. Dine on the Delta King paddlewheeler for a taste of river history. The **Delta King Pilothouse Restaurant**, 1000 Front Street, (916) 441-4440, offers fine continental cuisine. Bring your gold card.

    Frank Fats, 806 L Street, (916) 442-7092, is the place to throw a pricey eggroll at a state senator. For top quality traditional Italian fare, **Biba**, Capitol Street at 28th Street, (916) 455-2422, is the clear, but not cheap choice. It's located a block from Sutter's Fort. The beers are from the British Isles at **The Fox and Goose**, 1001 R Street, (916) 443-8825, but the menu strays pleasantly into California cuisine. Play some darts, dine, and then enjoy live music into the night.

LODGING

Several major highways and commercial avenues of Sacramento have concentrations of budget and chain lodging options. Many are found just north of the American River to the west of Business Interstate 80 on or near Arden Way (**Marriott, Hilton,** and **Red Lion**). Another cluster is found in Rancho Cordova (**Holiday Inn, Sheraton, Best Western, Motel 6,** and **Comfort Inn**), 12 miles west of downtown along U.S. 50. Use the numbers listed under "Resources" in the Practical Tips chapter to locate the one you prefer.

    My top choice by far for lodging in Sacramento is to book a state-room aboard the *Delta King*, an old paddlewheel riverboat permanently moored in the Sacramento River, 1000 Front Street (at the end of L Street) in Old Sacramento, (916) 444-5464 or (800) 825-5464. The smallish staterooms are a bargain from $110 to $150. The **Hyatt Regency**, 1209 L Street, (916) 443-1234 or (800) 233-1234, is Sacto's big hotel. Across from the capitol, it offers all the amenities. A drink in the top floor lounge is a nice way to finish the day. Rooms range from $130 to $210. The best B&B choice is the **Amber House** at 1315 22nd Street (near Capitol Avenue), (916) 444-8085 or (800) 755-6526. The lovely guest rooms are aptly named after classic artists. Rooms range from $130 to $250.

    There are some inexpensive to moderately priced options downtown as well. The **Quality Inn**, 818 15th Street, (916) 444 3980, has nice rooms for $60 to $80. The **Holiday Inn Capitol Plaza**, 300 J Street, (916) 446-0100, is just two blocks from Old Sacramento.

SACRAMENTO

Food

- **A** Biba
- **B** California Fats
- **B** Delta King Pilothouse Restaurant
- **C** The Fox and Goose
- **D** Frank Fats
- **E** Morton's of Chicago
- **E** River City Brewing Company

Lodging

- **F** Amber House
- **G** Americana Lodge
- **H** Best Western
- **I** Best Western Inn
- **H** Comfort Inn
- **B** *Delta King*
- **J** Hilton
- **H** Holiday Inn
- **K** Holiday Inn Capitol Plaza

Lodging *(continued)*

- **L** Hyatt Regency
- **J** Marriott
- **H** Motel 6
- **J** Red Lion
- **M** Quality Inn
- **N** Sacramento Hostel
- **H** Sheraton

Camping

- **J** Cal Expo RV Park
- **O** Sacramento Metropolitan KOA

Note: Items with the same letter are located in the same area.

Rooms range from $90 to $140. Four blocks north of the capitol is the **Best Western Inn**, 1100 H Street, (916) 441-1314. Rooms range from $70 to $90.

The **Sacramento Hostel** has a great location in the Williams Mansion at 900 H Street, (916) 443-1691. Beds are $15 to $16.

CAMPING

Three miles west of downtown, just off Interstate 80, is the **Sacramento Metropolitan KOA**, 3951 Lake Road, (916) 371-6771 or (800) KOA-2747. Take the West Capitol Avenue exit from Interstate 80. It's south of the freeway on Lake Road. Sites are $23 to $29; "Kamping Kabins" are $38. The **Cal Expo RV Park**, (916) 263-3187, is adjacent to the California Exposition Grounds, American River Parkway, and Waterworld. Take Arden Way east from Business Interstate 80, then head south on Ethan Way. RV sites are $20, and tent sites are available.

NIGHTLIFE

Near California State University Sacramento, **Bo Jangles**, 7042 Folsom Boulevard, (916) 386-0390, has live rock bands, deejay-driven dancing, and a youthful crowd. In Old Sacramento, you can immerse yourself in 19th-century memorabilia at **Fanny Ann's Saloon**, 1023 Second Street, (916) 441-0505. Stop in at **Java City**, 1800 Capitol Avenue, (916) 444-5282, for espresso, drinks, and tasty snacks. It's open until 11 p.m. (until midnight on weekends). For a nighttime view of the impressive capitol and bland cityscape, visit **Busby Berkeley's**, 1209 L Street, (916) 443-1234, at the top of the Hyatt Regency.

12
GOLD COUNTRY

James Marshall discovered gold in the American River on January 24, 1848, but it was entrepreneur and newspaperman Sam Brannan who ignited the Gold Rush five months later. On May 12, he walked the streets of San Francisco holding up a bottle of gold nuggets and shouting, "Gold, gold, gold, from the American River!" Almost all of San Francisco's 800 citizens immediately headed for the hills.

Within two years, tens of thousands of "forty-niners" from around the world were at work in the western Sierra foothills. They sluiced every cubic foot of likely river gravel and tunneled through the hard rock to reach every vein. When the easy gold was gone, most of the treasure seekers left, abandoning towns right and left. Poor James Marshall's initial luck was never followed up. He died penniless. The treasure trove in the area today is tourism.

The aptly numbered CA 49 links the key sights of the Gold Country in a ribbon of touristic interest. Whether it's a charming village, weathered ghost town, or strip-malled exurb, the towns along the way all have centers with nineteenth-century buildings and some degree of charm. Old mines, tailings, aqueducts, sluice boxes, and rusted hardware litter the land. The region features scores of abandoned, preserved, restored, and exploited historic sites.

There is a certain sameness to the history of Gold Country—each little town has a different variation on the same story. True buffs could spend weeks exploring. Most travelers will want to choose a segment that coincides with a larger travel plan. ◼

GOLD COUNTRY

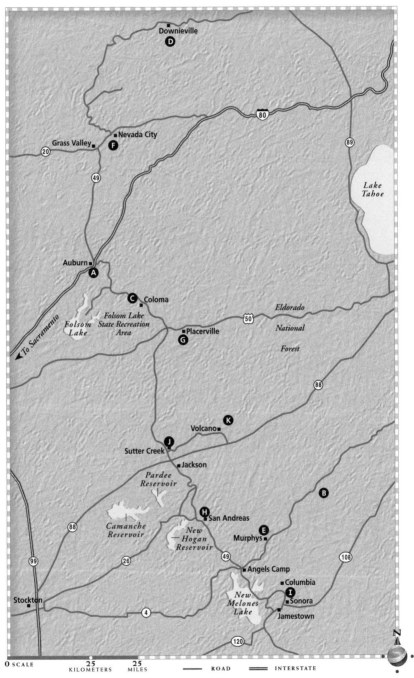

Downieville

D

80

89

Nevada City
Grass Valley ■
F

20

49

Lake
Tahoe

Auburn ■
A

Coloma
C

50

Eldorado

National

Forest

Folsom Lake
State Recreation
Area

Folsom
Lake

To Sacramento

Placerville
G

88

Volcano ■
K

Sutter Creek
J

Jackson ■

Pardee
Reservoir

B

Camanche
Reservoir

San Andreas
H

88

New
Hogan
Reservoir

Murphys ■
E

108

99

26

49

Angels Camp ■

Stockton
■

4

New
Melones
Lake

Columbia ■
I
■ Sonora

Jamestown ■

120

N

O SCALE   25   25
          KILOMETERS   MILES   ▬▬ ROAD   ≡≡ INTERSTATE

Sights

- Ⓐ **Auburn**
- Ⓑ **Calaveras Big Trees State Park**
- Ⓒ **Coloma/Marshall Gold Discovery State Historic Park**
- Ⓓ **Downieville**
- Ⓔ **Murphy's**
- Ⓕ **Nevada City Region**
- Ⓖ **Placerville**
- Ⓗ **San Andreas**
- Ⓘ **Sonora Region**
- Ⓙ **Sutter Creek Region**
- Ⓚ **Volcano**

A PERFECT DAY IN GOLD COUNTRY

My favorite segment of Gold Country is the Yuba River Valley between Grass Valley and Downieville. In the morning, visit Empire Mine State Historic Park. Travel on to Nevada City, one of the loveliest historic towns in the state. If you're not driving a huge RV or fifth wheel, visit Malakoff Diggins State Historic Park and the site of North Bloomfield. Drive up CA 49 as it winds into the cool, forested country of the Yuba River Canyon. Finish your sightseeing with a walk around the interesting town of Downieville. Spend the night in town, or head to the high country.

MINING FOR GOLD

Gold occurs with the mineral quartz in lodes, or deposits, near the edges of large, granite masses. As the mountains erode, gold is mixed into the sediments in placer deposits. Most of the individual miners and low-budget outfits of the past engaged in placer mining; that is, extracting the gold from deposited sediments—usually the silt, sand,

and gravels in and around streambeds. Hardrock mining, or deep mining, was much more expensive, requiring large investments of capital.

Gold's high density causes it to sink in moving water before lighter materials. Gold panners swirled grit and water in the bottom of shallow pans to sort out the good stuff. On a larger scale, streams were diverted to run through *sluice boxes*. Grit and gravel were shoveled in at the upper end, then washed down the length of the box. All would come out at the other end except the gold, which caught in the *riffles* along the bottom of the box. The largest operations used dredges to remove deposits from river bottoms or hydraulic jets to scrub sediments (and everything else) from the underlying bedrock, then all was sluiced.

The original hardrock mines utilized blasted, drilled, and hand-dug shafts to find lodes and to follow veins deep into the earth. Ore was removed and then crushed in *stamp mills* so it, too, could be sluiced.

SIGHTSEEING HIGHLIGHTS

★★★ **Nevada City Region**—Mining history receives a classic veneer in this charming, historic town. The blocks around Broad Street are loaded with interesting shops and restaurants. You can still see a show up the hill on Broad Street at the **Nevada Theater**, opened in 1865, the oldest in the state. The **Firehouse Museum No. 1** has heritage items, including relics from the Donner party. Details: 214 Main Street, Nevada City; (916) 265-5468; open daily from 11 a.m. to 4 p.m. April through October. Donations are accepted.

Four miles south on CA 49 is the very different town of **Grass Valley**, which reveals its history reluctantly. Exit the freeway and head to Main Street to see what there is. From Main, take Auburn Street under the freeway, then turn left on Empire Street to reach the **Empire Mine State Historic Park**. The deep rock Empire Mine was in operation until 1956 and produced nearly 190 tons of gold, all of which was extracted via 370 miles of tunnel. Stop at the visitor center for an overview and to sign on for a free, one-hour guided tour. Details: 10791 East Empire Street, Grass Valley; (916) 273-8522; open daily from 10 a.m. to 5 p.m. Admission is $3. (2 hours)

From CA 49, 12 miles north of Nevada City, go east 17 miles on Tyler-Foote Road to reach **Malakoff Diggins State Historic Park** and the townsite of **North Bloomfield**. The park preserves an area of devastation that resulted from hydraulic mining. With this method, water pressurized by pumps or gravity is shot through nozzles, washing everything, including gold-bearing placer deposits, from the surface to be sluiced. In North Bloomfield, a few restored buildings sit along the road, kept company by the marked sites of many more. Details: (916) 265-2740; park open daily from sunrise to sunset, museum open daily from 10 a.m. to 5 p.m. (open weekends only from 10 a.m. to 4 p.m. in winter). Day-use fee is $5. (1½ hours)

★★★ **Sonora Region**—The area around Sonora is ideal for exploring if you're on your way to or from Yosemite. CA 49 runs through the busy center of Sonora, but its historic charms are still intact. The **Tuolumne County Museum**, housed in the 1857 county jail, has the usual heritage displays. Details: The museum is located at 158 West Bradford Avenue, Sonora; (209) 532-1317; open Sunday, Monday, and Wednesday from 9 a.m. to 4 p.m., Tuesday, Thursday, and Friday from 10 a.m. to 4 p.m., and Saturday from 10 a.m. to 3:30 p.m. Admission is free. (1 hour)

Two miles north on CA 49 and another mile up Parrots Ferry Road is the wonderfully restored town of Columbia in the **Columbia State Historic Park**. The streets of Columbia are closed to cars, and historic businesses still sell old-time goods. Horse-drawn wagons roll through the streets. Two old hotels house guests, and a small theater offers period productions. Columbia is a great combination of living history museum and historic theme attraction. Details: Parrots Ferry Road, Columbia; (209) 532-4301; park shops are open daily from 10 a.m. to 5 p.m. Bars, hotel, and theater open into the evening. While individual attractions range in price, a walking tour is free. (2 hours)

Two miles south of Sonora is the town of **Jamestown**. Visit the splendid **Railtown 1897 Historic Park** to see the historic **Sierra Railway Depot**, used as a set in such movie and TV productions as *High Noon* and "Petticoat Junction." Explore the 26-acre collection of rail history and take a one-hour ride behind the **Mother Lode Cannon Ball**. Details: Fifth Avenue and Reservoir Avenue, Jamestown; (209) 984-3953; depot store and museum are open daily, 9 a.m. to 4:30 p.m. Guided tours run daily at ten minutes after the hour from 10:10 a.m. to 3:10 p.m. The train runs weekends only at 11 a.m. and 3 p.m. Guided tours are $2, train rides are $3. (2 hours)

South of Jamestown, at the junction of CA 49 and CA 120, is the virtual ghost town of **Chinese Camp** featuring the scattered shacks of

Chinese immigrant miners. Stop at the visitors bureau where Main Street meets CA 49 or look around on your own. Details: 10 miles south of Sonora on CA 49; (209) 984-4636 (visitors bureau); open anytime. (½ hour)

★★ **Calaveras Big Trees State Park**—Two marvelous groves of giant sequoia trees are preserved in this lovely state park. Hiking, fishing, camping, and swimming are enjoyed in the summer, while snowshoeing and cross-country skiing through the upper grove are popular with a few knowing souls throughout the winter. If you can't visit Sequoia National Park, this is a great place to enjoy these amazing trees. Details: On CA 4, 3 miles east of Arnold; open all day, every day; (209) 795-2334. All-day parking is $5. (2 hours)

★★ **Coloma/Marshall Gold Discovery State Historic Park**—This is where it all began. The park lies on either side of CA 49, on the banks of the American River. The centerpiece is a reconstruction of the sawmill where James Marshall spotted those first glitters in 1848. Up on the hill are Marshall's cabin and monument. Details: (916) 622-3470 for the park, (916) 622-1116 for the museum. The excellent visitor center and museum are open daily from 10 a.m. to 5 p.m. (until 4:30 p.m. in the winter). The park closes at dusk. Pay your $5 day-use fee at the first site you visit and make sure the receipt is visible in your windshield. (2 hours)

Coloma is also the center of white-water rafting in the region. Several outfitters rent equipment and lead trips (see "Fitness and Recreation" below).

★★ **Downieville**—This humble and historic town is particularly attractive for its setting, nestled on the Yuba River well up the canyon from the hot foothills. It's a great place to pan for gold and have a picnic. The 1852 **Downieville Museum** on Main Street has a miniature working stamp mill model, among other interesting items. Details: Main Street, Downieville; (916) 289-3423; museum open daily from 10 a.m. to 5 p.m. Memorial Day through mid-October. $1 donation is suggested. (½ hour)

Further up CA 49 is the **Kentucky Mine Park and Museum**, notable for its impressive, working tin stamp mill. Details: 1 mile north of Sierra City on CA 49; (916) 862-1310; open Wednesday through Sunday from 10 a.m. to 5 p.m. in summer (weekends in October). The tour costs $4. (1 hour)

★★ **Sutter Creek Region**—With its blend of history, charm, and hip romance, Sutter Creek is a popular destination for tourists and weekenders. The lovely town with its sheltered walks and historic storefronts is great for browsing. Iron was cast using waterwheel-powered machines at the **Historic Knight Foundry** until recently when it finally closed. Hopefully it will open again for visitors soon. Details: 81 Eureka Street, Sutter Creek; (209) 267-0201. (1 hour)

Two miles north of Sutter Creek on CA 49, the town of **Amador City** has a short, charming stretch of shops, many selling antiques. As the smallest incorporated town in the state, Amador City has trouble handling the thick highway traffic that rolls through downtown.

The large town of **Jackson** is 5 miles south of Sutter Creek on CA 49. As county seat, it's home to the **Amador County Museum**. The museum features a 1/12-scale, working model of the huge Kennedy mine which, along with the Eureka mine, dominated the scene until 1920. Details: 225 Church Street, Jackson; (209) 223-6386; open Wednesday through Sunday from 10 a.m. to 4 p.m. Tours of the model are offered Saturday and Sunday only, on the hour, from 11 a.m. to 3 p.m. Donations accepted, model tours are $1. (1 hour)

Visit **Kennedy Wheel Park** north of town to see huge mining wheels and other remnants of the Kennedy Mine. You can see the wheels from an overlook along CA 49.

★★ **Volcano**—This picturesque town gives a great feel for the way it once was. On Main Street, the St. George Hotel commands the scene. Shops and historic buildings, some unrestored, surround the town center. Nearby, **Daffodil Hill** is a magnificent sight in the springtime. Take Sutter Creek Road 14 miles east from Sutter Creek. It's worth it to wander off the beaten path to see this town.

Three miles to the south on Pine Grove-Volcano Road is **Indian Grinding Rock State Historic Park**. A rocky outcrop features numerous holes once used as bowls for the grinding of acorn meal. In addition, the rock face shows scores of historic petroglyphs. The **Chaw'Se Regional Indian Museum** has Miwok Indian heritage exhibits and a Miwok village. Details: Pine Grove-Volcano Road; (209) 296-7488; the park is open dawn to dusk, the museum is open from 11 a.m. to 3 p.m. Monday through Friday and from 10 a.m. to 4 p.m. weekends. Fee is $5 for day use. (1½ hours)

✫ **Auburn**—Auburn has been captured by the exurban expansion of
Sacramento. Deep within the sprawl, you will find the heavily touristed
historic district, with its wooden sidewalks, shops, restaurants, and
restored nineteenth-century buildings. Take Lincoln Street from CA
49. Visit the **Placer County Museum** in the courthouse for excellent
heritage exhibits. Details: Auburn; (916) 889-6500; open Tuesday
through Sunday from 10 a.m. to 4 p.m. Admission is free. (1 hour)

The fairgrounds host the **Gold Country Museum**, featuring historic mining and transportation exhibits. Details: 1273 High Street,
Auburn; (916) 889-4134; open Tuesday through Friday from 10 a.m. to
3:30 p.m., weekends from 11 a.m. to 4 p.m. Admission is $1. (1 hour)

A bit further south is the **Bernhard Museum**, a restored
Victorian house, winery, carriage house, and grounds that exhibit the
life of the times. Details: 291 Auburn-Folsom Road, Auburn; (916)
889-6500; open Tuesday through Friday from 11 a.m. to 3 p.m., weekends from noon to 4 p.m. Admission is $1. (1 hour)

✫ **Murphys**—With lovely Victorian homes, Murphys is a good place
to stroll and browse. Head 9 miles east on CA 4 from Angels Camp,
then left on Sheep Ranch Road. Stroll Main Street with your camera.

Another mile down on Sheep Ranch Road is **Mercer Caverns**,
famous for its outstanding examples of rare aragonite flos-ferri formations. One-hour tours depart every 20 minutes. Details: Sheep Ranch
Road, 1½ miles north of CA 4; (209) 728-2101; open from 9 a.m. to
8 p.m. daily from Memorial Day through Labor Day, from 10 a.m. to
4:30 p.m. Sunday through Thursday in the offseason (until 7 p.m.
Friday and Saturday). Admission is $7, $3.50 for kids. (1½ hours)

To the south of CA 4, beyond the town of Vallecito, is **Moaning
Cavern** which features a huge, vertical chamber accessed by a 100-foot
spiral staircase—the first arc-welded structure in California. Details: 2
miles south of Vallecito on Parrots Ferry Road; (209) 736-2708; open
daily from 9 a.m. to 6 p.m. in the summer (10 a.m. to 5 p.m. the rest of
the year). Tours last 45 minutes. Admission is $7.75, kids $4. (1 hour)

Continue south on Parrots Ferry Road for a view of **New
Melones Lake** and to reach Columbia. At the junction of CA 49 and
CA 4 is the community of **Angels Camp**, offering historic buildings in
the heart of town. If you're here during the third weekend in May, you
can experience the "Jumping Frog Jubilee," part of the celebrations of
the Calaveras County Fair. Mark Twain was inspired to write his
famous short story "The Celebrated Jumping Frog of Calaveras

County" while here. His legacy lives on in all its hokey glory. Details:
Call the Calaveras County Visitor Center for fair information; (800)
225-3764.

The large **Angels Camp Museum** features gold rush and
regional heritage items. Exhibits include a blacksmith shop, water-
wheel, and carriage house. Details: 753 South Main Street, Angels
Camp; (209) 736-2963. (1 hour)

☆ **Placerville**—As a gas and burger stop on the heavily traveled U.S.
50 to Tahoe, Placerville suffers a bit from growth and wear.
Fortunately, the highway bypasses Main Street, so browsing the historic center is relaxing. Placerville was once called "Hangtown" for a
spate of frontier justice that occurred during the Gold Rush. Notice
the hanging figure in front of the building that now sits over the stump
of the hanging tree. Both the historic **City Hall** and the free **Placerville
Historical Museum** are at the east end of Main Street. Details: (916)
626-0773; museum open Friday through Sunday from noon to 4 p.m.
(closed Friday in winter). Admission is free. (45 minutes)

The **El Dorado County Museum** is located 2 miles west of town
at the fairgrounds. It features historic buildings, farm implements, logging and mining equipment, and more. Details: 100 Placerville Drive,
Placerville; (916) 621-5865; open Wednesday through Sunday from 10
a.m. to 4 p.m. (from noon on Sunday). Admission is free. (1 hour)

Turn north on Bedford Avenue by the county courthouse and
drive 1 mile to **Hangtown's Gold Bug Park and Mine**. You can take
a self-guided, Walkman tour deep into an almost horizontal mine shaft.
Details: Bedford Avenue, Placerville; (916) 642-5207; open daily in the
summer, weekends in shoulder seasons, from 10 a.m. to 4 p.m.; closed
in the winter. Admission is $1. (45 minutes)

San Andreas—Check out the local heritage exhibits and California
native plant garden of the **Calaveras County Historical Museum**.
With the museum you'll find the courthouse where the infamous Black
Bart was tried and the jailhouse that held him. Other historic buildings
can be found on North Main Street. Details: 30 North Main Street;
(209) 754-6579; museum open daily from 10 a.m. to 4 p.m. Admission
is $1. (½ hour)

Ten miles east of town, on Mountain Ranch Road, are the beautiful **California Caverns** at Cave City. Details: Take Mountain Ranch
Road 8 miles east from San Andreas. Follow the signs for 2 more miles

on Michel and Cave City Roads to Cave City and the caverns; (209) 736-2708; cave tours last about 1½ hours, and depart hourly from 10 a.m. to 5 p.m. in summer, and from 10 a.m. to 4 p.m. in fall. Cost is $8, kids are $4.25. Guided spelunking tours also available. (1½ hours)

FITNESS AND RECREATION

One of the best hikes around is the 9-mile trail that leads through the South Grove of sequoias in **Calaveras Big Trees State Park**. The trailhead of the **South Grove Trail** is at the Beaver Creek Picnic Area, (209) 795-2334. The **Downieville Downhill**, a popular mountain biking route, follows Butcher Ranch and Third Divide trails in the hills near CA 49. Information, rentals, and trail shuttles are available from **Coyote Adventure Co.**, 123 Nevada Street, Nevada City, (916) 265-6909.

Coloma is a center for rafting, but other outfitters can be found across the Sierra foothills. **Earth Trek Expeditions** is located in Lotus, a stone's throw from Coloma on Lotus Road (from CA 49), (916) 642-1900 or (800) 229-8735. They offer half-to two-day rafting trips on several outstanding stretches of river for $70 to $250. **Whitewater Connections**, (800) 336-7238, has half-day to two-day trips, from $70 to $220. American River rafting trips are offered by **Whitewater Excitement** in Auburn. Call (800) 750-2386 for information.

FOOD

The gourmet pies at Nevada City's **Cowboy Pizza**, 315 Spring Street, (916) 265-2334, are out of this world. Try the "Popeye" with spinach, onions, garlic, feta cheese, and pine nuts. For fine dining, **Citronée Bistro & Wine Bar**, 320 Broad Street, (916) 265-0558, offers American cuisine with a Mediterranean influence.

In Auburn's historic heart, **Bootlegger's**, 210 Washington Street, (916) 889-2229, offers hearty American cuisine with a "gourmet flair." The **Shanghai Restaurant**, 289 Washington Street, (916) 823-2613, has been serving Cantonese dishes for almost 90 years.

At **Café Sarah's** in Placerville, Cathy will serve you monumentally huge pancakes or other large and tasty breakfast and lunch fare. It's next door to the hanging man at 301 Main Street, (530) 621-4680. **Lil' Mama D. Carlo's**, 482 Main Street, (916) 626-1612, is a classic and little Italian place serving tasty food.

In Sutter Creek, **Ron and Nancy's Palace**, 76 Main Street, (209) 267-1335, is the class act on historic Main Street. The building dates to 1884.

For fine dining in Jackson, try **Michael's Restaurant** in the National Hotel, 2 Water Street, (209) 223-3448.

In Murphys, head to the **Murphys Historic Hotel Dining Room**, 457 Main Street, (209) 728-3444, for an easy breakfast, lunch, or dinner. Visit **Grounds**, 402 Main Street, (209) 728-8663, for a great breakfast or lunch at a reasonable price.

In Columbia, step back in time at the **City Hotel Dining Room**, located in Columbia State Historic Park, (209) 532-1479, to enjoy cuisine described as "French preparation with California touches."

Sonora has a number of good spots, including the **Coyote Creek Café and Grill**, 177 South Washington Street, (209) 532-9115, with reasonably priced Southwestern-style dishes. **Good Heavens**, 49 North Washington Street, (209) 532-3663, has wonderful soups, sandwiches, and burgers.

LODGING

Budget and chain motel lodging are available on CA 49 in Grass Valley (**Best Western**), Auburn (**Best Western, Holiday Inn, Super 8**), Placerville (**Best Western, Days Inn**), Jackson (**Best Western**), Sonora (**Best Western**), Mariposa (**Best Western, Comfort Inn, Holiday Inn**), and Oakhurst (**Best Western**).

In the Lakes Basin on Gold Lake Road (N.F. 24), between Graeagle and CA 49 at Bassetts, the **Graeagle Lodge**, (916) 836-2511, is a beautiful place to get away from it all. The best feature is a wonderful swimming hole at the base of a small waterfall. Rooms are $170 for two people.

Downieville offers **Saundra Dyer's Resort**, (530) 289-3308 or (800) 696-3308, a down-home inn offering a good breakfast for $5. Rooms are $60, kitchen units $70 to $145. North on CA 89 is Sierra City and **Herrington's Sierra Pines Resort**, (916) 862-1151, a rustic lodge with a great Yuba River location. Rooms run from $50 to $90 (with kitchen units).

One of the nicest of the many B&B choices in Nevada City is the historic **Red Castle Inn**, 109 Prospect Street, (916) 265-5135 or (800) 761-4766, built in 1860 and overlooking Nevada City from the hills across the river. Rooms range from $70 to $140. The grand old

GOLD COUNTRY

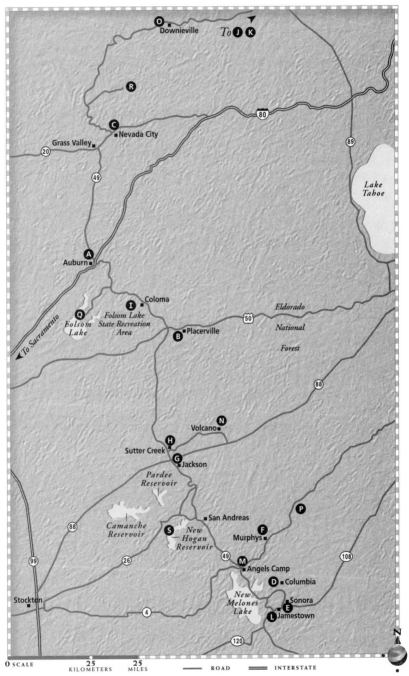

Downieville O

To J K

O

R

C Nevada City

Grass Valley

20

49

80

89

Lake Tahoe

A Auburn

Coloma I

Q Folsom Lake

Folsom Lake State Recreation Area

B Placerville

50

Eldorado

National

Forest

88

N

Volcano

H Sutter Creek

G Jackson

Pardee Reservoir

San Andreas

P

88

Camanche Reservoir

S New Hogan Reservoir

F Murphys

108

99

26

49

M Angels Camp

D Columbia

4

New Melones Lake

Sonora E

L Jamestown

Stockton

120

N

O SCALE   25   25
          KILOMETERS   MILES   ROAD   INTERSTATE

Food

- Ⓐ Bootlegger's
- Ⓑ Café Sarah's
- Ⓒ Citronée Bistro & Wine Bar
- Ⓓ City Hotel Dining Room
- Ⓒ Cowboy Pizza
- Ⓔ Coyote Creek Café and Grill
- Ⓔ Good Heavens
- Ⓕ Grounds
- Ⓑ Lil' Mama D. Carlo's
- Ⓖ Michael's Restaurant
- Ⓕ Murphys Historic Hotel Dining Room
- Ⓗ Ron and Nancy's Palace
- Ⓐ Shanghai Restaurant

Lodging

- Ⓑ Cary Hotel
- Ⓘ Coloma Country Inn
- Ⓕ Dunbar House
- Ⓓ Fallon Hotel
- Ⓙ Graeagle Lodge
- Ⓚ Herrington's Sierra Pines Resort
- Ⓛ Jamestown Hotel

Lodging (continued)

- Ⓜ Jumping Frog Motel
- Ⓕ Murphys Historic Hotel and Lodge
- Ⓖ National Hotel (Jackson)
- Ⓒ National Hotel (Nevada City)
- Ⓒ Red Castle Inn
- Ⓝ St. George Hotel
- Ⓞ Saundra Dyer's Resort
- Ⓔ Sonora Days Inn
- Ⓗ Sutter Creek Inn

Camping

- Ⓟ Calaveras Big Trees State Park
- Ⓘ Camp Lotus
- Ⓣ Coloma Resort
- Ⓠ Folsom Lake State Recreation Area
- Ⓓ 49er RV Ranch
- Ⓡ Malakoff Diggins State Historic Park
- Ⓢ New Hogan Lake Recreation Area

Note: Items with the same letter are located in the same town or area.

National Hotel at 211 Broad Street in downtown Nevada City, (916) 265-4551, is steeped in history. Rooms with private baths start at $68.

Near the heart of the Marshall Gold Discovery State Historic Park, the 1852 **Coloma Country Inn**, 345 High Street, (916) 622-6919, is a fine, historic option. The innkeepers offer rafting and hot-air ballooning trips, as well as use of their canoe on the nice pond.

The **Cary Hotel**, 300 Main Street, (530) 622-4271, in downtown Placerville offers history on a budget. Rooms at this landmark hotel range from $75 to $125 (suite).

Sutter Creek has several nice places, including the **Sutter Creek Inn**, right in town at 75 Main Street, (209) 267-5606. A few of the rooms have swinging beds (hanging from ceiling chains). Rooms start at $65 to $175 including a full country breakfast

The old **St. George Hotel** in Volcano, (209) 296-4458, has shared baths, no air conditioning or heat, and 130 long years under its belt. If that's OK with you, don't miss the chance to spend a quiet night in this town of yesteryear. Dinner and breakfast are included; call for rates.

In Jackson, the **National Hotel**, 2 Water Street, (209) 223-0500, has been in operation continuously since 1862. Many of the furnishings are original—as the plumbing seems to be. Rooms run from $50 to $80. Angels Camp has a good budget choice in the **Jumping Frog Motel**, (209) 736-2191, with basic rooms from $40 to $60.

Murphys has several B&Bs, including the historic **Dunbar House**, 271 Jones Street, (209) 728-2897, with rooms from $125 to $170. **Murphys Historic Hotel and Lodge**, 457 Main Street, (209) 728-3444, is a local landmark and gathering place. There are nine rooms in the original building, 20 in a motel addition, for $70 to $80.

Spend a night in another era at the **Columbia City Hotel**, right on the main street of the closed-to-vehicles town. Rooms cost from $85 to $105. Rooms at the associated **Fallon Hotel** range from $50 to $105. For reservations in either hotel, call (209) 532-1479.

In Sonora, the historic **Sonora Days Inn**, 160 South Washington Street, (209) 532-2400, has rooms from $50 to $140. In nearby Jamestown, the historic, restored **Jamestown Hotel**, 18153 Main Street, (209) 984-3902 or (800) 205-4901, is a great choice. Rooms all have private baths and range from $70 to $135, breakfast included.

CAMPING

There are several National Forest campgrounds along CA 49 and Gold Lake Road (N.F. 24), both north and south of Downieville.

Three reservoirs near CA 49 have one or more campgrounds. For **Folsom Lake State Recreation Area**, take Rattlesnake Bar Road from Pilot Hill south of Auburn. Roads from CA 49, CA 26, and CA 12 provide access to **New Hogan Lake Recreation Area** near Valley Springs. CA 49 crosses New Melones Lake south of Angels Camp. Campground access is from the highway on either side of the lake.

Near Nevada City, **Malakoff Diggins State Historic Park** (see "Sightseeing" listing for directions), (916) 265-2740 for information, (800) 444-7275 for reservations, has a campground with $7 tent sites and $15 cabins.

Calaveras Big Trees State Park on CA 4 above Arnold, (209) 795-2334 for information, (800) 444-7275 for reservations, has a nice campground next to a sequoia grove. Sites are $14 to $16.

The **Coloma Resort**, 6921 Mt. Murphy Road (from CA 49), (800) 238-2298, has RV sites and a few tent sites right on the American River, close to the attractions of the state historic park. Sites go for $29. Nearby, down Lotus Road, **Camp Lotus**, (916) 622-8672, has tent sites from $16 to $25. Half a mile from Columbia State Historic Park on Italian Bar Road (from Pacific Street) is the **49er RV Ranch**, (209) 532-4978, with nice shady sites for $23.

Scenic Route: High Sierra Pass Roads

Four ways cross the Sierras between Yosemite and Lake Tahoe: U.S. 50, CA 88, CA 4, and CA 108. Each climbs from the foothills of **Gold Country**, through the vacation cabins and pine forests, up into high ski and lake basins, and over the Sierra crest. Only U.S. 50, a main route to Tahoe, experiences truly heavy traffic.

CA 88, a designated **National Scenic Byway**, is perhaps the nicest of the four, with CA 4 and CA 108 close behind. CA 88 features beautiful **Caples Lake** and **Silver Lake**, as well as access to **Indian Grinding Rock Historic State Park** and **Volcano**, a virtual ghost town. CA 4 rides the high ridge above the **Mokelumne** and **Stanislaus** valleys and features wonderful sequoia groves in **Calaveras Big Trees State Park**. CA 108, the highest of the three roads at 9,624 feet, crosses **Sonora Pass**.

For those desiring a three- to six-day, 450-mile "Sierra sampler," take CA 120 through **Yosemite** with a tour of **Yosemite Valley**; U.S. 395 with stops at **Mono Lake** and a side trip to **Bodie**; CA 89 up to **Emerald Bay** on Lake Tahoe; and CA 88 across Carson Pass and down to Gold Country and CA 49. ◼

HIGH SIERRA PASS ROADS

13

LAKE TAHOE

S traddling the California-Nevada border at 6,229 feet above sea
level, beautiful Lake Tahoe attracts outdoor enthusiasts from all
over the world. A dozen ski resorts surround the basin, including
Squaw Valley U.S.A., which hosted events in the 1960 Olympics.
Tahoe is a top weekend getaway spot, both in winter and summer.
Don't get stuck on Interstate 80 and U.S. 50 at peak traffic times; that
is, eastbound on Friday evenings and westbound on Sundays. Spring,
fall, and midweek are the best times to be in the area.

Tahoe City on the northwest shore is the relaxed center for active
outdoor sports enthusiasts. Some of the most serious skiing is done at
Alpine Meadows and Squaw Valley just to the north on CA 89. The
southwest shore features beautiful state parks and wilderness access.
South Lake Tahoe hosts the largest concentration of accommodations
and vacation homes. Cross into Nevada on either the north or south
shores, and you shift immediately into the resort gambling scene.

Unless you're interested in gambling or specific Nevada sites,
don't bother circling the lake. CA 89 passes through the most scenic
areas. Your time is best spent in the hills, on the water, or at a café
table on a deck where the two meet.

North of Tahoe, the area around Truckee offers attractions relat-
ing to the history of gold and silver mining, the transcontinental railroad, and cannibalism in America—that's right, cannibalism! It was
around Donner Lake in the winter of 1846–1847 that some members
of the ill-fated Donner Party survived by eating their loved ones. ◣

LAKE TAHOE

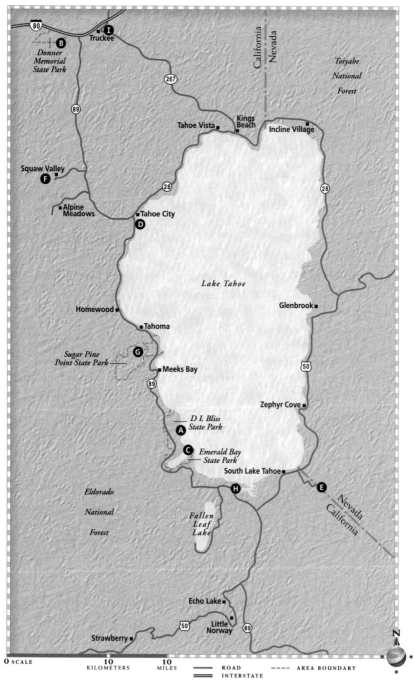

Truckee
80
I
B
Donner
Memorial
State Park
89
267
California
Nevada
Toiyabe
National
Forest
Tahoe Vista ■
Kings
Beach
Incline Village ■
28
Squaw Valley
F
28
■ Alpine
Meadows
Tahoe City ■
D
Lake Tahoe
Homewood ■
Glenbrook ■
■ Tahoma
Sugar Pine
Point State Park
G
50
■ Meeks Bay
89
Zephyr Cove ■
D L Bliss
State Park
A
C
Emerald Bay
State Park
South Lake Tahoe ■
Eldorado
National
Forest
H
E
Nevada
California
Fallen
Leaf
Lake
Echo Lake ■
Strawberry ■
50
Little
Norway
89
N

0 SCALE   10 KILOMETERS   10 MILES   ▬ ROAD   ---- AREA BOUNDARY
═══ INTERSTATE

Sights

- Ⓐ **D. L. Bliss State Park**
- Ⓑ **Donner Memorial State Park**
- Ⓒ **Emerald Bay State Park**
- Ⓓ **Gatekeepers Museum**
- Ⓔ **Heavenly Valley Tram**
- Ⓕ **Squaw Valley Gondola**
- Ⓖ **Sugar Pine Point State Park**
- Ⓗ **Tallac Historic Site**
- Ⓘ **Truckee**

A PERFECT DAY AROUND LAKE TAHOE

What's your pleasure? If you arrive in winter or spring, a day of downhill skiing at Alpine Meadows might be right. In summer or fall, a hike from Echo Lake into the edge of the Desolation Wilderness might fit the bill. If you're just passing through, follow CA 89. Stop in Truckee and Donner Memorial State Park for some history. Spend half a day hiking and enjoying the lake in D. L. Bliss and Emerald Bay State Parks. Pick a lakeside eatery to soak in the Tahoe scene. There's no place to go, you're already there.

SIGHTSEEING HIGHLIGHTS

✩✩✩ **D. L. Bliss State Park**—With the peaks of **Desolation Wilderness** looming above and the longest stretch of protected lakeshore below, this park should be at the top of your list. Walk the **Rubicon Trail** along the shore to find the patch of sand or granite boulder just right for basking. There are good spots to swim or to dive from the rocks. A 4-mile walk will take you to Vikingsholm in Emerald Bay State Park.

The parking lot at the beach is very small. At high times and during high season, you may have to walk an extra half or full mile from other areas closer to the highway. Try to arrive early, especially if your schedule puts you in Tahoe on the weekend. Details: CA 89 runs through the park, south of Meeks Bay; (530) 525-7277; open from 8 a.m. to dusk. Fee is $5 for day use. (2–4 hours)

✭✭✭ **Emerald Bay State Park**—Emerald Bay is one of the loveliest spots on this or any lake. Fed by a pristine stream draining from the Desolation Wilderness, a steady outflow assures that the water here will keep its crystal clarity, no matter how the larger lake fares in the long run. The bay's color is a feast for the eyes, the rich blue of the deeps blending into a turquoise that almost glows. CA 89 loops high above the bay, affording wonderful views. Details: On CA 89 south of Meeks Bay and D. L. Bliss State Park; (530) 525-7277; open dawn to dusk. Admission is free. (1–2 hours)

At the head of the bay is **Vikingsholm**, an imitation of a medieval Norse fortress built in 1929 by wealthy heiress Lora Josephine Knight. A steep, 1-mile path descends to the castle from the marked parking lot on the highway. Better yet, take the longer hike (about 4 miles) from the adjacent D. L. Bliss State Park to enjoy relative solitude and the best of the lakeside. Details: (530) 525-7982; open daily in summer from 10 a.m. to 4 p.m. Admission is $2. (3 hours)

✭✭ **Donner Memorial State Park**—In the spring of 1846, the Donners left Illinois with two other families, to be joined in Missouri by several others. The party was slowed in crossing the continent and became stranded by the shores of Donner Lake in one of the most bitter winters on record. Of the 87 who were snowbound, more than half died. Some resorted to cannibalism to survive.

In the forested flats around Donner Lake's eastern end, there's little to see besides plaques and a monument. However, don't miss the excellent **Emigrant Trail Museum** to gain a rich perspective of this compelling story. Details: (530) 582-7892; museum open daily from 9 a.m. to 5 p.m. (until 4 p.m. in winter), park open from sunrise to sunset. Admission is $2, free with payment of $5 day-use park fee. (1 hour)

✭ **Gatekeepers Museum**—You'll probably see a small crowd of visitors at this three-way attraction in Tahoe City. Features include the museum, the **Lake Tahoe Dam,** and the small **William B. Layton State Park**. It's hypnotic to watch the waters tumble over the small spillway that controls the lake level and serves as the headwaters of the Truckee River. The museum is a reconstruction of the original gatekeepers' log cabin in which dam attendants lived. There are good local heritage displays inside. Details: On CA 89 just south of the CA 89-CA 28 junction in Tahoe City; (530) 583-1762; open from 11 a.m. to 5 p.m. May 1 through early October, daily through the summer, and

Wednesday through Sunday in shoulder seasons. Donations are accepted. (45 minutes)

✻ **Sugar Pine Point State Park**—More developed and accessible than D. L. Bliss State Park, Sugar Pine has a popular beach, swimming dock, and tennis courts. There's an informative Nature Center near the water. Trails visit Sugar Pine Point, while a longer route climbs toward the high peaks through the large portion of the park that's above the road. Details: On CA 89, 1 mile south of Tahoma; (530) 525-7982; open from 8 a.m. to dusk. Fee is $5 for day use.

The star attraction is the **Ehrman Mansion**, a beautiful Queen Anne–style structure built in 1902. Details: 1 mile south of Tahoma; (530) 525-7982; mansion tours depart daily, on the hour, from 11 a.m. to 4 p.m., July 1 through Labor Day. Admission is free. (1 hour)

✻ **Heavenly Valley Tram**—For a spectacular, panoramic view of the lake basin without the challenge of a tough hike, take a tram ride. At the top you'll be 2,000 feet above the lake surface. Hiking trails can take you even higher. Details: Take Ski Run Boulevard south from U.S. 50 between South Lake Tahoe and the Nevada border; (702) 586-7000; a tram departs every 15 minutes from 10 a.m. to 9 p.m. daily in the summer (from 9 a.m. on Sunday, closed Sunday in shoulder season). Cost is $12. (1 hour)

✻ **Squaw Valley Gondola**—At the top of this 2,000-foot lift, there's a swimming pool, ice-skating rink, bungy-jumping tower, tennis courts, hiking and biking access, a restaurant, and more—as well as a fabulous view. Enjoy a cool drink as you soak in the alpine splendor. Details: 1960 Squaw Valley Road; (530) 583-6985 or (800) 545-4350; open daily, call ahead to make sure scheduled maintenance isn't underway. Tickets are $14. (1½ hours)

✻ **Tallac Historic Site**—Located on CA 89, 3 miles north of its junction with U.S. 50, the Tallac site features three historic estates on the shores of the lake. The **Pope Estate**, built between 1894 and 1913, serves as a visitor center and art gallery. The **Tallac Museum**, featuring heritage and Indian displays, is housed in the **Baldwin Estate**, built in 1921. **Valhalla** was constructed in 1924. Today the estates are used for tours, exhibits, and education programs. Call about the Valhalla Renaissance Festival held in June. Details: North of Camp

Richardson and South Lake Tahoe on CA 89; (530) 541-4975 (summer), (530) 542-4166 (winter); the site is open from dawn to dusk in the summer only. **Pope Estate Visitor Center** hours are 8 a.m. to 5 p.m. daily, summer only. (1½ hours)

✯ **Truckee**—The tracks for Northern California's main east-west rail route dominate this fine, historic town. Mining put Truckee on the map, and the completion of the transcontinental railroad through Donner Pass kept it there. Enjoy the shops, restaurants, and historic buildings while avoiding the outdoor chic of the lake and ski areas. (2 hours)

FITNESS AND RECREATION

There are many excellent skiing areas in the region. See the chart below for a breakdown.

Royal Gorge, (530) 426-3871, is the largest cross-country ski area in the nation, featuring 200 miles of trails. Take the Soda Springs exit from I-80, turn right at the flashing light, and follow the signs. Northeast of Tahoe City at the **Lakeview Cross-Country Ski Area**, 925 Country Club Drive, (530) 583-9353, the extensive network of trails starts on a never-finished golf course, then heads up into Burton Creek State Park. Take CA 28, turn onto Fabian at the Shell Station, take the first right onto Village, then turn left on Country Club. Trail fees range from $6 to $16, rentals $12 to $15. **Squaw Valley**, **Kirkwood**, **Northstar-at-Tahoe**, and other ski areas have cross-country trails as well.

A very nice bike path follows the north and west shores of the lake between Dollar Point and Sugar Pine Point State Park, with an extension down the Truckee River to Squaw Valley. Another designated path runs from South Lake Tahoe almost to Emerald Bay. For a major mountain bike ride, ask about the **Flume Trail** along the ridge in Lake Tahoe–Nevada State Park. The rental shops all have good information on rides. **Tahoe Paddle and Oar**, 8299 North Lake Boulevard, (530) 546-3535, in Kings Beach rents kayaks and offers guided kayak tours. A couple miles south of Tahoe City on CA 89 is Sunnyside, where you'll find **Cycle Paths**, 1785 West Lake Boulevard, (530) 581-1171, a good place to rent a bike. Guided day rides range from $30 to $50.

Just north of the posh homes of Tahoe Pines is the trailhead for **Eagle Rock**. A short, steep hike earns you marvelous views. It's a great way to spend an hour or so. The **Tahoe Rim Trail** circles the lake on the ridges, covering 150 miles in the process. There is access at several points. The **Desolation**, **Granite Chief**, and **Mount Rose Wilderness** areas have good trail systems.

LAKE TAHOE AREA SKIING

Name	Closest Tahoe Town	Phone	Vertical Drop	Lifts	Weekend$ *Day/Half
Alpine Meadows	Tahoe City	(800)441-4423	1,802'	12	47/35
Boreal	Truckee	(530)426-3666	600'	9	28/19
Diamond Peak	Incline Village	(800)468-2463	1,840'	6	38/28
Donner Ski	Ranch Truckee	(530)426-3635	750'	6	23/17
Heavenly	S. Lake Tahoe	(530)541-1330	3,500'	26	49/33
Kirkwood	S. Lake Tahoe	(209)258-6000	2,000'	12	43/32
Mount Rose	Incline Village	(800)754-7673	1,440'	5	38/26
Northstar	Kings Beach	(530)562-1010	2,280'	12	46/31
Sierra-at-Tahoe	S. Lake Tahoe	(530)659-7453	2,212'	10	43/29
Ski Homewood	Homewood	(530)525-2992	1,658'	8	35/26
Soda Springs	Truckee	(530)426-1010	650'	2	15/15
Squaw Valley	Tahoe City	(800)545-4350	2,850'	33	48/32
Sugar Bowl	Truckee	(530)426-3651	1,500'	12	42/27
Tahoe Donner	Truckee	(530)587-9444	600'	3	26/15

*1997–1998 prices

FOOD

In and around Tahoe, there's plenty of good food for the discerning and big food for the hungry.

In the Truckee Hotel, **The Passage**, 10007 Bridge Street (just off Commercial), (530) 587-7619, has great food with live music on weekends. The place is tiny, but the omelettes and sandwiches are giant and tasty at the **Squeeze In**, 10060 Donner Pass Road, (530) 587-9814.

In Kings Beach, the **Log Cabin Caffé**, 8692 North Lake Boulevard, (530) 546-7109, advertises the fact that they've been voted as having the best breakfast in Tahoe. I'll call it one of the best three which, in this restaurant-happy region, is close enough. At **Lanza's**, 7739 North Lake Boulevard, (530) 546-2434, pasta, pizza, and meat dishes are the real thing.

LAKE TAHOE

Truckee
Donner Memorial State Park
Kings Beach
Tahoe Vista
Incline Village
Toiyabe National Forest
California
Nevada
Squaw Valley
Alpine Meadows
Tahoe City
Lake Tahoe
Glenbrook
Homewood
Tahoma
Sugar Pine Point State Park
Meeks Bay
D L Bliss State Park
Zephyr Cove
Emerald Bay State Park
South Lake Tahoe
Eldorado National Forest
Fallen Leaf Lake
Nevada California
Echo Lake
Strawberry
Little Norway

80
267
89
28
28
50
89
50
89

0 SCALE
10 KILOMETERS
10 MILES
ROAD
INTERSTATE
AREA BOUNDARY

N

Food

- **A** Beacon
- **B** Captain John's
- **C** Fire Sign Café
- **D** Lanza's
- **B** Le Petit Pier
- **D** Log Cabin Caffé
- **E** The Passage
- **F** Red Hut Waffle Shop
- **G** Rosie's Café
- **E** Squeeze In
- **H** Stony Ridge Café
- **I** West Shore Café
- **G** Wolfdale's
- **B** Za's Pizza

Lodging

- **B** Beesley's Cottages
- **A** Camp Richardson Resort
- **F** Christiania Inn
- **B** Holiday House
- **F** Inn by the Lake
- **J** Sunnyside Lodge
- **G** Tahoe City Travelodge
- **G** Tahoe Marina Lodge
- **H** Tahoma Meadows Bed and Breakfast
- **E** Truckee Hotel

Camping

- **K** Bayview
- **A** Camp Richardson
- **L** D. L. Bliss State Park
- **M** Emerald Bay State Park
- **N** Fallen Leaf
- **O** Goose Creek
- **P** Granite Flat
- **Q** Kaspian
- **R** Meeks Bay
- **S** Nevada Beach
- **T** Silver Creek
- **U** Sugar Pine Point State Park
- **V** William Kent

Note: Items with the same letter are located in the same town or area.

There are two good fine dining options in Tahoe Vista. **Captain John's**, 7220 North Lake Boulevard, (530) 546-4819, features dinner entrées in the $16 to $20 range. Deck and pier seating is more casual. Next door, **Le Petit Pier**, 7238 North Lake Boulevard (CA 28), (530) 546-4464, is even more upscale, featuring Americanized French cuisine with a view. Entrées are in the $16 to $25 range.

The best known place in Tahoe City is **Rosie's Café**, 571 North Lake Boulevard (CA 28), (530) 583-8504. You can't go wrong, breakfast, lunch, or dinner. **Za's Pizza**, 395 North Lake Boulevard (CA 28), (530) 583-1812, hits the spot for lunch or dinner. For an upscale dinner, you can't do better than **Wolfdale's**, 640 North Lake Boulevard, (530) 583-5700.

Two miles south of Tahoe City in Sunnyside is the **Fire Sign Café**, 1785 West Lake Boulevard (CA 89), (530) 583-0871, another of the top three breakfast places around (good lunches too).

Across the highway from the Homewood Ski Area is the **West Shore Café**, 5180 West Lake Boulevard (CA 89), (530) 525-5200, featuring mixed-cuisine lunches from $10, dinner from $15, and great outdoor seating on the lake.

Third of the top three for breakfast is the **Stony Ridge Café** in Tahoma at the Tahoma Meadows B&B, (530) 525-0905.

Sit outside at the **Beacon**, 1900 Jamison Beach Road, (530) 541-0630, on the beach at Camp Richardson, just west of South Lake Tahoe. Enjoy a salad, sandwich, or seafood as you bask. There's live music, too. Drop in at the **Red Hut Waffle Shop**, 2723 Highway 50, South Lake Tahoe, (530) 541-9024, for breakfast or a burger. It's no-nonsense American fare done right. Enjoy the elegance and the fireplace at the Christiania Inn's dining room, 3819 Saddle Road, (530) 544-7337.

LODGING

Lodging at Lake Tahoe is often booked weeks in advance. Prices are generally highest in the summer, a bit lower in the winter, and much lower in the spring and fall shoulder seasons.

The **Truckee Hotel**, 10007 Bridge Street (just off Commercial), (530) 587-4444 or (800) 659-6921, offers a fine dose of history with all the comforts of a recent restoration. Shared-bath rooms range from $80 to $115, private-bath rooms from $100 to $140.

The biggest concentration of North Shore lodging options is in Tahoe Vista. Right on the water, the rooms of the **Holiday House**,

7276 North Lake Boulevard (CA 28), (530) 546-5857, have decks and lake views. There's a nice hot tub, and Alvina the friendly innkeeper offers windsurfing lessons. Rooms run $95 to $145. **Beesley's Cottages**, 6647 North Lake Boulevard (CA 28), (530) 546-2448, is clean, cute, on the beach, and family-friendly. Rooms and cottages range from $90 to $130 (closed in winter).

Tahoe City has several good places to stay. The **Tahoe Marina Lodge**, (530) 583-2365 or (800) 748-5650, is a nice beachfront motel with tennis courts and a pool. Rooms start at $91 midweek in the shoulder season and climb to $235 in August. **Tahoe City Travelodge**, 455 North Lake Boulevard (CA 28), (530) 583-3766 or (800) 578-7878, next to the golf course, is more reasonable with rooms from $50 to $115.

The moderately luxurious **Sunnyside Lodge**, 1850 West Lake Boulevard (CA 89), (530) 583-7200 or (800) 822-2754, at the Sunnyside Marina has rooms from $90 to $200—cheapest in spring and fall, priciest in the summer.

The cozy cabins of **Tahoma Meadows Bed and Breakfast**, 6821 West Lake Boulevard, Tahoma, (530) 525-1553 or (800) 355-1596, have that Tahoe "feel"—a fine place with a great breakfast. Cabins run from $110 to $150.

West of South Lake Tahoe, the **Camp Richardson Resort**, (530) 541-1801 or (800) 544-1801, has nightly rentals in a lodge, condos, or rustic cabins ranging from $70 to $125. The resort is next to the Tallac Historic Site and features a marina, the Beacon Bar & Grill, and a private beach.

South Lake Tahoe is motel central. A number of budget and chain motels are found along U.S. 50. Others are clustered near the state line and casino action. Use the numbers listed under "Resources" in the Practical Tips chapter to contact the chains. For general reservation assistance, call the South Lake Tahoe Visitors Authority at (800) 288-2463. The **Inn by the Lake** at 3300 Lake Tahoe Boulevard (U.S. 50), (530) 542-0330, has nice rooms from $85. Near the base of the Heavenly Valley ski lifts is the **Christiania Inn**, 3819 Saddle Road, (530) 544-7337, with a range of rooms and romantic suites from $55 to $195.

CAMPING

Each of the three main state parks have very nice campgrounds. **Sugar Pine Point State Park**, located above the highway, (530) 525-7982, has

access to mountain trails, is open year-round, and costs from $14 to $16.
D. L. Bliss State Park, (530) 525-7277, has easy access to the lakeshore
and Rubicon Trail, and costs from $14 to $20. **Emerald Bay State Park**,
(530) 541-3030, or (800) 444-7275, has great sites on Eagle Point at the
south side of Emerald Bay and costs from $14 to $16.

Several National Forest campgrounds are located around Lake
Tahoe and along the Truckee River. Many more are nearby, especially
along CA 89, both north and south of the lake, and along CA 88
between Nevada and Silver Lake. Between Truckee and Tahoe City on
CA 89 are: **Granite Flat** (fairly large and close to Truckee), **Goose
Creek** (the nicest of the three because it's set back from the highway),
and **Silver Creek** (closest to Squaw Valley and the lake).

Around the lake, you'll find: **William Kent** (above CA 89 just
south of Tahoe City), **Kaspian** (close to Eagle Rock, above Tahoe
Pines, with shore access across the road), **Meeks Bay** (in the trees next
to Meeks Bay resort with beach access), **Bayview** (undeveloped sites
above Emerald Bay with access to great views and rocky climbs),
Fallen Leaf (at the end of lovely Fallen Leaf Lake, take Fallen Leaf
Lake Road from Camp Richardson), **Camp Richardson** (beach access,
near South Lake Tahoe), and **Nevada Beach** (just over the Nevada
border with great beach access). Prices range from $11 to $17. Some
sites are reservable, call (800) 280-2267 ($7.50 per reservation).

NIGHTLIFE

Down by the lake in Tahoe City, behind the Safeway, the **Pierce
Street Annex**, 950 North Lake Tahoe Boulevard (CA 28), (530) 583-
5800, has a full line of drinks with deejay dancing Thursday through
Saturday. Across the road is **Humpty's**, 877 North Lake Boulevard
(CA 28), (530) 583-4867, a bar, grill, and rock 'n' roll club with good
bands and a bad attitude. **Pete and Peter's**, 395 North Lake
Boulevard, (530) 583-2400, is a good sports bar in the heart of town.
Truckee offers a small concentration of watering holes in the town
center. Cross the Nevada border to **Stateline** in the south and **Incline
Village** in the north to reach the casinos.

14

OWENS VALLEY AND MONO LAKE

E ast of Yosemite, the land drops steeply into the shallow, undrained Mono Lake Basin. The surrounding land is dry and desolate, a sagebrush-tufted home to coyotes and jackrabbits. Here, at the heavily faulted and fractured edge of the Sierra range, volcanic formations attest to the molten rock that hovers near the surface. Few people live in the region, though it once crawled with miners.

South of Mono Lake, no road crosses the High Sierra for almost 200 miles. At all times, an unbroken jagged line of 12,000-foot to 14,000-foot peaks frown down upon you, rising as much as two vertical miles above the Owens River. Nowhere else in North America can you find such a precipitous drop from ridgecrest to valley floor. Owens Valley is the deepest on the continent.

The steep valleys of the Eastern Sierra hide treasures of beauty and wonder. Short miles above the dusty basins, sparkling waterfalls dance and tumble into forested defiles, spilling across alpine meadows. Hot springs well up, flowing into pools and channels created by grateful bathers across the years. Barren cinder cones pepper the slopes. Atop a high ridge to the east, trees still grow that were alive when the first Egyptian pyramids were no more than plans scratched in the sand.

If you take U.S. 395 through the valleys east of the Sierra, you'll discover the magnificent land outside California's back door. Relatively few travel this way—be one of the few if chance allows. ∎

OWENS VALLEY AND MONO LAKE

Carson City

Walker River
Indian
Reservation

Grover
Hot Springs
State Park

Toiyabe

Walker
Lake

D 89
HOT SPRINGS RD

National

Walker ■

Forest

D Fales 395
Hot Springs ■ Bridgeport **B**

Nevada
California

270
Bodie State
Historical Park

G
Mono
Lake

Lee
Vining

Yosemite

Mono Craters

F 120

120
National

158

6

Inyo

Park

June Lake

National

D Casa Diablo
Hot Spring

Forest

C **D** 203
E
Mammoth
Lakes

Devil's Postpile
National
Monument

H

WHITE MOUNTAIN RD

A

Sierra

■ Bishop

National

H 168

Forest

Glacier Lodge ■

■ Big
Pine

N

O SCALE   30   30
        KILOMETERS   MILES   ▬▬▬ ROAD   ━ ━ ━ AREA BOUNDARY
                              ✕━ PLACE OF INTEREST

Sights

- Ⓐ Ancient Bristlecone Pine Forest
- Ⓑ Bodie State Historic Park
- Ⓒ Devil's Postpile National Monument
- Ⓓ Hot Springs
- Ⓔ Mammoth
- Ⓕ Mono Craters
- Ⓖ Mono Lake
- Ⓗ Sierra Valleys

A PERFECT DAY IN THE EASTERN SIERRAS

Enjoy the overlooks and scenic drives down from Tahoe on CA 89 or from Yosemite on CA 120. Walk among the ghosts in Bodie State Historic Park, then head to Lee Vining for a picnic lunch with a view of Mono Lake. Choose an afternoon activity—perhaps a walk in the South Tufa Reserve on Mono Lake's southern shore, a visit to Devil's Postpile, a hike or horseback ride in a high valley of the eastern Sierra, or a tour of volcanic sites. Climb out of Big Pine on CA 168 for a sunset view at 11,000 feet and camping near the ancient bristlecone groves.

SIGHTSEEING HIGHLIGHTS

★★★ **Ancient Bristlecone Pine Forest**—Making sure you have half a day available and a full tank of gas, take CA 168 east from the town of **Big Pine** to reach the forest. The road winds from the valley floor to the crest of the **White Mountains**, 11,000 feet above sea level. Two main groves of the stubby, gnarled bristlecones, some over 4,000 years old, can each be explored in one to three hours. The views westward of the **Owens Valley** and **Sierra Crest** are fabulous. **Grandview** is the highest and the best of five campgrounds along the highway. Details: Located north of CA 168 on Westgard Pass Road; (760) 873-2500; open daily from June through October. (½ day)

★★★ **Bodie State Historic Park**—Seven miles south of Bridgeport on U.S. 395, desolate CA 270 heads off eastward through an empty landscape, 13 miles to the site of historic Bodie. After it was discovered in 1859, more than $100 million worth of gold came from the area surrounding this rough-and-ready boom town. Some 10,000 people lived here at one time, working one of the 700 mining claims or serving those who did. Scores of bars and brothels satisfied the baser instincts of the residents—Bodie was known as much for sin and violence as it was for precious metal.

Though the buildings that still stand are only a small percentage of the original, they have never been vandalized or restored, and have been preserved by isolation and dry climate. Almost as important, no modern commercial enterprises or structures of any kind are to be found nearby. No other ghost town in the West will give you a better feel for the past.

For a bit of adventure, return to U.S. 395 via Cottonwood Canyon Road—a 20-mile back route over a low pass and down a winding arroyo to Mono Lake. It's a good gravel road that cuts up to the right just before you reach the Bodie entrance kiosk. There are no services of any kind off U.S. 395, so make sure you have at least 70 miles' worth of gas in the tank when you leave Lee Vining or Bridgeport. The Bureau of Land Management land surrounding Bodie State Historic Park is open to free, dispersed camping, though you need a permit for a campfire. Details: Located 13 miles east of U.S. 395 on CA 270; (760) 647-6445; open daily from 9 a.m. to 7 p.m. (8 a.m. to 4 p.m. in winter). Day-use fee is $2 per person. (3 hours)

★★★ **Mono Lake**—This lonely, unique lake, the remnant of an ancient inland sea, appears to be the oldest continuously filled body of water on the continent. It has been saved from extinction by rulings that limit the level of diversion from its feeder streams. Having no drainage, the lake is naturally alkaline and mineral rich. Its islands provide breeding sites for most of the world's California gulls, which feast on the brine shrimp that thrive in the lake. (3 hours)

Weird crystalline formations called tufa rim the lake. Formed underwater, the tufa has been exposed by the gradual shrinkage of the lake's volume. A special reserve has been established to protect the moderately delicate formations. It is possible to walk among the best formations from access points in the **South Tufa Reserve** on the southern shore of the lake. Details: Take CA 120 east from U.S. 395, south of Lee Vining; (760) 647-6595. Admission is free. (1½ hours)

The town of Lee Vining, near the junction of U.S. 395 and CA 120, is the only town of consequence in the basin. Stop at the fine visitor center just north of town for information on lake access and a panoramic view. (3 hours)

✵ **Devil's Postpile National Monument**—The 80-foot, multisided basalt columns of Devil's Postpile are joined together into a scarp ¼-mile long. The formation, set in pleasant **Red's Meadow** in the **San Juaquin River Valley**, was created after the slowly cooled innards of a lava flow were exposed by time. The column tops show the shine and striations of a good polish by a glacier. A 1½-mile trail leads to lovely, 100-foot **Rainbow Falls** near the monument's south end. There are hot springs to enjoy in Red's Meadow, as well as a pack station. Five National Forest campgrounds line the river and Minaret Road.

From the end of CA 203 at **Minaret Summit** above **Mammoth Lakes**, a narrow road descends to the monument and San Juaquin River. The road is closed in the winter. During much of the summer it is closed from 7:30 a.m. to 5:30 p.m. to private vehicles without campground reservations. Shuttles leave twice an hour from the Mammoth Mountain Inn, stopping at several spots on the way, including the parking area for the Minaret Summit viewpoint where you can enjoy a magnificent view as you wait. Details: (209) 565-3341; open from June to October. Round-trip shuttle is $7. (½ day)

✵ **Mammoth**—Perhaps more properly called **Mammoth Lakes**, the region refers to the area around **Mammoth Mountain**, an old volcanic peak. There are indeed several lakes, the town of Mammoth Lakes, and access to the Ansel Adams Wilderness and Devil's Postpile National Monument. The famed **Mammoth Mountain Ski Area** has 27 lifts plus two gondolas. The mountain and lifts are open in the summer to mountain bikers, some of whom ride in the "Kamikaze Downhill" at the end of June—a race for the somewhat less than sane. In both winter and summer, Mammoth attracts people who like to play hard, day and night.

The lakes and wild country draw plenty of hikers, bikers, fishers, and vacationers throughout the summer. Take Lake Mary Road from CA 203 near the top of the village to enjoy the lakes. Drive CA 203 to its end at Minaret Summit for a fantastic view of the San Juaquin Valley and jagged Minarets. The **Mammoth Scenic Loop Road** links CA 203, a mile above town, with U.S. 395. Either take the road down from CA 203 or watch carefully for the sign a few miles above the U.S. 395 and CA 203 junction. This scenic road goes through an interesting volcanic region. Stop at the **Earthquake Fault** for a walk into a fascinating crevasse created by the forces that give Mammoth its precarious reputation. (2–4 hours)

✦ **Mono Craters**—South of Mono Lake, a distinct volcanic ridge of cinder cones parallels U.S. 395 to the east. A trailhead along CA 120 near the north cone and a couple of National Forest roads allow close inspection of these black and rust-colored rock piles. Good views are available from the roadside along U.S. 395. (15 minutes–3 hours)

✦ **Sierra Valleys**—South of the Mammoth Lakes junction, several spur roads climb quickly up to high valleys and lake basins below the Sierra crest. Drives up into any one of these valleys, or those further south, are short and rewarding. Just up from the arid valley floor are lakes, waterfalls, rushing streams, and alpine scenery. Most of the valleys have pack stations for trail rides and hiking access to high passes and remote basins.

CA 7, the **Convict Lake Road**, leads three short miles to a beautiful lake named for murderous escapees who hid there for a time. **Rock Creek Road** passes upward through a beautiful valley to lovely **Rock Creek Lake**. Twelve National Forest campgrounds can be found on or near the road, which climbs to 10,000 feet above sea level. Farther south, **Pine Creek Road** would be similarly beautiful if not for the mammoth tungsten mine at the head of the valley. Still, the contrast of mineral extraction and pristine splendor is quite impressive. CA 168, out of Bishop, climbs to lakes with views of the 14,000-foot **Palisade** peaks. A café overlooking **Lake Sabrina** is a great place for lunch or a snack. **Glacier Lodge Road** leads to charming **Glacier Lodge**, (760) 938-2837, campgrounds, and views of **Palisade Glacier**. (2 hours per road)

Hot Springs—The Mammoth area is one of the most seismically active in California. Volcanic features are common throughout the eastern Sierra, and dire predictions of pending eruptions are frequent. Certainly, the abundance of hot springs in the region is pleasant proof that plenty of hot rock lies not far below the surface.

Grover Hot Springs State Park gathers warm waters into a family-style fenced pool. Details: Located 3 miles west of Markleeville, off

CA 89 on Hot Springs Road; (916) 694-2248; open from 9 a.m. to 9 p.m. Memorial Day through Labor Day and winter weekends, from 2 to 9 p.m. winter weekdays (closed two weeks in September for cleaning). Admission is $5 per car, plus $4 for adults and $2 for kids. (2–3 hours)

Primitive and pleasant **Buckeye Hot Springs** are about 10 miles southwest on Buckeye Road, which meets U.S. 395 4 miles north of Bridgeport. Continue up Buckeye Road to reach four National Forest campgrounds and Twin Lakes Road, which returns you to Bridgeport or to Twin Lakes. Try **Hot Creek Geological Site**, a state park a short way north of the main Mammoth Lakes junction. Caution: the water is really hot, and sudden temperature changes can be dangerous. In **Red's Meadow** next to Devil's Postpile, mineral baths are available at a nominal charge.

FITNESS AND RECREATION

Excellent hikes into the Sierras leave from the end of every road that heads up into a valley. In the bristlecones, the **Methuselah Trail** starts at Schulman Grove, looping 4¼ miles through the oldest of the old.

For a guided canoe tour of Mono Lake, join the nonprofit **Mono Lake Committee** on their summer weekend trips, departing at 8, 9:30, and 11 a.m. Saturday and Sunday. Trips are $15. Call (760) 647-6595 for information.

Caldera Kayaks, (760) 935-4942, offers rentals and guided tours on Mono Lake. They're located at the Crowley Lake Marina south of Mammoth on U.S. 395.

Most of the eastern Sierra valleys have pack stations offering trail rides. Near Grand Lake on the June Lake Loop, **Frontier Pack Station**, (760) 648-7701, has rides ranging from one hour to all day for $20 to $70. **Rock Creek Pack Station** is at the Rock Creek Resort up Rock Creek Road west of U.S. 395, south of Mammoth, (760) 935-4170. Take CA 168 above Bishop to reach South Lake and the **Rainbow Pack Station**, (619) 873-8877. One-hour to one-day rides range from $20 to $75.

FOOD

Two miles south of Coleville, you'll find the **Meadowcliff Restaurant**, 110411 U.S. 395, (530) 495-2180, offering American and Mexican food for breakfast, lunch, and dinner.

OWENS VALLEY AND MONO LAKE

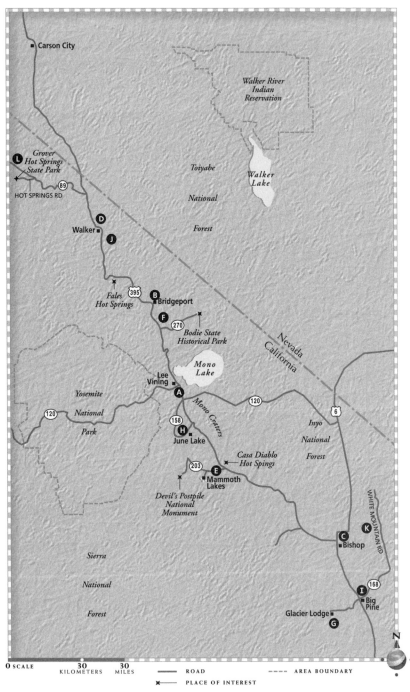

- Carson City

Walker River
Indian
Reservation

Grover
Hot Springs
State Park

Totyabe

Walker
Lake

HOT SPRINGS RD

National

Forest

Walker

Fales
Hot Springs

Bridgeport

Bodie State
Historical Park

Mono
Lake

Lee
Vining

Yosemite

Mono Craters

National

Park

Inyo

June Lake

National

Casa Diablo
Hot Springs

Forest

Mammoth
Lakes

Devil's Postpile
National
Monument

Sierra

WHITE MOUNTAIN RD

National

Bishop

Forest

Big
Pine

Glacier Lodge

N

0 SCALE

30

30

KILOMETERS   MILES   ROAD   ---- AREA BOUNDARY

PLACE OF INTEREST

Food

- **Ⓐ** Bodie Mike's Pizza
- **Ⓑ** Bridgeport Inn
- **Ⓒ** Erick Schat's Bakkery
- **Ⓓ** Meadowcliff Restaurant
- **Ⓐ** Nicely's
- **Ⓔ** Paul Schat's Dutch Bakery
- **Ⓔ** Slocum's Italian American Grill
- **Ⓔ** Tiger Bar
- **Ⓕ** Virginia Creek Settlement
- **Ⓒ** Whiskey Creek

Lodging

- **Ⓑ** Cain House
- **Ⓗ** The Four Seasons
- **Ⓐ** Gateway Motel
- **Ⓖ** Glacier Lodge
- **Ⓗ** June Lake Villager Motel
- **Ⓓ** Meadowcliff
- **Ⓔ** North Village Inn
- **Ⓑ** Silver Maple Inn
- **Ⓘ** Starlight
- **Ⓙ** Toiyabe Motel

Camping

- **Ⓒ** Brown's Town
- **Ⓚ** Grandview Campground
- **Ⓛ** Grover Hot Springs State Park
- **Ⓔ** Mammoth Mountain RV Park
- **Ⓕ** Willow Springs Motel and RV Park

Note: Items with the same letter are located in the same town or area.

Bridgeport has Bridgeport Inn, (760) 932-7380, for fine dining. It's been in business since 1877, so you know they're doing something right.

Look for the Virginia Creek Settlement south of Bridgeport. The restaurant has pizzas from $8, Italian dinners and steaks from $9 to $15.

In Lee Vining, basic nourishment, steady coffee, and good service can be had at Nicely's, (760) 647-6477. For pizza and beer, drop in at Bodie Mike's Pizza, (760) 647-6432.

The **Tiger Bar**, (760) 648-7551, in Mammoth Lakes is a favorite après-ski place for a bite and a beer. **Paul Schat's Dutch Bakery**,

3305 Main, (760) 934-6055, is a good stop for breakfast. Down the street, **Slocum's Italian American Grill**, 3221 Main, (760) 934-7647, has good dinners.

In Bishop, Paul's kinsman has a place called **Erick Schat's Bakkery**, 763 North Main Street, (760) 873-7156, that people crowd into with zeal. You can come out with a strange mix of goodies, like a cup of soup, decaffeinated espresso, and a birthday cake. **Whiskey Creek**, 524 North Main Street, (760) 934-2555, has a good patio for enjoying the fading evening over dinner and a pint of site-brewed beer.

LODGING

A mile south of Coleville is the lonely **Meadowcliff**, (916) 495-2255. It's a pleasant bargain with a pool. Rooms range from about $40 to $50. There are clean rooms and teepees at the **Toiyabe Motel** in Walker, (916) 495-2281. Rooms are $27 to $47.

In the charming little town of Bridgeport, try the **Silver Maple Inn**, (760) 932-7383. Rooms range from $60 to $80 (closed in winter). For a more pampered setting, indulge yourself next door at the **Cain House**, (760) 932-7040 or (800) 433-2246, a lovely B&B. Rooms run from $85 to $140.

The town of Lee Vining has surprisingly expensive basic motels. The **Gateway Motel**, (760) 647-6467, offers winter rooms for $45, summer rooms for $95 (the same rooms). Maybe it's the view of Mono Lake.

Along the June Lake Loop, **The Four Seasons** features A-frame cabins with splendid views of the High Sierras. Rates range from $80 (up to three people) to $200 (seven people, peak season). Look for the signs south of Silver Lake, (760) 648-7476. The **June Lake Villager Motel**, in the town of June Lake, (760) 648-7712 or (800) 655-6545, has rooms a nice notch up from basic at $35 to $80 and up.

In Mammoth, the **North Village Inn**, 103 Lake Mary Road, (760) 934-2525 or (800) 257-3781, is a great alternative to the big hotels on the strip. It's located just up Lake Mary Road from CA 203. Rooms are $50 to $125 in the summer, $30 more in the winter.

Big Pine has several motels, including the **Starlight,** 511 South Main, (760) 938-2011, a clean, nicely kept place with HBO, and rooms for $35 and $45.

West of Big Pine up Glacier Lodge Road is **Glacier Lodge**, (760) 938-2837, nestled in a gorgeous valley at 8,000 feet with views of Palisade Glacier. Rustic rooms are $65 to $75.

CAMPING

National Forest campgrounds are renowned for their quality, and there are many along the eastern Sierras. Every road that climbs west from U.S. 395 has at least one. They don't offer hookups and only occasionally do they have pull-throughs, but the sites are almost always spacious and set away from neighbors. Areas where several campgrounds are concentrated together include CA 89 north of Markleeville, CA 120 above Mono Lake, the June Lake Loop Road, Mammoth Lakes, Rock Creek Road, and CA 168 above Bishop. Sites usually cost from $8 to $11.

Grover Hot Springs State Park, (916) 694-2248 for information, (800) 444-7275 for reservations, offers a nice campground and easy access to the hot springs pool.

If you need a camping night near Bodie, the friendly keepers of **Willow Springs Motel and RV Park**, (760) 932-7725, will take care of you. There's a campfire every evening and diversions for the kids. It's 5 miles south of Bridgeport on U.S. 395. Rooms are $45 to $65, and campsites are $18.

Mammoth Mountain RV Park, (760) 934-3822, has some good tent sites too. There are a pool, Jacuzzi, and recreation hall. Van tours and shuttles are available. Tent sites are $17, and RV sites are from $24 to $28.

For an entertaining camp, stay at **Brown's Town**, 1 mile south of Bishop on U.S. 395, (760) 872-6911. Most sites are shady, and there's a mock-up of an old Western town to explore. Rates are $10, or $13 with hookups. The **Grandview Campground**, at the edge of the Ancient Bristlecone Pine Forest, is a great place to spend a night if you're not bothered by high altitude (over 10,000 feet). The views are astronomical. Free camping opportunities abound in the National Forests and BLM lands that make up most of the region.

Scenic Route: June Lake Loop

As you cruise through the sagebrush basins and dry pine forests along U.S. 395, it's hard to imagine the alpine wonders to be found above. All along the eastern Sierra, streams and rivers drain into forested valleys and beautiful lake basins. The June Lake Loop (CA 158) offers easy access to such an area.

The northern end of CA 158 meets U.S. 395 6 miles south of **Lee Vining**. Very quickly the land changes character as the road enters the foothills. Large **Grant Lake** seems to spill out of the high hills into a sage-dotted basin. The road enters a beautiful gorge, circling through a resort and recreation area to Silver Lake. From here, you drive through a pine forest with occasional views of the high peaks of the **Ansel Adams Wilderness**.

At the high point on the road, **June Mountain Ski Basin** rises above the town of **June Lake**, the site of some lodging and dining options. Go for a swim at the **June Lake Swimming Beach**, and enjoy the gorgeous mountain backdrop. From here the road slips back down to the highway. ◼

JUNE LAKE LOOP

YOSEMITE

During the long high season, many thousands of people visit Yosemite every week. While most settle for snapshot viewpoints, the wisest escape the crowds and hit the trails. Be among the wise and find yourself a quiet spot. You will know without a doubt that you are in one of the most beautiful places on earth.

In May, Yosemite Falls, the tallest falls in North America, bursts from the valley rim to fall almost a half mile to the rocks below. In October, delicate Bridalveil spills a light stream over the edge, much of it blowing to mist before it can reach the valley floor. Incomparable walls of granite soar 3,000 feet above the gentle meadows along the Merced River. Only the perspective provided by the dots of red-jacketed climbers gives a sense of scale to the scene.

Despite the glory, there is a sadness to the valley. It is truly and utterly exhausted by overuse, overexposure, and the endless accolades it receives. You must visit Yosemite Valley, but it helps to imagine it as it once was—silent except for the sounds of wind and water, and empty but for a small Indian group or two living along the river.

Fortunately, the glories of the park are not in the valley alone. The remarkable hard granite of the valley cliffs is found throughout the high country. Marvelous domes have surfaces that bootsoles stick to like velcro. Alpine meadows filled with wildflowers sprawl near the Tioga Pass Road. Lonely passes and lake basins are reached by over 800 miles of hiking trails. Besides, the valley is just as beautiful, if not more so, from the viewpoints and overlooks you earn with a couple of hours of hiking. ◣

YOSEMITE

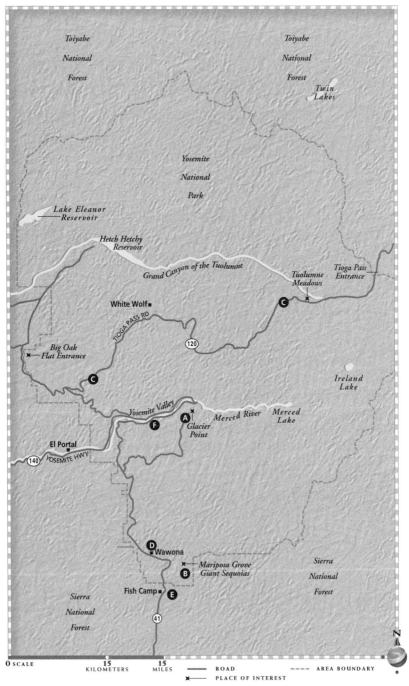

Toiyabe

National

Forest

Toiyabe

National

Forest

Twin
Lakes

Yosemite

National

Park

Lake Eleanor
Reservoir

Hetch Hetchy
Reservoir

Grand Canyon of the Tuolumne

Tuolumne
Meadows

Tioga Pass
Entrance

White Wolf■

C

TIOGA PASS RD

(120)

Big Oak
Flat Entrance

C

Ireland
Lake

Yosemite Valley

F **A**

Merced River

Glacier
Point

Merced
Lake

El Portal■

(140) YOSEMITE HWY

D ■Wawona

Mariposa Grove
Giant Sequoias

B

Sierra

National

Forest

Fish Camp■ **E**

Sierra

National

Forest

(41)

N

0 SCALE 15
KILOMETERS 15
MILES ——— ROAD ----- AREA BOUNDARY
✕— PLACE OF INTEREST

Sights

- **Ⓐ** Glacier Point
- **Ⓑ** Mariposa Grove
- **Ⓒ** Tioga Pass Road
- **Ⓓ** Wawona
- **Ⓔ** Yosemite Mountain Sugar Pine Railroad
- **Ⓕ** Yosemite Valley

A PERFECT DAY IN YOSEMITE

Pick a challenge that matches your ability and walk. Hike from the Tioga Pass Road into Mono Pass for stunning views from the crest of the divide. Loop from Lambert Dome to Ragged Lakes, then back to Tuolumne Meadows. Hike to Harden Lake from White Wolf to reach views of Hetch Hetchy. Bus to Glacier Point and take a three-waterfall loop down the Panorama and John Muir Trails to Happy Isles. Take a modest hike from the valley to Yosemite Falls, Mirror Lake, Vernal Fall, or Inspiration Point. Stroll quietly along the Merced. Stop, sit, think, breathe, and smile.

INFORMATION AND THE FUTURE

At press time, it was still uncertain what new plan would be implemented for improving conditions in Yosemite Valley. The pressure has been mounting to exclude all private vehicles from the valley, requiring visitors to leave their cars at the edge of the park and ride shuttle buses to the sights, lodgings, and campgrounds. To complicate matters, it can often be frustrating to get updates about the park by phone. Some contact numbers listed below offer only recorded information. Seek news elsewhere, or visit the Yosemite Web site at www.nps.gov/yose.

Valley Visitor Center/General Information	(209) 372-0200
Lodging Reservations	(209) 252-4848
Wilderness Permit Information	(209) 372-0310
Public Information Office	(209) 372-0265
Campground Reservations	(800) 436-PARK

SIGHTSEEING HIGHLIGHTS

★★★ **Yosemite Valley**—The three western highway approaches to the park all lead into Yosemite Valley. A one-way loop road takes visitors through the heart of the valley along the Merced River. As you drive in, the mighty mass of El Capitan anchors the north wall, rising 3,000 feet above the valley floor. To the south, Bridalveil Fall gushes during the spring snowmelt but is reduced to a windblown wisp of its former self at the end of the dry season. After passing the spires of the Cathedral Rocks, views of Yosemite Falls will begin to open out. At 2,450 feet, the Upper and Lower Falls together are the tallest in North America. In the springtime, the flow over the canyon rim is truly spectacular.

The services and accommodations in Yosemite Valley are clustered below Yosemite Falls. The Valley Visitor Center is located in Yosemite Village, above the outbound one-way road. Next door is the Yosemite Museum Gallery and Indian Cultural Exhibit. Details: Open daily from 9 a.m. to noon and from 1 p.m. to 4:45 p.m. Admission is free. (1½ hours)

Fairly short hikes lead out of the valley to **Vernal Fall** and **Nevada Fall** on the Merced, **Illilouette Fall** on Illilouette Creek, **Mirror Lake** below Half Dome, and the base of **Lower Yosemite Falls**. Trails are marked on the park map issued to all visitors. Try the Inspiration Point trail for a great view of the whole valley.

East of Yosemite Falls, the valley splits, climbing up through beautiful, glacier-carved valleys and into granite basins. Inviting trails lead off in several directions. Dominating the area is mighty **Half Dome**, its rounded summit looking 5,000 feet down to the valley floor. Half Dome's vertical north face, a daunting wall above the **Tenaya Creek**, looks as though it were sliced with a heavenly cleaver. With a 93-percent grade, it is the sheerest cliff on the continent. The numbers matter little; it is a stunning rock and the centerpiece of the park. Several views are particularly memorable, including the one from **Sentinel Bridge** just south of the village and from **Mirror Lake** at the base of the north face in **Tenaya Canyon**.

Open tram tours, ranger-led walks, evening programs, and other park-sponsored activities are available. Current schedules, locations, and reservation information are printed in the park literature that all visitors receive. The Valley Visitor Center is your best source for personal assistance. (all day)

★★★ Glacier Point—As you exit the Yosemite Valley, loop back to the south side road after you pass Valley View to reach the Wawona Road, and follow it as it climbs away from the Merced and up to a low pass at Chinquapin Junction. From here, take Glacier Point Road 16 miles up to Glacier Point for a sheer view 2,600 feet down into Curry Village. The valleys spread out before you: **Tenaya**, **Merced**, and **Illilouette**. Half Dome seems only a stone's throw away. You'll hear the echoes of roaring waters. So, too, will you hear the honking of horns, the straining of diesels, and, even, on a calm day, the calls of exuberant visitors.

For an even better view, take the **Pohono Trail** to the **Sentinel Dome Trail** and climb to **Sentinel Dome**. At 900 feet above the level of Glacier Point, you'll notice that you're a notch closer to the divine. The round-trip hike is about 2 miles from where the Pohono Trail crosses the road, about ¼ mile before the parking lot. (4 hours)

★★★ Tioga Pass Road—CA 120 passes through the heart of the Yosemite high country, crosses the Sierra crest at **Tioga Pass**, and

Yosemite Valley

drops steeply down into the Mono Lake Basin. At its western end, CA 120 enters the park at Big Oak Flat and passes near the sequoias of **Merced Grove** and **Tuolumne Grove**. Both are a short walk from well-marked turnouts. The road winds up the divide between the Merced and Tuolumne basins through evergreen forest. There is good hiking access to the north rim of the valley from **Tamrack Flat** and **Yosemite Creek Campgrounds**.

Olmstead Point affords a magnificent view down the sculpted Tenaya Canyon to the head of the valley, with Half Dome presiding over all. Walk the short path out to the small granite knob opposite the parking area for a better look and feel. There are many points along the road where you can walk on the rocks. The granite of Yosemite is exceptionally "clean" rock, with little grit or sand to make you slip. You can walk right up steep grades without fear of slipping—though falling is still entirely possible if you're out of your league. Enjoy **Tenaya Lake** as you regret that the road couldn't have passed a bit farther from its shores.

The **John Muir Trail** comes up from the valley to meet the **Pacific Crest Trail** in **Tuolumne Meadows**. The meadows cluster around the confluence of several streams as they merge into the Tuolumne River. The meadows are still lovely, but boot traffic over the years has taken "pristine" out of the description. The visitor center can provide information on the several trails that fan out from here into the high country. If you're walking to Canada, start here.

Just over Tioga Pass, the scene changes radically. The road hugs a well-engineered grade as the land drops from sculpted highlands through a plunging valley to the basins of the eastern Sierras. (all day)

★★ **Mariposa Grove**—The Mariposa Grove is the largest of the three sequoia groves in Yosemite. You can drive or take a free shuttle from Wawona to the grove parking lot. From here, you can see the grove via open air tram or on foot. A free museum in the grove has exhibits on the sequoia. Details: Daily tram tours leave from the parking areas on the hour, from 9 a.m. to 6 p.m., May through October. The tram follows a 2-mile loop and includes a stop at the museum. Cost is $7.

If you're looking for solitude among these amazing trees, visit in winter or in midweek during the spring and fall—or visit groves outside of the park. (2 hours)

★ **Wawona**—Twenty miles south of the valley mouth on CA 41, the Wawona Road, you'll come across a 120-year-old hotel set amid meadows, open forest, and a golf course. Wawona is Yosemite's southern gateway and the first site developed in the park. The **Pioneer Yosemite History Center**, a living history museum, is the chief attraction for non-golfers. Buildings from the area dating back to the 1850s are on display. Crafts and other demonstrations are scheduled throughout the summer, along with stagecoach rides. Details: At Wawona on CA 41; open Thursday through Sunday from 9:30 a.m. to 4:30 p.m. Admission is $3. (2 hours)

Yosemite Mountain Sugar Pine Railroad—On CA 41 in Fish Camp, you can take a short excursion on a narrow gauge rail line. There are also dinner packages and moonlight rides available. Details: Fish Camp; (209) 683-7273. The schedule has several variations, so call ahead; regular rides leave every half hour from 9 a.m. to 4 p.m., March 21 through October (closed in winter). Cost is $6.75. The **Logger**, a steam locomotive, departs less frequently. Cost is $10.50. (1 hour)

FOOD

In Yosemite Valley, you can dine at the rustically elegant **Ahwahnee Hotel Dining Room**, (209) 372-1489. Men are requested to wear a jacket and tie for dinner. Reservations are usually necessary. The **Mountain Broiler Room** in Yosemite Lodge is casual in atmosphere, but upscale in price and menu. Curry Village has the nice **Terrace Lounge** and the budget **Dining Pavilion**. Yosemite Village goes Italian at the **Pasta Place**.

The **Wawona Hotel**, (209) 375-6556, is the place for breakfast and dinner in Wawona. Reservations are needed for dinner.

On the Tioga Road, you can eat at **White Wolf** or **Tuolumne Meadows**. Both are easy and casual. Groceries and snacks are available at Yosemite Village and Tuolumne Meadows. Call (209) 252-4848 for all general lodging and food information.

LODGING

Yosemite Valley has choices from luxurious to rustic. The fabulous **Ahwahnee Hotel** is at the top end with rooms for $210. The Ahwahnee is easily the finest of its kind and is worth a visit even if you aren't staying the night. It's a big step down to the **Yosemite Lodge**. Rooms here are $82, $61 with shared bath. **Curry Village** looks

YOSEMITE

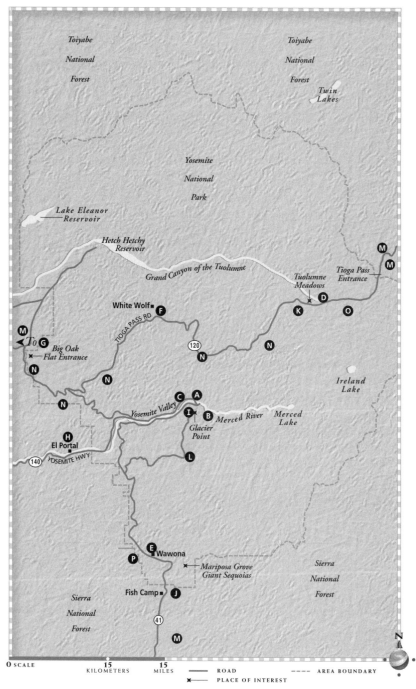

Toiyabe National Forest

Toiyabe National Forest

Twin Lakes

Yosemite National Park

Lake Eleanor Reservoir

Hetch Hetchy Reservoir

Grand Canyon of the Tuolumne

Tuolumne Meadows

Tioga Pass Entrance

White Wolf ■ **F**

M
M

K **D** **O**

TIOGA PASS RD

To **G**
Big Oak Flat Entrance

M

N

N

120
N

N

Ireland Lake

C **A**

Yosemite Valley

I **B** Merced River Merced Lake

Glacier Point

H
El Portal

140 YOSEMITE HWY

L

E ■ Wawona

P

Mariposa Grove Giant Sequoias

Sierra National Forest

Fish Camp ■ **J**

Sierra National Forest

41

M

N

0 SCALE
15
KILOMETERS
15
MILES
——— ROAD
- - - - AREA BOUNDARY
✕——— PLACE OF INTEREST

Food

- **Ⓐ** Ahwahnee Hotel Dining Room
- **Ⓑ** Dining Pavilion
- **Ⓒ** Mountain Broiler Room
- **Ⓐ** Pasta Place
- **Ⓑ** Terrace Lounge
- **Ⓓ** Tuolumne Meadows
- **Ⓔ** Wawona Hotel
- **Ⓕ** White Wolf

Lodging

- **Ⓐ** Ahwahnee Hotel
- **Ⓖ** Buck Meadows Lodge
- **Ⓗ** Cedar Lodge Motel
- **Ⓑ** Curry Village
- **Ⓖ** Groveland Motel
- **Ⓘ** Housekeeping Camp
- **Ⓙ** Narrow Gauge Inn
- **Ⓙ** Tenaya Lodge
- **Ⓚ** Tuolumne Meadows Lodge
- **Ⓔ** Wawona Hotel
- **Ⓕ** White Wolf Lodge
- **Ⓒ** Yosemite Lodge
- **Ⓗ** Yosemite View Lodge

Camping

- **Ⓛ** Bridalveil Creek Campground
- **Ⓑ** Lower Pines Campground
- **Ⓑ** Lower River Campground
- **Ⓜ** National Forest Campgrounds
- **Ⓑ** North Pines Campground
- **Ⓝ** Tenaya Lake Campground
- **Ⓞ** Tuolumne Meadows Campgrounds
- **Ⓑ** Upper Pines Campground
- **Ⓑ** Upper River Campground
- **Ⓟ** Wawona Campground

Note: Items with the same letter are located in the same town or area.

almost like a military camp with its cabins lined up in nice rows. The wooden ones are $53, while tent cabins go for $40. **Housekeeping Camp** has more tent cabins at $42.

In Wawona, the historic **Wawona Hotel** is an elegant choice for lodging. Rooms start at $90, $70 for shared bath.

On the Tioga Road, **White Wolf Lodge** is a very pleasant alternative to the busy valley. Cabins with a bath are $62; tent cabins are $42. The **Tuolumne Meadows Lodge** has tent cabins for $42. Reservations for all of the above sites are made via **Yosemite Reservations,** (209) 252-4848.

Several options are found along CA 41 near the Wawona entrance. The **Narrow Gauge Inn,** 48751 CA 41, (209) 683-7720, is close to the station of its namesake, the Yosemite Mountain Sugar Pine Railroad. This rustic inn has great rooms, a pool, a whirlpool, and a pleasant woodsy setting. Rooms range from $85 to $130. On CA 41, just outside the park, the luxurious **Tenaya Lodge,** (209) 683-6555 or (800) 635-5807, has the works. The lofty lobby with its grand fireplace sends an immediate message. More resort than hotel, the Tenaya has room service, indoor pool, weight room, and more. Rooms range from $70 (winter) to $260 (summer, suite).

Outside the park entrance on CA 140 is the motel village of El Portal. The **Yosemite View Lodge,** (209) 379-2681, has rooms from $100 to $140. Nearby, the **Cedar Lodge Motel,** (209) 379-2612, has rooms from $70 to $100. Further down the valley, Mariposa has several chain motels.

Sonora also offers several chain motels to those entering the park via CA 120. In Groveland, the **Groveland Motel,** (209) 962-7865, has basic rooms for $60. Closer to the park, the **Buck Meadows Lodge,** (209) 962-5281, has rooms from $70 to $80.

Outside the park's east entrance, rooms are available in the town of Lee Vining (see chapter 14).

CAMPING

Yosemite Valley has quite a few campgrounds. All of the sites in the valley must be reserved through **Parknet** by calling (800) 436-7275. There's no reservation fee beyond the cost of the campsite. If you want to stay in the valley anytime from spring through fall, you should definitely make reservations well ahead of time. Though the size and even the existence of the following campgrounds may change when the new park development plans are initiated, the following description is the best available at the time of publication.

Three **Pines Campgrounds, Upper, Lower,** and **North,** are farthest from the village traffic and closer to valley trailheads. **Lower River** and **Upper River** are on either side of the main loop and seem more crowded. None of them are particularly nice compared to National Forest or state park campgrounds.

Bridalveil Creek Campground on the Glacier Point Road is nice for its relative isolation and easy access to south rim sunsets.

There are seven campgrounds between the Big Oak Flat entrance and Tioga Pass along CA 120. High country campgrounds don't open until they are largely clear of snow, sometimes as late as July. First-come, first-served sites may be available at one or more of these camp-grounds, but it still pays to use the free reservation service. **Tenaya Lake** (walk-ins, $3) and **Tuolumne Meadows Campgrounds** are both good choices for their accessibility to the lovely granite dome country. **Wawona Campground** is an option at the south end of the park.

Many good National Forest campgrounds are located outside of the park. From Cedar Valley on CA 41, take Sky Lakes Road to reach four such campgrounds. On CA 140, the two Sierra National Forest campgrounds near Incline and Briceburg are administered by the Park Service. Call (800) 436-7275 for reservations. Five campgrounds are strung along CA 120 between Groveland and the Big Oak Flat entrance. Beyond the east entrance, six campgrounds are located in the beautiful basins above Mono Lake. Several of these campgrounds take reservations. Call (800) 280-2267 ($7.50 per reservation).

16

SEQUOIA AND KINGS CANYON NATIONAL PARKS

Together, the vast parkland of Sequoia and Kings Canyon National Parks preserves the tallest mountain in the lower 48, a canyon that dips deeper than any other on the continent, and the largest living thing on the earth. All this, yet it receives relatively few visitors. For one thing, the park is well off the beaten track, too far from urban areas for most weekenders, and not on the way to or from anywhere else. For another, it is primarily wilderness. The main access road barely reaches into the park, while two others are slow, winding roads that few follow.

The most rugged stretch of the High Sierra Mountains is found in the park. No American peak outside of Alaska is taller than Mount Whitney, at 14,495 feet above sea level. Several other peaks over 14,000 feet are found along the Sierra crest, along with many exceeding 13,000 feet. The Pacific Crest National Scenic Trail passes through the parks, hugging the heights. With sheer-faced granite peaks, glacier-gouged cirques and canyons, and miles of maintained trails, it's a backpacker's paradise.

What most visitors come to see is the mighty *Sequoia giganteum*, the shorter and thicker cousin of the coastal redwood tree, (*Sequoia sempervirens*). Sequoias grow only in about 130 groves on the slopes of the western Sierras between Lake Tahoe and Bakersfield. Groves range from 1 to 4,000 acres in size. Though other species may grow taller, older, or bigger at the base, nothing contains more living mass. ◼

SEQUOIA AND KINGS CANYON NATIONAL PARKS

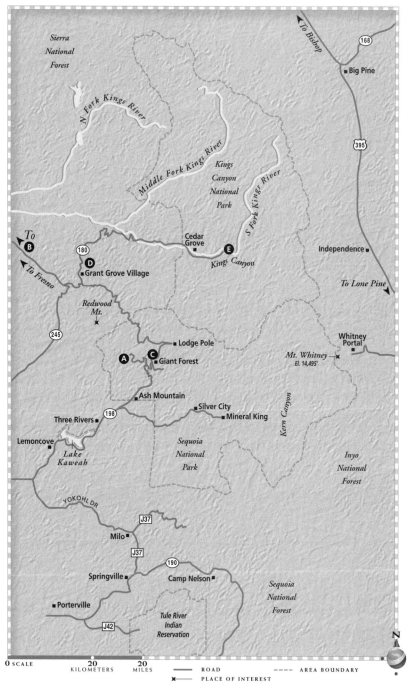

Sierra National Forest

To Bishop

168

Big Pine

N. Fork Kings River

395

Middle Fork Kings River

Kings Canyon National Park

S Fork Kings River

Cedar Grove

E

Kings Canyon

Independence

To B

180

D

Grant Grove Village

To Fresno

To Lone Pine

Redwood Mt.

245

A

C

Lodge Pole

Giant Forest

Whitney Portal

Mt. Whitney →
El. 14,495'

Ash Mountain

Silver City

Three Rivers

198

Mineral King

Kern Canyon

Lemoncove

Lake Kaweah

Sequoia National Park

Inyo National Forest

YOKOHL DR

J37

Milo

J37

190

Springville

Camp Nelson

Sequoia National Forest

Porterville

J42

Tule River Indian Reservation

N

0 SCALE

20 KILOMETERS

20 MILES

——— ROAD

---- AREA BOUNDARY

✕— PLACE OF INTEREST

Sights

Ⓐ Crystal Cave

Ⓑ Forestiere Underground
Gardens

Ⓒ Giant Forest

Ⓓ Grant Grove

Ⓔ Kings Canyon

A PERFECT DAY IN THE HIGH SIERRA

From your campsite or lodge room in Kings Canyon, drive to Roads
End and hike along the South Fork of the Kings River to Mist Falls or
even up into Paradise Valley. Enjoy a picnic lunch along the Kings
River, then drive the winding road back up to Grant Grove. Register
for your cabin or campsite (reserved weeks ago if you're traveling in
high season), then drive on to Giant Forest to enjoy an afternoon walk
along the easy Congress Trail. Gaze at the General Sherman Tree,
granddaddy of 'em all, returning along one of the many quieter loops
through the large grove. After a late picnic, drive or hike the mile and
a half to Moro Rock. Struggle up the steep steps to the top for an
unbeatable sunset panorama.

SIGHTSEEING HIGHLIGHTS

★★★ **Forestiere Underground Gardens**—Most visitors to Sequoia
and Kings Canyon arrive via Fresno and the hot highways of the
Central Valley. Few want to seek out the charms of valley towns and
cities, but there's one strange and compelling attraction that qualifies
as a must-see on my list.

In the early 1900s, Baldasare Forestiere, an immigrant from
Sicily, built himself a small room below ground level to escape from
the heat. By the time he died in 1946, he had completed scores of
rooms, niches, passageways, gardens, skylights, patios, a chapel, and an
800-foot auto tunnel—all below the surface, and all without plans or
heavy equipment. Touring the site, you imagine a man with rare vision
and passion.

The site of the gardens resembles an overgrown vacant lot with a
chain link fence around it. Once a rural road, Shaw Avenue has long

since attracted fast food joints and ugly storefronts. Somehow, this just adds to the magic of what you find beneath it all. Details: 5021 West Shaw Avenue. Take the Shaw Avenue exit from CA 99, about 8 miles northwest of central Fresno. Go two blocks east and look for the sign on your right. (209) 271-0734; tours are hourly from 10 a.m. to 4 p.m. (closed in winter, call for current schedule). Admission is $6. (1 hour)

★★★ **Giant Forest**—Here, in the largest sequoia grove of all, you'll find the **General Sherman Tree**, the largest living thing in the world at approximately 2,770,000 pounds. Trails thread through the forest, taking you well away from the road if you wish—though the traffic in Giant Forest is nothing compared to that in Yosemite. The **Congress Trail** is an easy link between the General Sherman and the remnant of **Giant Forest Village**. In the spring, the white blooms of tiny dogwood trees contrast marvelously with the huge, rust-colored trunks of trees that are as much as 3,000 years old.

South of the village, a short spur road leads through a portion of the grove to **Moro Rock**. From the parking area, a steep, narrow path of carved steps climbs a ¼ mile to the summit. From the top of this bald, granite dome, the views up and down the **Kaweah River Valley** are magnificent. To the southwest, the deep valley gentles, finally opening out through the foothills into the **Central Valley**, some 20 miles distant. To the east, the valley climbs swiftly to the high cirques and basins below the **Great Western Divide**. Hidden beyond this range of 12,000-foot peaks, the amazing **Kern Canyon** drains a wilderness watershed watched over by Mount Whitney, the highest peak in the contiguous U.S.

Note that the Giant Forest Village is being phased out as a site of services, a process that should be complete by 1999. Village buildings are a threat to the health of several sequoias—and a falling sequoia could well be a threat to the health of the village buildings and those they contain. Details: Located 16 miles southeast of the park entrance on the General's Highway; (209) 565-3134; open year-round. Admission is $5 per vehicle. (½ day)

★★★ **Kings Canyon**—Driving north from Grant Grove on CA 180, you enter **Sequoia National Forest**. The road soon begins a long, winding descent down into the canyon of the **South Fork of the Kings River**. The drop to the river from **Spanish Mountain**, the ridgeline summit you can see across the river, is more than 8,200 feet, making this segment of the valley the deepest canyon in the country.

The valley floor broadens as you enter the park and arrive in the **Cedar Grove** area. Though the Kings River can rage with snowmelt after a wet winter, its flow is often gentle. The hike through open forest lands along its banks is quite relaxing. At **Roads End**, the valley splits around a great spur. Trails lead up **Bubbs Creek** toward the **Kings-Kern Divide** and up beautiful Kings Canyon into **Paradise Valley** and beyond. (½ day)

✦✦ **Grant Grove**—Near the junction of the Kings Canyon and Giant Forest Roads, Grant Grove offers campgrounds, a ranger station, and the chance for wonderful walks through the sequoias. Here, open parkland areas are found in parts of the grove, enhancing the majesty of the giants. Details: **Grant Grove Visitor Center** is located 3 miles from the park entrance on CA 180; (209) 565-3134; open daily from 8 a.m. to 5 p.m. Admission is $10 per vehicle (good for one week). (1½ hours)

✦ **Crystal Cave**—A narrow road climbs to the cave; allow 20 minutes for the drive from Giant Forest. Stalagmites, stalactites, curtains, "cave bacon," and other formations can be seen. Details: Take Spur Road 2 miles south of Giant Forest Village; (209) 565-3134; tours start on the hour from 8 a.m. to 4 p.m., May through September. You must obtain your reservation and $5 ticket for a tour at either the Lodgepole or Ash Mountain visitor center. (2 hours)

FITNESS AND RECREATION

A beautiful day hike through the large, roadless **Redwood Mountain Grove** is the best way to get a real feel for the primeval sequoia tree. A trail runs down Redwood Creek from the General's Highway, about 6 miles south of Grant Grove Village. Two side trails circle across the slopes to the east and west of the valley path, allowing for loop choices of between 5 and 12 miles or so.

Another good hiking option is from **Kings Canyon** into **Paradise Valley**. The 2½-mile hike to the **Mist Falls** is an easy option. The additional 2 miles to Paradise Valley involves a 1,000-foot elevation gain.

FOOD

The **Giant Forest Village Cafeteria**, (209) 565-4040, is open for breakfast, lunch, and dinner, and offers basic American fare. Picnic

SEQUOIA AND KINGS CANYON NATIONAL PARKS

Sierra National Forest

To Bishop

168

Big Pine

395

N Fork Kings River

Middle Fork Kings River

Kings Canyon National Park

S Fork Kings River

Cedar Grove

180

C Grant Grove Village

A

Kings Canyon

To Fresno

Independence

To Lone Pine

Redwood Mt.

J

245

H

Whitney Portal

D Lodge Pole

Mt. Whitney
El. 14,495'

B Giant Forest

M

I

Ash Mountain

Kern Canyon

F 198

E

Silver City

Three Rivers

Mineral King

L

Lemoncove

Sequoia National Park

Inyo National Forest

Lake Kaweah

K

G

YOKOHL DR

J37

Milo

J37

190

Springville

Camp Nelson

Sequoia National Forest

Porterville

J42

Tule River Indian Reservation

N

O SCALE

20
KILOMETERS

20
MILES

—— ROAD

---- AREA BOUNDARY

✕— PLACE OF INTEREST

Food

- Ⓐ Cedar Grove Snack Bar & Market
- Ⓑ Giant Forest Village Cafeteria & Market
- Ⓒ Grant Grove Restaurant & Market
- Ⓓ Lodgepole Deli & Market

Lodging

- Ⓔ Buckeye Tree Lodge
- Ⓐ Cedar Grove
- Ⓒ Grant Grove
- Ⓕ Lazy J Ranch & Motel
- Ⓖ Mesa Verde Plantation Bed & Breakfast
- Ⓗ Stony Creek

Camping

- Ⓘ Buckeye Flat
- Ⓐ Cedar Grove
- Ⓙ Dorst
- Ⓒ Grant Grove
- Ⓚ Lake Kaweah
- Ⓖ Lemon Cove Sequoia Campground
- Ⓓ Lodgepole
- Ⓛ Mineral King
- Ⓜ Potwisha
- Ⓗ Stony Creek

Note: Items with the same letter are located in the same town or area.

supplies can be purchased at the **Giant Forest Market**. Both are open daily in the summer from 8 a.m. to 7 p.m., though one or both may be closed as part of the phaseout of Giant Forest Village.

The Lodgepole area has the **Lodgepole Market,** open daily from 10 a.m. to 6 p.m.; and the **Lodgepole Deli**, serving sandwiches and pizza from 11 a.m. to 7 p.m.

In Grant Grove, the **Grant Grove Restaurant**, Highway 180 at Grant Grove Village, (209) 335-5500, is somewhat nicer than the rest, serving three meals a day and offering cocktail service in the evening. It's open from 7 a.m. to 9 p.m. The **Grant Grove Market**, at the same location as the restaurant, has food and other supplies. It's open from 8 a.m. to 9 p.m.

Cedar Grove, in Kings Canyon, has a snack bar and a market at the Cedar Grove Lodge, and is open daily from 7 a.m. to 9 p.m. Hours for all facilities are shorter before Memorial Day.

LODGING

Sequoia and Kings Canyon National Parks offer lodging locations with several options. In **Grant Grove**, cabins are $35 to $75 in the high season, $30 to $60 in the low season. Lodge rooms in **Cedar Grove** are around $90 (summer only). In **Stony Creek**, rooms are about $100. Reservations are made through Sequoia Guest Services, (209) 561-3314.

When approaching the park from CA 198 from Visalia, there are several good lodging options. The **Mesa Verde Plantation Bed & Breakfast**, 33038 Sierra Highway (CA 198), Lemon Cove, (209) 597-2555 or (800) 240-1466, has nice rooms and a lovely yard. Prices are very reasonable at $60 to $100. In Three Rivers, the **Lazy J Ranch & Motel**, 39625 Sierra Drive (CA 198), (209) 561-4449 or (800) 341-8000, has a wonderful, sprawling lawn with a pool, shade trees, and nice rooms from $50 to $80. A minute from the park entrance, the **Buckeye Tree Lodge**, 46000 Sierra Drive (CA 198), (209) 561-5900, is right on the Kaweah River, with a pool and rooms from $50 to $80.

Those approaching via CA 180 and the General's Highway will find that Fresno has many chain motels. They include **Best Western**, **Marriott**, **Days Inn**, **Hilton**, **Holiday Inn**, **Ramada**, **Sheraton**, **Super 8**, and **Motel 6**. Most are concentrated at exits from CA 99.

CAMPING

The park has campgrounds at **Lodgepole**, **Grant Grove**, **Mineral King**, and **Cedar Grove**, as well as two campgrounds along the General's Highway, **Stony Creek** and **Dorst**; and two in the Kaweah Valley, **Buckeye Flat** and **Potwisha**. Grant Grove is the busiest area and is very close to the actual Grant Grove sequoia grove. Dorst has a trailhead for the 2-mile walk to Muir Grove. All four Cedar Grove campgrounds are along the Kings River. Lodgepole is the closest to Giant Forest.

Outside of the park, there are several good campgrounds. Four National Forest campgrounds are near Grant Grove, two to the north in the Kings Valley, and two to the east along the road to Big Meadows and Horse Corral Meadow (from the General's Highway). On CA 198 below Three Rivers, **Lake Kaweah** has a campground operated by the U.S. Army Corps of Engineers. Also on CA 198, the **Lemon Cove Sequoia Campground**, 32075 Sierra Drive, (209) 597-2346, is quiet and shady, with sites from $15 to $20, a store, and a pool.

APPENDIX

METRIC CONVERSION CHART

1 U.S. gallon = approximately 4 liters
1 liter = about 1 quart
1 Canadian gallon = approximately 4.5 liters

1 pound = approximately $\frac{1}{2}$ kilogram
1 kilogram = about 2 pounds

1 foot = approximately $\frac{1}{3}$ meter
1 meter = about 1 yard
1 yard = a little less than a meter
1 mile = approximately 1.6 kilometers
1 kilometer = about $\frac{2}{3}$ mile

90°F = about 30°C
20°C = approximately 70°F

Planning Map: Northern California

You have permission to photocopy this map.

INDEX

Alcatraz, 37, 38, 44
Ancient Bristlecone Pine
    Forest, 21, 29, 229, 233,
    237
Anderson Valley, 28, 123,
    128, 138, 139, 141, 147
Angel Island, 63
Año Nuevo State Reserve,
    18, 87–89, 98
Arcata, 159, 163, 164, 167,
    170, 171
Armstrong Redwoods
    State Reserve, 147, 149
Auburn, 206, 208, 209, 213
Audubon Canyon Ranch,
    65
Austin Creek State
    Recreation Area, 147,
    149, 156
Avenue of the Giants, 160,
    161, 167

Bale Grist Mill State
    Historic Park, 125, 129
BART (Bay Area Rapid
    Transit), 29, 30, 47, 84
Bay Model, 66
Bear Flag Republic, 14,
    123, 192
Berkeley, 15–17, 21, 24,
    30, 72, 73–84
Berkeley Marina, 75, 78,
    80, 82, 83
Big Basin Redwoods State
    Park, 87, 89, 93, 98
Big Sur, 21, 23, 28, 104,
    113–122
Big Sur (town), 117, 120
Bodega, 148, 149
Bodega Bay, 141, 144, 145,
    148, 149, 152, 153, 155
Bodie State Historic Park,
    29, 229, 230, 237
Bolinas, 61, 65, 70, 146

Cable Cars, 37, 40, 44, 46

Calaveras Big Trees State
    Park, 21, 204, 208, 213,
    214
California Marine
    Mammal Center, 62
California State Capitol,
    187, 189, 190
Calistoga, 123, 125, 126,
    128, 129, 132, 133, 136,
    138, 139
Camera Obscura, 43
Cannery Row, 103, 104,
    106–109, 112
Capitola, 87, 90, 91, 95, 99
Carmel, 17, 101, 103, 104,
    106, 108, 109, 113, 116
Castle Crags Wilderness,
    176, 180
Central Valley, 13, 18–20,
    25, 29, 30, 123, 173, 178,
    187–198, 253, 254
Chico, 177, 191
Chinatown, 13, 16, 37, 39,
    47, 50, 53
Civic Center (San
    Francisco), 40, 41, 50, 52
Coit Tower, 37, 41
Coloma/Marshall Gold
    Discovery State Historic
    Park, 204, 208, 212, 213
Crescent City, 160, 161,
    162, 167, 170
Crocker Art Museum, 187,
    189, 192
Crystal Cave, 257

D. L. Bliss State Park,
    217–219
Devil's Postpile National
    Monument, 229, 231,
    233
Donner Memorial State
    Park, 217, 218
Downieville, 201, 204,
    208, 209, 213

East Bay, 13, 21, 63, 73–84
El Pueblo de San Jose de
    Guadalupe, 92
elk (animal), 19, 63, 161,
    190

Emerald Bay State Park,
    214, 217, 218, 226
Eureka, 24, 25, 28, 157,
    159–163, 167, 170, 171

Ferndale, 157, 159, 164,
    170, 172
Filoli, 91
Fisherman's Wharf
    (San Francisco), 37, 43,
    44, 50, 53, 56
Fisherman's Wharf
    (Monterey), 103,
    105–108
Forestiere Underground
    Gardens, 253
Fort Bragg, 141, 143–149,
    152, 153, 155
Fort Point, 38, 39, 41, 45,
    47
Fresno, 28, 193, 253, 254,
    259

Garberville, 164, 167
Gatekeepers Museum, 218
Ghirardelli Square, 37, 44
Giant Forest, 253–258
Glacier Point, 241, 243
Glen Ellen, 125, 126, 129,
    130, 137
Gold Country, 23, 28,
    199–214
Gold Rush, 15, 26, 28, 76,
    101, 177, 187, 191, 199,
    207, 230
Golden Gate Bridge, 13,
    38, 39, 41, 45, 47, 61, 62
Golden Gate National
    Recreation Area, 38, 42,
    62, 64
Golden Gate Park, 41, 42,
    47, 57
Governor's Mansion State
    Historic Park, 187, 192
Grant Grove, 255, 258
Gualala, 149, 152, 154, 156

Healdsburg, 126, 128, 131,
    133, 137
Hearst Castle, 115, 116,
    121

Henry Miller Memorial Library, 115, 117
Hershey Chocolate Factory, 193
hot springs, 232
Humboldt Redwoods State Park, 21, 157, 160, 161, 164, 166, 171, 172
Hyde Street Pier, 37, 44

Indians, 14, 89, 161, 165, 186, 205

Jack London Square, 79, 80, 83
Jack London State Historic Park, 125, 129, 133
Jackson State Forest, 143, 149
Joseph D. Grant County Park, 98
Julia Pfeiffer Burns State Park, 116, 120
June Lake Loop, 233, 236–238

Kings Beach, 221
Kings Canyon National Park, 20, 21, 28, 251–259

Lake Almanor, 29, 177
Lake Tahoe, 13, 20–23, 25, 29, 176, 214–226, 229
Lands End, 42
Lawrence Hall of Science, 79
Lee Vining, 229–231, 235, 236, 238, 248
Leggett, 160, 161, 164, 165
Leland Stanford Jr., 90, 194
Leland Stanford Mansion, 187, 194
Living Memorial Sculpture Garden, 176, 185
Loomis Museum, 176
Lower Klamath National Wildlife Refuge, 185
Lucia, 115, 120, 121, 122

Luther Burbank Home and Gardens, 131

M.G. Vallejo, 14, 125, 130
M. H. de Young Memorial Museum, 42
MacKerricher State Park, 146, 155
Mammoth Lakes, 21, 29, 231–237
Manchester State Park, 146, 155
Marin County, 13, 16, 17, 21, 59–72
Marin County Civic Center, 66
Marin Headlands, 38, 39, 61, 62, 64
Mariposa, 209, 248
Mark Abbott Memorial Lighthouse, 89
Marshall Gold Discovery State Historic Park, 212
Mendocino, 17, 123, 141, 143, 144, 147–149, 152, 154, 155, 157
Mendocino Coast, 23, 28, 141–156
Mendocino Coast Botanical Gardens, 143, 144
Mendocino Headlands State Park, 143, 144
Mill Valley, 64, 65, 70, 71, 72
Mission Dolores, 47
Mission Santa Clara de Asis, 91
Mono Craters, 232
Mono Lake, 29, 214, 227–238, 244
Monterey, 13, 14, 22, 25, 28, 101, 103–109, 112, 113
Monterey Bay, 89, 94, 99, 101, 103, 106
Monterey Bay Aquarium, 103, 107
Monterey Peninsula, 13, 17, 23, 101–112
Monterey State Historic Park, 104, 105, 106, 107

Mount Diablo, 76
Mount Lassen, 20, 173, 175, 176
Mount Shasta, 13, 20, 21, 28, 29, 173, 175–180, 185, 186
Mount Shasta (town), 173, 177, 180, 181, 184
Mount Tamalpais State Park, 64, 71, 72
Mount Whitney, 20, 251, 254
Muir Woods, 38, 61, 64, 65
Murphys, 206, 209, 212
Musée Mechanique, 43

Nacimiento Road, 115, 122
Napa, 123, 126, 136, 137
Napa Valley, 22, 25, 123, 125–127, 132, 138
Napa Valley Wine Train, 136
Natural History Museum (San Francisco), 42
Navarro River Redwoods State Park, 147
Nevada City, 28, 201–203, 208, 209, 212, 213
New Brighton State Beach, 99
New Marine World Theme Park, 131
North Bloomfield (ruins), 201–203
North Coast, 13, 17, 21, 22, 31, 141–156

Oakland, 13, 16, 17, 21, 24, 27, 29, 30, 73–84
Oakland Museum of California, 75, 76
Old Sacramento, 187, 189, 191, 194, 195, 198
Owens Valley, 19, 29, 227–238

Pacific Grove, 101, 103, 106–109
Palace of Fine Arts, 38, 43

Palo Alto, 85, 87, 90, 94, 95, 99
Patrick's Point State Park, 159, 161, 171
Peninsula Coast, 21, 85–100
Petaluma Adobe State Historic Park, 130
Pfeiffer Big Sur State Park, 117, 120
Philip Burton Wilderness Area, 63, 64
Pinnacles National Monument, 21
Placerville, 207–209, 212
Point Arena, 145, 152, 154, 155
Point Arena Lighthouse, 145
Point Bonita Lighthouse, 38, 62
Point Lobos State Reserve, 116
Point Reyes National Seashore, 14, 21, 61–64, 67, 71, 72
Point Sur State Historic Park and Light Station, 116
Presidio (Monterey), 101, 106, 107
Presidio (San Francisco), 38, 39, 45, 47

Red Bluff, 192
Redding, 173, 178, 179, 180, 181, 186
Redwood National and State Parks, 157–172
Redwood National Park, 21, 160, 161, 166
Redwoods, 25, 64, 65, 85, 89, 94, 141, 147, 157, 159, 160
Robert Louis Stevenson, 105, 132
Rockefeller Forest, 160, 161
Rodeo Valley, 62, 64, 67, 71

Rosicrucian Egyptian Museum and Planetarium, 91
Russian Gulch State Park, 147, 155
Russian River Valley, 23, 123, 128, 133, 139, 141, 147, 153

Sacramento, 13, 16, 27, 187–198, 206
Sacramento Delta, 19, 20, 190
Sacramento National Wildlife Refuge, 192
Saint Helena, 132
Sam Brannan, 129, 187, 199
Samuel P. Taylor State Park, 61, 64, 65, 72
San Andreas Fault, 62, 88, 146
San Francisco, 13, 15–17, 21–23, 25, 27, 28, 30, 35–57, 63, 64, 65, 73, 78, 123, 141, 162, 199
San Francisco Maritime National Historical Park, 43, 44
San Francisco Museum of Modern Art, 46
San Jose, 13, 16, 24, 25, 85, 91–95, 98, 99
San Juan Bautista, 88, 95, 98
San Rafael, 61, 66, 70, 71, 72
San Simeon, 113, 116, 120, 121
Santa Cruz, 18, 21, 22, 87–95, 98–100, 106
Santa Cruz City Museum of Natural History, 89
Santa Rosa, 131, 137, 139
Sausalito, 61, 62, 65, 66, 70, 71
Scotia, 161, 164, 167
Sequoia National Park, 20, 21, 28, 30, 251–259
Sequoias, 19, 204, 208, 213, 244, 251, 254, 255

Seventeen-Mile Drive, 101, 103, 105
Shasta Caverns, 178
Shasta State Historic Park, 179
Sierra Nevada, 13, 19, 21, 22, 25, 26, 28, 29, 176, 214–259
Silverado Museum, 132
Skunk Train, 148
Sonoma, 14, 123, 125, 126, 128, 130, 137, 138
Sonoma Coast, 23, 141–156
Sonoma Coast State Beaches, 148, 155
Sonoma State Historic Park, 130
Sonoma Traintown Railroad, 130
Sonoma Valley, 123, 125–127, 133, 138, 139
Sonora, 203, 204, 209, 212, 248
South Bay, 13, 85–100
South Lake Tahoe, 219, 220, 224, 225
St. Helena, 127, 129, 131, 132, 136, 138
Stanford University, 85, 87, 90, 99
Stinson Beach, 38, 64–66, 70, 71
Sugar Pine Point State Park, 219, 220, 225
Sutter Creek, 205, 209, 212
Sutter's Fort State Historic Park, 187, 189, 193

Tahoe City, 215, 218, 220, 224–226
Telegraph Avenue (Berkeley), 75, 76, 80, 83, 84
Tiburon, 61, 63, 66, 70
Towe Ford Museum, 193
Trinidad, 162, 165, 167, 171
Trinity Alps Wilderness, 21, 173, 177, 180

Truckee, 215, 217, 220, 221, 224, 226
Tule Lake National Wildlife Refuge, 185
Tuolumne Meadows, 241, 244, 245, 248, 249
Twin Peaks, 38, 46

U.S.S. *Jeremiah O'Brien*, 46
Union Square, 37, 45, 46, 51, 52
University of California at Berkeley, 73, 76, 77

Van Damme State Park, 143, 148, 149, 155
Volcano, 205, 212, 214

Wawona, 244, 245, 248, 249
Weaverville, 177, 178, 180, 181
Weed, 173, 176–178, 183, 185
Wells Fargo History Museum, 187
Whale Watching, 108, 141, 144, 145
Whiskeytown-Shasta-Trinity National Recreation Area, 178
Wilder Ranch State Park, 87
Winchester Mystery House, 93
Wine Country, 13, 17, 23, 28, 31, 123–139

Yerba Buena Gardens, 37, 46
Yosemite Mountain Sugar Pine Railroad, 245, 248
Yosemite National Park, 13, 21, 28–30, 176, 203, 214, 227, 229, 239–249, 254
Yosemite Valley, 13, 20, 25, 214, 239, 242–245, 248
Yreka, 178, 179, 181, 183

Map Index

Berkeley, Sights/Food/Lodging/Camping, 74
Big Sur, Food/Lodging/Camping, 118; Sights, 114

Gold Country, Food/Lodging/Camping, 210; Sights, 200

High Sierra Pass Roads, Scenic Route, 214

June Lake Loop, Scenic Route, 238
Lake Tahoe, Food/Lodging/Camping, 222; Sights, 216
Lava Loop, Scenic Route, 185

Marin County, Food/Lodging/Camping, 69; Sights, 60
Mattole Road, Scenic Route, 172
Monterey Peninsula, Food/Lodging/Camping, 110; Sights, 102

Nacimiento Road, Scenic Route, 122
North Coast, Food/Lodging/Camping, 150; Sights, 142

Oakland, Sights/Food/Lodging, 81
Owens Valley and Mono Lake, Food/Lodging/Camping, 234; Sights, 228

Planning Map: Northern California, 10–11, 260–261

Redwood Parks, Food/Lodging/Camping, 168; Sights, 158

Sacramento, Food/Lodging/Camping, 196; Sights, 188
San Francisco, Food/Lodging, 48; Nightlife, 54; Sights, 36
Sequoia and Kings Canyon National Parks, Food/Lodging/Camping, 256; Sights, 250
South Bay and Peninsula Coast, Food/Lodging/Camping, 96; Sights, 86
Suggested Itineraries, 3–8; Arts and Culture Tour, 5; Best of Northern California Tour, 3; Best of the Bays Tour, 7; Family Fun Tour, 6; High Sierras Tour, 8; Nature Lovers' Tour, 4

Volcanoes, Food/Lodging/Camping, 182; Sights, 174

Wine Country, Food/Lodging/Camping, 134; Sights, 124

Yosemite, Food/Lodging/Camping, 246; Sights, 240

You'll Feel like a Local When You Travel with Guides from John Muir Publications

CiTY-SMarT™ GUIDEBOOKS

Pick one for your favorite city: *Albuquerque, Anchorage, Austin, Calgary, Cincinnati, Cleveland, Denver, Indianapolis, Kansas City, Memphis, Milwaukee, Minneapolis/St. Paul, Nashville, Portland, Richmond, San Antonio, St. Louis, Tampa/St. Petersburg, Tucson*

Guides for kids 6 to 10 years old about what to do, where to go, and how to have fun in: *Atlanta, Austin, Boston, Chicago, Cleveland, Denver, Indianapolis, Kansas City, Miami, Milwaukee, Minneapolis/St. Paul, Nashville, Portland, San Francisco, Seattle, Washington D.C.*

TRAVEL✦SMART®

Trip planners with select recommendations to: *Alaska, American Southwest, Carolinas, Colorado, Deep South, Eastern Canada, Florida Gulf Coast, Hawaii, Kentucky/Tennessee, Michigan, Minnesota/Wisconsin, Montana/Wyoming/Idaho, New England, New York State, Northern California, Ohio, Pacific Northwest, South Florida and the Keys, Southern California, Texas, Western Canada*

Rick Steves' GUIDES

See *Europe Through the Back Door* and take along country guides to: *France, Belgium & the Netherlands; Germany, Austria & Switzerland; Great Britain & Ireland; Italy; Russia & the Baltics; Scandinavia; Spain & Portugal;* or the *Best of Europe*

ADVENTURES IN NATURE

Plan your next adventure in: *Alaska, Belize, Costa Rica, Guatemala, Honduras, Mexico*

JMP travel guides are available at your favorite bookstores. For a FREE catalog or to place a mail order, call: 800-888-7504.

John Muir Publications • P.O. Box 613 • Santa Fe, NM 87504

ABOUT THE AUTHOR

Paul Otteson *knows* Northern California. He has been exploring Northern California and the American West for more than 20 years, and he's covered thousands of miles on foot, exploring scores of parks and wilderness areas and wandering the highways and backroads of the West. It's no surprise that he feels a special affinity for Northern California—an area that he also calls home.

Otteson's international journey led to his first book, *The World Awaits: A Comprehensive Guide to Extended Backpack Travel*, a classic for those planning independent travel overseas. His other works include *Alaska: Adventures in Nature*—a complete guidebook for active and environmentally aware travelers to the 49th state, and *Kids Who Walk on Volcanoes*—a children's book on the lives of kids in the Central American highlands.

Otteson and his wife Mary live in the San Francisco Bay Area. He hosts an extensive travel Web site at www.worldawaits.com featuring travel advice, stories, and resources, as well as information on his books and a catalog of his photos. He can be reached through John Muir Publications or by e-mail at editor@worldawaits.com.

Cater to Your Interests on Your Next Vacation

**The 100 Best Small Art Towns in America
3rd edition**
Discover Creative Communities, Fresh Air, and
Affordable Living
U.S. $16.95, Canada $24.95

**The Big Book of Adventure Travel
2nd edition**
Profiles more than 400 great escapes to all corners
of the world
U.S. $17.95, Canada $25.50

Cross-Country Ski Vacations
A Guide to the Best Resorts, Lodges, and Groomed
Trails in North America
U.S. $15.95, Canada $22.50

Gene Kilgore's Ranch Vacations, 4th edition
The Complete Guide to Guest Resorts, Fly-Fishing,
and Cross-Country Skiing Ranches
U.S. $22.95, Canada $32.50

Indian America, 4th edition
A traveler's companion to more than 300 Indian
tribes in the United States
U.S. $18.95, Canada $26.75

Saddle Up!
A Guide to Planning the Perfect Horseback
Vacation
U.S. $14.95, Canada $20.95

Watch It Made in the U.S.A., 2nd edition
A Visitor's Guide to the Companies That Make Your
Favorite Products
U.S. $17.95, Canada $25.50

The World Awaits
A Comprehensive Guide to Extended Backpack
Travel
U.S. $16.95, Canada $23.95

**JMP travel guides are available
at your favorite bookstores.
For a FREE catalog or to place a
mail order, call: 800-888-7504.**

John Muir Publications ◆ P.O. Box 613 ◆ Santa Fe, NM 87504